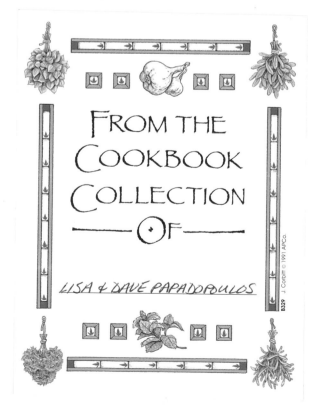

From the Cookbook Collection —Of—

LISA & DAVE PAPADOPOULOS

B329 J. Corbitt © 1991 APCo.

FRENCH COOKING

En Famille

FRENCH
COOKING
En Famille

JACQUES BURDICK

Fawcett Columbine
New York

A Fawcett Columbine Book
Published by Ballantine Books
Copyright © 1989 by Jacques Burdick

LIBRARY OF CONGRESS CATALOGING-IN-PUBLICATION DATA

Burdick, Jacques.
French cooking en famille/Jacques Burdick.
p.   cm.
Includes index.
ISBN: 0-449-90303-6
1. Cookery, French.   2. Menus.   I. Title.
TX719.B9248   1989
641.5944—dc20   88-92244
                                          CIP

Designed by Beth Tondreau Design/Jane Treuhaft
Manufactured in the United States of America
First Edition: September 1989
10 9 8 7 6 5 4 3 2

—à ma famille partout

ACKNOWLEDGMENTS

My debt of gratitude is vast. Indeed, I could not list the names of all those who helped me in the preparation of this little book. I thank each one. However, I owe special thanks to a few: to my faithful friend and fellow cook, Anne Casale, who suggested I write the book; to my brilliant editor, Joëlle Delbourgo, and her fine staff, whose wise suggestions, passionate interest and sustaining vision informed the book; to my constantly supportive literary agent, Amy Berkower; to my pals, Janet Waller and Selma Dreiseszun, whose sharp eyes caught many snarls in my text; finally, to my large family of friends, colleagues and students, who sampled the recipes and enthusiastically endorsed them.

Contents

Foreword

This is a book about how ordinary French householders prepare good, simple, economical food in their own urban and farmhouse kitchens for themselves, their families, and occasional guests. It is a book written especially for those United States householders who love good food and are willing to invest a little time in learning how most French homemakers plan, shop, prepare, and serve family meals.

Today it is almost impossible to find true French home cooking in United States restaurants. Traditional French dishes, once familiar items on the menus of good French restaurants, have almost disappeared in favor of new creations made of exotic, trendy, and costly ingredients. For those who love traditional French food and want it often, the order is clear: make it yourself. For most Americans, the thought of preparing French meals on a day-to-day basis is a daunting prospect. If you feel a little overwhelmed at that thought, take courage! I have written this book for you.

I remember that same overwhelming feeling. Forty years ago when I arrived in France as a student from my native Texas, all I knew about most French food was that I loved it and wanted to learn all about it. As a student I could not afford costly meals in great restaurants. However, in those days Americans were in favor in France, and I was lucky to be invited often to dine in many households where the food was excellent. I always made a point of getting to know the cooks in those households. It was those wonderful cooks who taught me the basics of French home cooking. They literally took me by the hand and led me step by step through their favorite recipes, while lavishing on me an endless wealth of regional food lore and kitchen wisdom. They were often demanding and authoritarian in their instructions, but they were always warm, convivial, and often affectionate with me. I feel a deep obligation to hand on, whenever I can, what they entrusted to me. For forty years I have cooked as they taught me to. Naturally, many of their attitudes have become mine, so please forgive me if, in the course of guiding you through the recipes in this book, I sometimes become authoritarian. I consider cooking a joyful but serious business. Like my teachers, I think that spoiling good food through ignorance, haste, or inattention is a kind of impiety; it diminishes the potential enjoyment of the entire household. It is also wasteful.

I love every recipe I have included here. I think of these recipes as old friends. In most cases I have framed the recipe with an anecdote, a bit of food lore, a suggestion or two about how the recipe may be enhanced or modified in some useful way.

Back in 1951, Hannah Mathieu, my high-spirited, food-loving landlady in Aix-en-Provence, scribbled this *dédicace* on the flyleaf of a book of regional recipes she gave me:

> *En attendant de taquiner*
> *la queue de la poêle*

In literal translation it loses much of Madame Mathieu's earthy wit and Rabelaisian humor:

> *While waiting to tease*
> *the handle of the frying pan*

In plain American words the sentiment is fitting for American beginners who want to learn about French home cooking through this book:

> *While you're waiting to*
> *take over the kitchen!*

Ready? Then let's do some home cooking *à la française*!

FRENCH COOKING

En Famille

An Introduction to French Household Cooking

As a young Texan arriving in provincial France forty years ago, I was astonished at the consistently fine quality of everyday food in French households. A bit later, when I was permitted to enter the kitchens of those homes, I was even more astonished at how such fine food was prepared, day in, day out, with so little equipment, so few appliances, and in such close, often tiny quarters. Even in large French houses, the kitchen was sometimes no larger than a hallway and was often badly lighted. By American standards the stove was usually very small and often without a stationary oven. The sink was a block of marble with a circular declivity in the center about twelve inches in diameter and no more than an inch deep. In the middle was a small hole for a drain. The running water came from a single tap directly above the shallow sink. Hot water had to be heated in kettles on the stove. If there happened to be a hot-water heater, it was tiny and could be lighted for only a few minutes to allow the interior coils to heat the water as it ran through. The heater had to be extinguished immediately after each use, or the steam buildup would burst the pipes. As a comfort-loving American; I marveled. My admiration for those devoted cooks grew immeasurably as I understood how much they did to produce those fine meals from scratch. French kitchens have changed a great deal since those days. Even today, however, the kitchens in most French homes are not pleasant, cheerful places where the family gathers, as they are in most homes in the States. Of course, there are exceptions, but I can't remember very many.

It was a great lesson to me in 1950 to see the consistently wonderful food that came from those poky kitchens. I learned then and there that great home cooking depends upon devoted cooks and good, fresh ingredients, not a great store of equipment. Those resourceful cooks taught me how to prepare a fine meal, using only the tiny alcohol burner I kept in my room for making my morning coffee. The knack was simple. It consisted of choosing food that could be done quickly and simply on such a tiny burner.

I do not mean to suggest by what I have said that the French household kitchens where I learned French home cooking were not equipped to prepare the food they cooked. All of them had exactly what they needed—no more, no less. The menus were always well thought out, always carefully budgeted, and the shopping was done daily and with great attention. Generally speaking French household cooks plan much more shrewdly than most of their American counterparts. If devotion to good food is a French characteristic, so is thrift. The classic game plan in French homes is to provide excellent food daily and manage to save a few francs in the bargain. That requires a good knowledge of ingredients and their preparation, alert shopping, and tenacious bargaining. Supermarkets everywhere have reduced the possibilities of bargaining, but my French friends never hesitate to ring the butcher's bell in the supermarket to ask for a special cut and request that a marrow bone or piece of suet be thrown in for good measure. They usually get it.

Before discussing the basic equipment in a French household kitchen, I want to speak about the daily schedule of meals in an ordinary French home and their relative importance. Except on farms, where those who do heavy work usually eat more heartily, breakfast in most French households is not an important meal. The family rarely sits down to eat breakfast together. A pot of coffee is brewed by the first breakfaster and poured into a saucepan. Milk is heated in another. Both are left on the stove so that each breakfaster may reheat them and serve himself as he likes. A package of *biscottes* or rusks, a basket of grilled, leftover bread, a cut of sweet butter, and a pot of jam or honey are usually laid out on the kitchen table. You will not find hot croissants, brioches or fresh bread or rolls there unless someone has run out to fetch them from the neighborhood bakery. This simple breakfast is no more than that: a "breakfast."

French household cooks often use the free time that results from such a serve-yourself system to draw up the menus for lunch and dinner. They quickly calculate the available time, schedule it, and hurry off to do the shopping. Early morning is still the French nation's favorite time to shop for food. Every neighborhood has its beef butcher, its pork butcher, poulterer, and fishmonger. There will be a neighborhood bakery, a pastry shop, a greengrocer, a fruit shop, wine, tea, and coffee shops. In most neighborhoods an itinerant market will set up its stalls in the early morning several times a week and disappear by noon.

With such an array of provisioners, French household cooks can afford to be shrewd and demanding. Shopkeepers must be on their toes. Even the stallkeepers in the street markets must beware of giving short measure or selling faulty merchandise. The exchanges between the buyers and sellers are lively, often quite loud. Offended customers sounding off can be disastrous for business. Vendors can expect to have their merchandise poked, squeezed, and handled. Merchants who protest are commonly answered with a sharp remark or a lost sale. But the exchange between shopkeepers and shoppers often takes the form of a bit of food lore, a recipe, or a word of advice about how an article in question is best prepared. In a French market or shop you become aware very soon that both buyers and sellers adore food and that they will discuss food and its preparation with the greatest enthusiasm at the drop of a hat.

The household cook returns home laden with the day's provisions, puts them away, thinks carefully of what has to be started at once, and gets it underway. The French have their lunch at noon. It used to be their largest meal. Though they eat far less than they used to at noon, most French people still take two hours for lunch. Shops usually close for two hours and so do many businesses. At school classes are suspended for two hours as well. To compensate for this noon break, most French people work until 6:00 or 6:30 P.M. Dinner is usually served at 8:00 P.M., so children are given a light snack called a *goûter* as soon as they return home from school.

In a French home lunch and dinner normally consist of several courses: an hors d'oeuvre or soup, the entrée or main course, with its accompanying vegetables, followed by a green salad. Meals finish with cheese, fruit, or a dessert. These dishes are served in sequence, rarely together. Wine and mineral water are traditionally drunk at all principal meals, but you may be served cider instead of wine in the northwest, or light beer in the northeast.

French cooks rarely attempt to prepare at home a dish that requires highly specialized training or expensive equipment not found in the ordinary home kitchen. Why try making puff paste or pâté at home when the local pastry cook and *charcutier* prepare them daily and will sell them to you by the gram? No French household cook of my acquaintance would think of baking bread at home.

In the United States, we love to try out the most difficult cooking techniques. We go to cooking schools or get our instructions from the plethora of cooking lessons on television, and we sometimes produce food fit for the best restaurants. French cooks, on the other hand, al-most never make at home what can be easily bought in their neighborhood. The exception is an occasional fruit tart, a special pâté during the Christmas–New Year holidays, or a special cake never found in the local pastry shop. For that reason, in this book I have not tried to introduce complicated techniques that belong more to the glorious world of French restaurant cooking than to French household cooking. The recipes I have chosen to present here are those that many French cooks prepare at home in their modest kitchens, those that I feel you can manage in your own kitchen.

There may be some kitchen tools or special pots and pans that the French householder uses that you may not have in your kitchen. I do not recommend that you rush out and buy them all at once. You should think carefully about how often you will use the piece of kitchen equipment you are considering.

There follows a list of some of the standard items regularly found in a French home kitchen. Most of them can be found in United States department stores and specialty shops. If you have a poorly equipped kitchen, outfit it a little at a time, making sure what you buy will serve you often and well. Also worth thinking about is where you will store a new piece of kitchen equipment when it is not in use.

Standard Kitchen Equipment for French Household Cooking

French home cooking came to its apogee in the latter part of the nineteenth century when as a symbol of their success and affluence the wealthy middle class began to emulate the fabulous restaurant cooking of the period. In that epoque, which Roger Shattuck has called "The Banquet Years," family celebrations were synonymous with sumptuous meals of eight to ten courses. It was customary to serve a different wine with each course, and champagne flowed like fountains. In the 1950s I met many octogenarians in the Midi who spoke eloquently of the period before World War I when feasts that took days to prepare and days to consume were regularly offered in their own households for weddings, christenings, first communions, confirmations, and anniversaries.

By 1950, when I arrived in France, most of the elaborate kitchen equipment used in preparing such feasts had disappeared from the household kitchens I knew, but mountains of it could still be seen in the flea markets of Aix: gigantic mortars of Aubagne marble with their billyclub-size pestles; curious nests of tarnished baroque pâté and pastry molds of every size and shape, held together with ornate cotter pins; long-handled toasting forks; blackened salamanders for flash-browning soft meringues and crystalizing glazes on custards and creams without curdling them; crystal and silver vinaigrettes, windlassed coffee roasting drums; little coffee grinders that had to be held securely between the thighs while using them; titanic serving platters; latticed and pierced flatware; and so forth. All that equipment, of course, required hectares of storage space and a retinue of servants to clean and maintain it.

The age of live-in servants passed and with it the sumptuous household feasts and the elaborate household kitchen equipment. Fortunately, much of the afterglow of the great age of nineteenth-century bourgeois cooking remains. Meals have grown smaller, more reasonable, and very carefully budgeted. But the quintessential foodsmanship remains. Compared to everyday meals in most United States households, the daily meals in most French homes still seem marvelously ample. In this age of one-dish meals, the devotion to good food and its preparation still prevails as an almost universal cultural phenomenon. However, at present that devotion is practiced with far less kitchen equipment than it once was. If you are interested in cooking, perhaps you already have most of the standard equipment needed for French household cooking in your own kitchen. Here is a minimal checklist.

For cutting, slicing, and chopping:

One 12-inch chef's knife
One 6-inch paring knife
One 8-inch narrow-bladed boning or filleting knife
One 10-inch narrow-bladed ham knife for slicing (optional)
One 6-inch vegetable peeler with swivel blade

1 knife sharpener
1 hardwood or polyurethane chopping block
1 knife block with a slot for each knife
1 pair heavy kitchen shears (optional)
1 metal pastry scraper (optional)

Good knives are always expensive. It pays to buy the best quality you can afford and treasure them as a good investment. Take the time to examine each knife carefully before you buy it. The blade should be of the best steel, in one solid piece from the point to the very end of the handle or tang. The heel of the blade should be well recessed at the bolster, where the blade enters the handle, so that you can grasp the handle and chop vigorously without touching your knuckles to the chopping board.

Good kitchen knives should be used only for the purpose for which they were designed. They should be sharpened properly and often, cleaned and dried after each use, and stowed in such a way that their points and cutting edges are prevented from striking or touching metal. If you haven't a knife storage block or a proper rack and must keep your sharp knives in a drawer, protect them as the French sometimes do by running the point and the middle of the cutting edge into bottle corks. The French save corks as many of us save bits of string. They are generally used for waxing tiles and furniture, but they have many other handy uses, one of which is safeguarding the points and cutting edges of kitchen knives.

For measuring:

1 glass measuring cup
1 set metal measuring cups
1 set measuring spoons

2 sieves (1 small, 1 large),
  preferably stainless steel

For mixing, beating, and whipping:

1 nest stainless steel mixing bowls
1 wooden spoon

1 wooden, plastic, or rubber spatula
One 9-inch-long whisk

For sautéing and frying:

2 heavy-bottomed frying pans,
  1 medium-sized, 1 large

1 long-handled fork
1 pair kitchen tongs

For simmering, boiling, and braising:

1 heavy-bottomed 1-quart saucepan
  with lid
1 heavy-bottomed 2- to 3-quart
  saucepan with lid

1 heavy-bottomed braising pan with
  lid
One 4-quart kettle with lid
1 dutch oven with lid

For baking and grilling:

Assorted crock, Pyrex, or porcelain
  ovenware in various shapes and
  sizes
1 pie tin
1 shallow 12-inch tart tin
2 cookie sheets

1 rectangular loaf pan
One 8- to 10-inch springform cake
  tin
1 porcelain terrine with lid
1 pastry brush

For washing and draining:

1 colander   1 vegetable brush
1 salad dryer

For puréeing, crushing, and emulsifying:

1 Mouli food mill   1 mortar
1 potato masher   1 pestle

You will also need:

1 skimmer   Paper towels
1 ladle   Cotton kitchen string
1 slotted spoon   Cotton cheesecloth
1 four-sided grater   Dish towels
1 kitchen timer   Dish cloths
Aluminum foil   Aprons
Wax paper

NOTE: The French kitchens where I learned to cook forty years ago had neither a food processor, a blender, nor an electric beater/mixer. If you possess any or all of these wonderful inventions, by all means use them. They will save you worlds of time and, in many cases, do a better job.

SEASONING NEW CAST-IRON POTS AND PANS

In the old days, long before Teflon antistick coatings, household cooks in my part of the country knew how to season their cast-iron cooking pots and pans so that their cooking surfaces became more and more impervious to sticking. I used to see my great-grandmother "cure" a new cast-iron skillet or frying pan by first boiling it in a kettle of water to which she had added a fistful of baking soda. Then she would give it a good "country" scrubbing with a corncob, sand, and wood ashes to remove the protective coating the manufacturer had used to prevent rusting on the store shelf. After rinsing the piece well, she would dry it and grease it with a ham or bacon rind. She then heated it on top of the range. She would repeat this last step many times until she was satisfied it was cured of its tendency to stick. I saw her curing all of her cast-iron pots and pans until they took on a handsome mat black patina. Once the pots and pans were cured, she could fry an egg or a pancake on them with almost no oil or fat and they would never stick. She was as careful with cured pots as she could possibly be, and she was as likely to allow you to use them as she was to loan you her favorite brooch.

Many years later, when I went to live in France, I was delighted to discover that French household cooks went about seasoning their cast-iron cookware in the very same fashion. They, too, were reluctant to allow their seasoned pots to be used—or even washed—by a visitor who might not be aware of their patiently developed seasoned surfaces and how easily those surfaces could be destroyed.

Teflon and Silverstone coatings have made it unnecessary to season most pots and pans, but uncoated cast-iron pots and pans must still be seasoned. It is useful for a present-day household cook to know how to cure those rough-surfaced pots and pans of sticking, for stick they will! They cannot do otherwise. Their surfaces are incredibly pitted and rough, though the naked eye cannot see it. These pits and rough patches must be filled in with grease or oil topping just as a rough road full of potholes and ruts must be filled in with asphalt. Heat forces apart the surface molecules. That is why even a well-cured pan, if allowed to overheat with nothing in it, may need to be seasoned again, since the grease and oil can burn off or sink into the pits. Detergent, bleach, and rough scrubbing will also remove the seasoning. The ruined surface must then be reprocessed. That explains why cooks who prize their seasoned pots are reluctant to allow others to use them or wash them. All that explained, here is how to cure your cast-iron pots of sticking:

1. Boil the cast-iron piece for 10 to 15 minutes in a kettle of water containing 2 tablespoons of baking soda. (If the piece is too large to submerge in a large kettle, or if the handle of the piece is damageable, simply fill the piece with water and a little soda and boil it on the top of the stove for 10 to 15 minutes.)
2. Rinse the piece well and let it cool.
3. Scrub the cooking surface of the piece with fine steel wool and strong scrubbing powder to remove all the industrial protective coating.
4. Rinse the piece well and dry it.
5. Grease or oil the cooking surfaces lightly and heat the piece for 5 minutes over a moderate flame or in the oven.
6. Repeat the greasing and heating step at least once.
7. Wipe the piece with paper towels or a piece of soft cloth and hang it up or store it upside down in a dry place. It is now seasoned and ready to use.

N O T E : If you use oil to season the piece, do not choose safflower or corn oil. Both leave a varnishlike residue on the surface of the piece that must inevitably be scrubbed off.

It is preferable to wipe out rather than wash newly seasoned pots. If for some reason a seasoned pot should stick, rub away the bits that have stuck to the surface with a soft cloth dipped in a little vegetable oil and a little coarse salt. Carefully remove all the salt and lightly oil the surface of the pot before storing it.

CHAPTER TWO

Sauces

Introduction

One of the cardinal elements of French cooking that distinguishes it from any other ethnic cooking is the importance it assigns to sauces. All French cooking concerns itself with sauces, whether it be the thrifty cooking of French households or the extravagant cuisine of great French restaurants. French households usually lack the time, equipment, kitchen space, personnel, and food budget for preparing the elaborate sauces that are the pride of great French restaurants. The pride of the French home cook, on the other hand, is the choice of sauces appropriate to the individual household's budget and tastes.

While no French cook I know would refuse an invitation to dine in a great French restaurant, there is a very widespread belief among home cooks that the *petits plats cuisinés*—the "labored-over dainties"—of great restaurants, if eaten often, can bring on *le mal au foie*, the infamous Gallic liver attack. The French joke about it, yet it remains the bogeyman of French overindulgence. However, having said that, I must quickly repeat that all French cooking is planned with great attention to appropriate sauces, and that food-loving French householders want their food served up with the appropriate sauces. While the rich, elaborate sauces of great restaurants may be inappropriate for the food served in a modest French home, that household will prepare its own repetoire of appropriate sauces. Those sauces, like their rich cousins, the restaurant sauces, have common origins: they are all based on half a dozen basic French sauce-making techniques, techniques that produce the "mother sauces" from which the whole, vast genealogy of French sauces derives.

I have tried to keep the presentation of sauce making as simple, rudimentary, and straightforward as possible here. I have set down a few of the most widely used techniques, suggesting only a few of the dozens of ways in which they may be elaborated for the special accent or twist appropriate to the dishes for which they are being created. Sauces were never made to exist on their own. They exist to enhance specific dishes. For that reason I have scattered sauce recipes throughout the book, placing them, where I felt it appropriate, next to the dishes to which they most often belong, rather than collecting them all in one place. For quick reference, look in the index under Sauces.

Stocks and Broths

LES COURTS BOUILLONS, LES BLANCS, ET LES FONDS

Stocks or broths account in large measure for the full-bodied flavor of many French sauces. They are so fundamental to the economy of French cooking that the generic term *fonds*, which designates a full-bodied broth, or "treasury of tastes," can be applied equally to an investment or fund, just as the word *stock* in English is both a culinary and a banking term. To a household cook a few containers of good stock deposited in the freezer are like money in the bank. Making a proper stock takes hours, but that time is an investment in French cooking that is never lost; you get the investment back with interest when you use the stock.

In our busy lives we cannot easily add a day of stock-making to the schedule when planning a gala meal. That is why I believe it is important to use a free day once or twice a year to make and freeze a good amount of stock, just as I take a day or two in high summer to preserve the best summer tomatoes, make tomato sauce, and freeze fresh basil. The investment, as I have said, pays off with interest on a bleak day in winter.

A WORD ABOUT COURTS BOUILLONS

The culinary term *court bouillon* means an aromatic liquid consisting principally of water, wine, or both, or beer, milk, fruit juice, or an already prepared stock, in which meat, fish, fowl, or vegetables are soaked, poached, seethed, simmered, boiled, or blanched. The flavoring depends upon what is to be marinated or cooked in it. The flavorings or aromatics are chosen to enhance the taste of the meat, fish, fowl, or vegetable, balance its flavor, lighten it, or impose upon it a calculated bouquet. Often, a court bouillon is used as a marinade to leach out or tame a wild or strong taste, in which case it is usually discarded. Courts bouillons known as *blancs* often contain acidic elements such as lemon juice, vinegar, or verjuice—the juice of green grapes—to prevent delicate vegetables from darkening as they cook. Such *blancs* are also useful in helping poached vegetables retain their bright, fresh color.

In the practical world of French household cooking, the most important role of courts bouillons is to furnish the *fonds* or "treasury of tastes" for soups or sauces. If courts bouillons are not used at once, they are strained and carefully kept in the refrigerator for a sauce or soup for the following day.

I am including four recipes for basic stocks here. Three of them are "quick method" recipes that do not take much time. The fourth is a recipe for simple brown stock that takes six hours. However, it makes three quarts of good, stout, brown stock. Freeze it in small containers and it will last a long time.

Rapid Method Clear Veal Stock

LE FONDS BLANC

MAKES ABOUT 1½ CUPS

1 pound veal shank
1 pound lean ground veal
3 large sprigs fresh parsley
1 large carrot, scraped and cut into several pieces

1 medium-sized onion, unpeeled and studded with 1 clove
2½ cups water

1. Heat the oven to 325°.
2. Put all the ingredients in a heavy kettle with a cover, put the covered kettle in the oven, and allow mixture to cook for 1¾ hours.
3. Strain the broth through a sieve lined with 2 thicknesses of dampened cheesecloth.
4. Place the stock in a porcelain or glass container, cover with cheesecloth or foil pierced in several places, and chill.
5. Remove every vestige of fat that has surfaced and solidified.

NOTE: The stock is now ready to use. It will be pale yellow and rather insipid until you add salt and whatever flavoring you deem appropriate. If you do not plan to use the stock at once, place it in a sealed container and freeze it. Veal stock is unusually subject to spoilage, so if you plan to keep it in the refrigerator more than 24 hours, make certain that you bring it to a boil every 24 hours to prevent its souring. I do not counsel refrigerating veal stock for many days, even if you keep boiling it each day; it is a very delicate stock which, like sweet butter and heavy cream, will pick up the taste of any food you may have stored in the refrigerator.

This lovely, light *fonds blanc* is excellent for delicately flavored soups and sauces.

Rapid Method Vegetable Stock
LE FONDS DE LEGUMES
MAKES 4 CUPS

This is the basic soup stock that so many cooks in France habitually make each day so that it can be quickly converted into le potage du soir, *what Lewis Carroll might have had in mind when he had his characters sing ". . . beautiful soup of the evening." Beautiful it is!*

2 tablespoons sweet butter
2 medium-sized carrots, scraped, trimmed, and cut into 1-inch pieces
1 large leek, white part only, cut lengthwise, well washed, and finely sliced
1 medium-sized onion, peeled, trimmed, and coarsely chopped

2 ribs celery, well scrubbed and finely sliced
1 plump clove garlic, peeled and halved
1 bouquet garni consisting of 3 sprigs fresh parsley, 1 sprig thyme, and 1 bay leaf, tied together with cotton string
1 quart water

1. Heat a 2- to 3-quart saucepan and melt the butter gently.
2. Sauté all the vegetables, stirring them well to coat them with the melted butter, for 7 to 10 minutes, or until they begin to wilt and become transparent.
3. Add the bouquet garni and the water and simmer for 30 to 40 minutes, skimming off the froth from time to time.
4. Strain the broth. It is now ready to use.

NOTE: If this broth is to be the dinner soup, add 2 medium-sized potatoes, peeled and cut into small pieces. Instead of discarding the vegetables, run them through a food mill and use them as a thickener for the soup. Adjust the seasoning with salt and pepper. Shredded cabbage and a turnip or two, peeled and cut up in small pieces, are often added with the potatoes. It makes a delicious first course at dinner.

Clear Fish Stock

LE FUMET BLANC DE POISSON

MAKES ABOUT 7 CUPS

This makes a very delicate fish broth that is excellent as a base for light soups and sauces to accompany or bind fish dishes. Remember that the stock must be salted and flavored to suit the dish in which you use it.

2 medium carrots, scraped, trimmed, and thinly sliced

1 rib celery, well scrubbed and cut into 3-inch pieces

1 large onion, peeled, trimmed, and coarsely chopped

1 bouquet garni consisting of 1 small bay leaf, 3 sprigs fresh parsley, 1 sprig thyme, and 3 black peppercorns, tied up in cheesecloth

5 pounds of bones, tails, heads (with gills removed), and trimmings of nonfatty fish such as flounder, sole, sea perch, monkfish, or the like

2 cups dry white wine

1 teaspoon freshly squeezed lemon juice

½ teaspoon fennel seed

5 cups water

1. Arrange the sliced carrots, celery, onion, and the bouquet garni over the bottom of a large kettle.
2. Arrange the fish bones and trimmings over the vegetables.
3. Add the wine, lemon juice, fennel seed, and water.
4. Bring the liquid to a boil, reduce to a simmer, and allow to cook for 40 minutes, skimming off the froth as it rises.
5. Remove the kettle from the fire and allow the broth to cool.
6. Strain the broth through a very fine sieve, discarding all the solids.
7. Use the *fumet* at once or pour it into small containers, seal, and freeze for future use.

Simple Brown Stock
LE FONDS BRUN DE VEAU
MAKES ABOUT 3 QUARTS

This is a very fine basic brown stock. Use it in any of the recipes that call for broth or water. It can also be used for full-bodied, clear soups. Half a cup of it will strengthen and extend pan juices. The stock lacks a distinctive taste because it contains no salt, but the taste will become distinct and rich as soon as salt is added. You may also use this stock as an excellent brown sauce or meat glaze by reducing it to 1/3 its volume. If you make such a reduction, don't salt it until after you have reduced it.

2 pounds veal bones, cut or broken into small pieces (ask your butcher to do this for you)

3 pounds stewing veal

1 calf's foot, sawed in two lengthwise, then cut into 2- to 3-inch pieces (the butcher should do this for you, as well)

3 tablespoons vegetable oil

1 quart degreased, unsalted chicken or veal stock (you may elect to use tinned broth, but choose an unsalted one)

3 medium-sized carrots, scraped, trimmed, and cut in thin roundels

1 bouquet garni made up of two 6-inch pieces of celery, 2 sprigs fresh parsley, 1 sprig thyme, and 1 bay leaf, tied up with cotton string

3 medium-sized onions, unpeeled, spiked with 3 cloves

3 quarts cold water

1 jigger dry sherry or Madeira (optional)

1. Heat the oven to 350°.
2. Brush the bones and meat with oil.
3. Place the bones and meat in a shallow pan and allow them to brown well in the oven, turning them from time to time.
4. Pour half the chicken or veal stock over the bones and let it reduce to a syrupy consistency.
5. Pour in the other half of the stock and repeat the reduction. Then remove the pan from the oven and turn off the heat.
6. Choose a large 4- to 5-quart kettle with a lid and cover the bottom with the carrot roundels. Place the bouquet garni and the onions in the center and surround them with the bones. Put the meat nearest the top.

7. Pour some of the water into the roasting pan and stir it with a wooden spatula, dislodging any bits that have stuck to the bottom of the pan. Empty the contents of the roasting pan into the kettle, add the rest of the water, cover the pot, and allow to braise for 5 to 6 hours at the very lowest heat. During the first hour skim off the froth that rises.

8. When braising is finished, remove and discard the bones, the bouquet garni, and the onions.

9. Strain the stock through a sieve lined with several thicknesses of cheesecloth that has been rinsed in cold water and wrung out.

10. Add the wine and allow the stock to cool uncovered. Then chill it and carefully remove all the fat that has risen to the surface.

11. The stock will jelly when chilled. Heat it again to liquefy it, then pour it into small containers, seal, and freeze for future use.

Natural Gravy
LE JUS

The simplest, often the very best sauce for a chop, steak, roast, or fowl is the juice those meats produce while they are cooking. These valuable, nutritious juices pack a wallop to the taste buds, and when reduced to a thick, syrupy concentrate they are hard to beat as a simple accompaniment for the meat that produced them. They are also highly prized for flavoring boiled rice or pasta.

1. Remove the juices from the tray or pan in which the meat or poultry was cooked. If any of the juices have browned and stuck to the bottom of the pan, just add a little water, put the pan over a gentle fire, and scrape back and forth over the bottom with a wooden spatula until all the adhered juice has dissolved in the liquid. This is a basic technique in French cooking known as *déglaçage*, literally "deglazing."

2. Add ½ wineglass of liquid for each person. The liquid may be dry white or red wine, a mixture of water and wine, or stock.

3. Reduce the liquid to ⅓ its volume by boiling it down. This basic technique in French cooking is referred to as *réduction*. It not only thickens the juices, it also concentrates their taste. For that reason juices should not be salted or highly flavored until after they are reduced.

4. Remove and discard any fat that rises to the surface. Use a spoon for most of it, then finish the job with a folded piece of paper towel. This is another essential technique in French cooking, called *dégraissage*. The most efficient way of removing the fat from a broth or sauce is by chilling it overnight in the refrigerator. The fat then forms a solid layer on top that can be removed in one piece, and the surface of the jellied juice underneath can then be completely cleaned with a piece of paper towel. If there isn't time to leave the broth overnight, you can do your *dégraissage* by skimming and blotting.

5. Adjust the seasoning with salt and pepper and whatever other aromatics or herbs you choose and serve the sauce in a warm sauceboat.

NOTE: You can experiment and improvise on this basic *jus de viande* with various appropriate additions as long as you keep them subtle and don't overpower the wonderful, natural taste of the juices. A mirepoix—a slowly browned mass of coarsely chopped vegetables—is a standard addition that adds a hearty bouquet to this natural gravy. (The recipe for mirepoix follows.) Other excellent additions are a tablespoonful of Cognac, Madeira, or dry sherry. If the juice is from lamb, add a handful of bruised fresh mint leaves, skimming them out of the sauce just before you serve it up.

La Mirepoix
THE NATURAL FRENCH FLAVORING AND COLORING AGENT

There is a jingle from the Ariége region near the Spanish border that runs:

> *Quel que soit l'âge,*
> *Pas de joie*
> *Dans le potage*
> *Sans mirepoix.*

It means: At whatever age, the soup won't be a joy without mirepoix.

Mirepoix is a dandy little sauté of chopped vegetables and ham or bacon, slowly browned until it is almost a purée. The recipe is thought to have originated in the area around Foix in the Pyrenees, but its use is now widespread in French household cooking. In some kitchens it is called a brunoise. *It adds a hearty flavor and a beautiful brown color to soups and sauces, and raises the status of a simple brown gravy to something special.*

1 tablespoon sweet butter
⅓ cup chopped ham or bacon
2 medium-sized carrots, scraped, trimmed, and coarsely chopped
1 small onion, peeled, trimmed, and finely chopped
1 medium-sized white turnip, peeled and finely chopped

1 rib celery, scubbed and finely chopped
1 teaspoon granulated sugar
1 sprig thyme
1 bay leaf
⅛ teaspoon freshly ground black pepper
½ teaspoon coarse salt

1. Heat a sautéing or frying pan and gently melt the butter.
2. Sauté the bacon or ham until it is almost transparent.
3. Add the chopped vegetables and stir them about, coating them with the hot fat.
4. Add the sugar, thyme, bay leaf, pepper, and salt and stir well. Cover and cook very gently for 45 minutes.
5. Discard the thyme and bay leaf. The mirepoix is now ready to add to your soup or sauce.

Cooking Techniques for Thickening Sauces

LES LIAISONS

The French household cook uses several standard techniques for thickening sauces other than simply reducing them. The most commonly used liaison is *le roux*, literally "reddish-brown," which consists of a small amount of flour fried, or simply whisked, in fat. The fat, depending upon the region and usage, may be butter, oil, or, in the case of Creole or Cajun cooking, pork lard or dripping. The flour may be simply beaten with the fat to prevent it from forming lumps, or it may be fried until it turns a pale ivory color, hazelnut, cinnamon, or a deep, chocolate brown for Creole and Cajun sauces. Continental French household cooking rarely browns a roux past the "hazelnut" stage because both butter and oil would burn in the process. The only fat that will not burn long before the roux becomes a deep chocolate brown is pork lard or pork dripping. Since we are primarily concerned here with French household cooking, I have not included any recipes that require dark roux.

Le Roux

MAKES ABOUT 1 CUP

In the United States sauces are often thickened by mixing a little flour or cornstarch with cold water and adding the paste to the boiling sauce. The one exception I can think of in regional American cooking is the making of cream gravy. When my mother used to make it in Texas, she always used, though she never called it that, the roux technique, as did every cream gravy maker I knew as a child. Authentic French roux is produced by frying the flour in the hot fat and adding stock, milk, wine, or water, depending upon the dish that is being prepared.

1½ tablespoons sweet butter 1 cup liquid
  1 tablespoon flour Salt and pepper to taste

1. Heat a saucepan and gently melt the butter.
2. Add the flour and stir it well into the hot butter, using a wooden spatula.
3. For a white sauce, fry the flour for about 30 seconds; for a brown sauce, fry it until it is darker, stirring it constantly to prevent it from scorching.
4. Add the liquid, stirring vigorously or whisking it to prevent lumps from forming. Continue to cook the sauce for 5 to 7 minutes, stirring it to prevent sticking. Season as appropriate.

N O T E : Mixing the flour with the fat prevents the flour from making lumps. Be sure you taste the finished sauce to make sure it doesn't taste of raw flour. If you can still taste the flour, simply return it to the pan and let it cook a few minutes more. The flour taste will disappear.

Béchamel Sauce

MAKES ABOUT 2 CUPS

This is a basic white sauce that can be used for fish, meat, fowl, or vegetables. If you have it, use stock that is appropriate to the finished dish. A fish fumet is more suitable for making a fish dish, and veal stock is better for a meat dish, than plain water. If you haven't an appropriate stock, I suggest you use another cup of milk rather than water.

1 stick (8 tablespoons) sweet butter	¼ teaspoon freshly ground white pepper
3 tablespoons flour	½ teaspoon coarse salt
1½ cups whole milk	⅛ teaspoon freshly grated nutmeg
1 cup stock	

1. Heat a heavy-bottomed saucepan and gently melt the butter.
2. Add the flour and stir it well into the melted butter with a wooden spatula. Let the mixture fry gently for 1 minute, stirring it constantly.
3. Meanwhile, heat the milk to the scalding point, then remove it from the fire.
4. Add the milk to the roux of flour and butter, stirring well to prevent lumps from forming.
5. Add the stock and simmer the sauce for 7 to 10 minutes, stirring it from time to time to see that the sauce does not stick to the bottom.
6. Add the pepper, salt, and nutmeg.

N O T E : *Béchamel* can be quickly converted to a *sauce Mornay* by whisking in ½ cup freshly grated Gruyère cheese and thinning the sauce with a little cream. This famous cheese sauce works well over poached fish, poached eggs, or for a gratin of any sort. If you make a gratin, use plenty of the *sauce Mornay* to dress the ingredients in the baking dish. Sprinkle the surface liberally with more grated cheese and breadcrumbs. You will find that the sauce browns beautifully and forms a delicious crust. *Béchamel* may be made ahead of time and refrigerated. If you decide to do this, melt a little butter and cover the surface so that it does not form a skin. Alternatively, you may cut a piece of foil or plastic wrap the size of the surface and float it on the surface. Refrigerated *Béchamel* becomes quite thick. Warm it up before using it.

THICKENING SAUCES WITH EGG YOLKS

Beaten egg yolks are often used in a French kitchen instead of a roux to thicken a sauce. This adds quite a lot of richness to the sauce, so those who must watch their cholesterol intake should beware. Also, it is important to remember that egg yolks must not be heated to the boiling point or they will scramble and sabotage your sauce.

Savory Sabayon Sauce
LA SAUCE SABAYON
MAKES ABOUT 2 CUPS

This is a very, very delicate sauce and yet it is quite tasty. It is splendid over poached fish, chicken breasts, or vegetables.

2 cups boiling stock
3 egg yolks, at room
    temperature, beaten until
    light and lemon-colored with
    1 tablespoon water

½ teaspoon freshly squeezed
    lemon juice
Salt to taste

1. Remove the stock from the fire and let it cease boiling.
2. Whisk a few tablespoons of the hot stock into the egg yolks, and then whisk the yolks into the rest of the stock.
3. Place the whisked yolks and stock in a saucepan.
4. Place the saucepan in a pan of warm water over gentle heat.
5. Continue to whisk the sauce as it heats, never allowing the water in the pan to boil. In about 7 minutes the sauce will have thickened like a custard sauce. Remove it immediately from the fire and whisk in the lemon juice.
6. Season the sauce appropriately and serve it at once in a warm sauce-boat.

N O T E : If you wish to reheat the sauce, do it carefully by once more whisking the sauce over hot water. (Old hands at making sauces with egg yolks often make them without setting the saucepan in water, but they are extremely careful about taking the saucepan off the fire from time to time to make sure the sauce doesn't curdle from too much heat.)

THICKENING SAUCES WITH
HEAVY CREAM

In Normandy, where there are plenty of dairy products, sauces are often thickened with heavy cream. The cream is added and the sauce is allowed to reduce to about one-third by gently cooking it over low heat. When a rich sauce is appropriate, this technique is a good one to know. The principle is very simple: 1 cup of heavy cream at room temperature to ½ cup of stock. Whisk the stock and the cream together and continue whisking as the sauce reduces over a low fire. This may take 7 to 10 minutes, but be vigilant: cream boils up and over the sides of the pan if it is not whisked as it heats, making a terrible mess to clean up. A rich, beautifully textured sauce is the reward for patient whisking during the reduction. Adjust the seasoning as appropriate.

There are many ways of flavoring this Norman favorite. In Normandy it is often flavored with a spoonful of Calvados, the aromatic regional applejack. A dash of Cognac and ½ teaspoon freshly cracked black pepper make a sauce for a Norman-style pepper steak that is both celestial and diabolical! It also combines well with a tablespoon or so of good Dijon mustard, finely chopped parsley, and a little chopped scallion to make a *sauce piquante* for boiled beef or cold poached fish or chicken.

Butter-Based Sauces

Sweet butter is the base for two branches or families of sauces in French household cooking. The first of these is made by incorporating various fresh or dried herbs, aromatics, or other highly flavored ingredients with the fresh butter. These flavored butters, called *les beurres composés*, are rolled up and sliced in coin-shaped bits that are plopped down to melt on top of a freshly grilled chop, steak, or fish fillet. The technique is easily learned. I explain it here with anchovy butter, one of the great favorites; then you can try it with various other ingredients, arriving at your own preferences.

• • •

Anchovy Butter
LE BEURRE AUX ANCHOIS
MAKES 8 ROUNDELS

2 to 3 crushed fillets of anchovy
or 1 tablespoon commercial
anchovy paste
1 tablespoon finely chopped
flat-leaf parsley
1 teaspoon freshly squeezed
lemon juice

¼ teaspoon finely grated lemon
peel
¼ teaspoon freshly ground black
pepper
¾ stick (6 tablespoons) sweet
butter, at room temperature

1. Pound the ingredients together in a mortar until they are evenly mixed. A food processor will do it in 3 to 6 pulses.
2. Cool the mixture slightly in the refrigerator.
3. Roll the mixture up like a roll of dimes in a piece of aluminum foil or wax paper and chill until ready to serve.
4. At serving time, unwrap the roll, cut it into ¼-inch-thick roundels, and place one roundel on the top of each hot serving. Serve at once before the butter melts completely.

Browned Butter Sauce
LA SAUCE AU BEURRE NOIR
MAKES ABOUT ½ CUP

This beautifully simple, very appetizing sauce can be mastered in 5 minutes. It is usually served over poached fish, especially raie *or skate, but it turns fried eggs into a dish fit for a king. Because the dark sauce on the fried eggs makes a rather startling contrast, a funny metaphor was born. Now the expression for a black eye in French is* un oeil au beurre noir: *an eye in browned butter sauce! Don't be put off by the metaphor. The combination is mouth-watering.*

¾ stick (6 tablespoons) sweet
butter
1 tablespoon coarsely chopped
flat-leaf parsley

2 tablespoons wine vinegar
½ teaspoon freshly squeezed
lemon juice

1. Heat a frying pan and melt the butter over medium heat until it is amber-colored, but not burnt.
2. With a wooden spatula, stir the butter about, adding the parsley, vinegar, and lemon juice, and remove at once from the fire.
3. Spoon the warm sauce over the portions while the servings are still hot, and serve at once.

Melted Butter and Parsley Sauce
LA SAUCE A LA MEUNIERE

MAKES ABOUT ½ CUP

This is probably the best known and most loved of all the melted butter sauces. To my mind no better sauce has ever been discovered for fried fillet of sole. Try it on lightly floured, quickly sautéed sea scallops; the combination is equally wonderful.

¾ stick (6 tablespoons) sweet
   butter
1 teaspoon freshly squeezed
   lemon juice

⅛ teaspoon freshly ground white
   pepper
¼ teaspoon coarse salt
1 tablespoon finely chopped
   flat-leaf parsley

1. Melt the butter over gentle heat.
2. Strain the butter through a fine sieve, taking care to exclude both the milk solids and the few drops of milk that usually sink to the bottom of the pan.
3. Wipe out the pan with a piece of paper towel and heat the clarified butter a little.
4. Remove from the heat and quickly whisk in the lemon juice, pepper, and salt.
5. Spoon the sauce over the freshly fried fish while it is still sizzling. Sprinkle with parsley and serve at once.

• • •

The Other Branch of Butter-Based Sauces

The other branch of butter-based sauces used in French household cooking is the emulsions, in which butter—and sometimes oil—is suspended with flavored liquids and egg yolk by whipping them together. The technique produces a rich sauce that can be served as a soft, velvety solid that quickly melts and coats warm foods. We are more familiar with mayonnaise, made of oil and egg yolk, than with the butter emulsions, but the latter, such as béarnaise and hollandaise, are among the great accomplishments of French sauce making.

Béarnaise Sauce

LA SAUCE A LA BEARNAISE

MAKES A LITTLE OVER 1 CUP

A perfect béarnaise sauce is an achievement. It is not difficult, but it requires great attention to detail when making the emulsion. The sauce is generally served with a thick grilled chop or steak. It is a perfect sauce for boiled vegetables served up steaming hot.

1 large shallot, peeled, trimmed, and sliced paper-thin
1 tablespoon coarsely chopped tarragon leaves or ½ teaspoon dried tarragon leaves, crumbled
1 tablespoon fresh chervil leaves, coarsely chopped
1 sprig thyme
1 small bay leaf
¼ teaspoon coarse salt
¼ teaspoon freshly cracked black pepper

¼ cup dry white wine
¼ cup vinegar
3 large egg yolks
1 tablespoon water
1 stick (8 tablespoons) sweet butter, at room temperature, cut into pat-size pieces
½ teaspoon freshly squeezed lemon juice
$^{1}/_{16}$ teaspoon ground cayenne pepper

1. Put the shallot, tarragon, chervil, thyme, bay leaf, salt, cracked pepper, wine, and vinegar in a saucepan and boil over gentle heat until mixture is reduced to about 2 tablespoons of liquid.

2. Strain the concentrate into a small saucepan and place the saucepan in another pan of hot water over the lowest heat.
3. Beat the egg yolks with the 1 tablespoon water until they are light and lemon-colored.
4. Stir the beaten yolks and water into the warmed concentrate with a wooden spoon, always stirring in the same direction.
5. Add the bits of butter, stirring them in a few at a time and making certain that each lump of butter is incorporated before adding others. Be sure the water in the lower saucepan never boils.
6. When the sauce has absorbed all the butter, remove from the fire and stir in the lemon juice and cayenne.
7. Pour the sauce into a warm sauceboat and serve at once.

N O T E : Should the sauce curdle and separate while you are adding the butter, don't be alarmed; it is reparable. The standard rescue is simple: Quickly chill a bowl in the freezer (a stainless steel mixing bowl is excellent for this). When the bowl is cold, add a little lemon juice and slowly stir in the curdled sauce. The sauce should reemulsify. Béarnaise sauce should be served warm, but don't heat it up over the fire. Simply put the sauce container in a bowl or pan of very hot—not boiling!—water and let it warm gently.

Hollandaise Sauce
LA SAUCE A LA HOLLANDAISE
MAKES ABOUT 1 CUP

A well-made hollandaise sauce, though it contains several egg yolks and much butter, should appear as light as a buttercup. It is a perfect sauce for poached fish, steamed vegetables and poached eggs. Despite its light, silken appearance and its delicate flavor, hollandaise sauce is not recommended for those who must watch their cholesterol count.

Because the sauce is such a delicate emulsion and curdles easily, even some experienced cooks resist making it. Don't let that prevent you from trying it. If you follow the steps carefully, you should be able to turn out an exemplary hollandaise on the first try. Just don't get in a hurry; never allow the water in the bain-marie *to simmer; and rest assured that the proper consistency for this sauce is gossamer-soft, somewhat runny and not stiff and immobile like a well-stabilized mayonnaise.*

1½ sticks sweet butter cut into
    pat-sized pieces
¼ cup good white wine vinegar
¼ teaspoon salt
¼ teaspoon finely ground white
    pepper

3 large egg yolks at room
    temperature (Save the
    whites for another purpose.)
1 tablespoon water
1 tablespoon freshly squeezed
    lemon juice
⅛ teaspoon finely ground
    cayenne pepper

1. Melt the butter gently and put it aside to cool. It works best for this recipe when tepid.
2. Mix the vinegar, salt and white pepper in a Pyrex or enamelware pan and reduce the liquid over high heat to about 2 tablespoons.
3. Let the reduction and the pan cool to just warm.
4. Improvise a *bain-marie* by heating ½-inch water in a heavy skillet.
5. Whisk the egg yolks, water and reduction together lightly in the same pan in which you did the reduction. Don't overwhisk at this point.
6. Making certain that the water never simmers, put the pan in the water and begin to whisk the egg mixture. Continue whisking until the eggs take on a whitish appearance and begin to thicken like heavy cream.
7. Remove the pan from the water at once and begin to whisk in the melted butter, a drop at a time. Take your time.
8. When the sauce has accepted all the butter, whisk in the lemon juice and the cayenne pepper.
9. Whisk in a few drops of tepid water to stabilize the emulsion.
10. If the sauce seems too thin, return the pan to the hot water, but take care to remove it from time to time as you whisk, until you think the consistency is right. Should it become a little too thick, add a few drops of water and whisk it to the proper consistency.
11. Heat a fine-meshed sieve by pouring hot water through it, dry it, then pass the sauce through the warmed sieve.
12. Serve up the sauce in a warm, dry sauceboat. It should be served while warm.

Les Hors D'oeuvre

The term *hors d'oeuvre* has an interesting history. It is invariable, whether used in the singular or plural, and it began as an architectural term at the end of the sixteenth century, when it meant a small room detached from the main building. Gradually it came to mean food that was served to guests as an appetizer before they went in to dine. That food has nothing in common with the hot and cold dishes wheeled about in carts in some restaurants in the States, hot and cold dishes that are often so sumptuous and heavy, I might add, that they seem destined to kill the appetite before the main course arrives. At present hors d'oeuvre are served in a French household as the first course of a meal. They are always light and meant to serve as "openers" for the appetite.

Most French householders keep their liquor cabinets well stocked, but they rarely drink before meals unless there are guests or the occasion is festive and seems to call for it. In those instances you will be invited to have a drink, and out will come a few tiny crackers, some olives, and a small plate of nuts. Of all the nibble food offered with drinks in a French household, my favorite is a handful of those blanched, roasted almonds that the provident household cook prepares and keeps hidden away for special occasions. They are neither salty nor oily.

Blanched, Roasted Almonds
LES AMANDES GRILLEES

These roasted almonds are a handy staple. I use them to enhance cakes and cookies. Set out a plate of them with drinks. They are the perfect accompaniment to a glass of good sherry.

1 pound shelled raw almonds	2 tablespoons freshly squeezed
4 cups hot water	lemon juice
4 cups cold water	

1. Place the almonds in a colander and wash them under cold running water. Discard any discolored or broken ones.
2. Put the washed almonds in a heavy pan. Cover them with 4 cups hot water and boil them for 5 minutes until the skins begin to loosen.
3. Drain the almonds and rinse them again under cold running water.
4. Remove each almond from its skin by pressing it gently between the thumb and forefinger and catching it with the other hand when it pops out. Drop each skinned almond into a glass or ceramic bowl containing 4 cups cold water and the lemon juice.
5. When you have finished husking all the almonds, discard the husks and dry the almonds well with paper towels.
6. Preheat the oven to 225°.
7. Line a cookie sheet with aluminum foil and spread the almonds over it in one layer. Roast almonds until they turn a pale ivory color. Then remove them immediately from the oven and allow them to cool completely.
8. Store the almonds in a sealed tin or jar and keep them in the refrigerator. They will stay fresh for months, but once your family has tasted them they are likely to disappear very quickly.

A WORD ABOUT FRENCH SALADS

The French are famous for their salads. They know how to make many kinds from both raw and cooked ingredients, and those salads range from the ubiquitous all-time favorite, the plain green salad in its simple vinaigrette sauce, to the more complicated mixed salads that they refer to as *salades composées.* The French believe that a few leaves of salad greens dressed with vinaigrette are a decided aid to the digestion. For that reason they prefer serving green salad after the main course rather than before it, though they usually do not object to serving more substantial salads as a first course. In fact, in summer a large mixed salad may be served as the principal course for lunch.

French food-shoppers are usually very fastidious about salad greens. They insist that salad greens be crisp and fresh enough to break, and they prefer that the greens have an almost aggressively fresh aroma. Though the shopkeepers often protest, I have never known a French shopper who could be dissuaded from forcing apart the outer leaves of a head of lettuce to get a good look at the inner leaves to make sure there was no hidden rust. Every French household cook knows that it is a point of honor to serve only first-rate, fresh, crisp, well-washed, well-cleaned, and well-dried salad greens. They also know that most metal knives will cause the delicate greens to oxidize and turn brown, so they prefer preparing the greens with their hands, tearing them apart rather than using even a stainless steel knife on them.

To prepare salad greens, the French will discard any tough, bruised, or discolored leaves. The others are washed free of dirt, grit, and foreign matter under cold running water and immediately set to soak for 5 minutes in lightly salted cold water. This not only crisps the greens, it dislodges any insects or slugs that may be hiding in the leaves. The greens are then washed once more under cold running water and carefully dried on kitchen towels or in a centrifugal extractor. In the old days, the greens were put in a wire basket called a *saladière.* This basket was taken out into the yard and swung about until the water was entirely extracted. Any children, animals, or fowl who happened to be near the kitchen door when the cook came out to swing the *saladière* would run for cover to escape being showered. The cook would swing the basket until every drop of water had been flung off the leaves. It is still a strict rule in French households that salad greens must never be presented wet at table. It prevents the sauce from adhering to the leaves.

The usual dressing for green salad in France is a simple vinaigrette, and it is usually made right in the salad bowl and left there with the well-washed, well-dried leaves piled on top until the moment comes to toss and serve the salad. Tossing the greens ahead of time causes them to wilt and go limp. Very often one of the guests will be asked to toss the salad right at the table, especially if the guest is unmarried. The point is to toss the salad without allowing any of the leaves to fall on the tablecloth. It is said that the number of leaves dropped on the tablecloth corresponds to the number of years that must pass before the salad-tosser marries. It is a charming French custom, but I suspect its origin lies primarily in the practical concern for not staining the table linen.

Classic French Salad Dressing
LA SAUCE VINAIGRETTE

MAKES ½ CUP

French cooks are fond of repeating this old saw: To make the perfect vinaigrette one must assume the guise of a miser when measuring the salt, a banker when measuring the vinegar and mustard, and a spendthrift when adding the oil.

1 plump clove garlic, peeled, trimmed, and crushed to a paste with
   ½ tablespoon coarse salt
2 tablespoons wine vinegar
⅛ teaspoon granulated sugar (optional)

1 teaspoon Dijon mustard
6 to 8 tablespoons light olive oil at room temperature
⅛ teaspoon freshly ground white pepper

1. Place the garlic and salt paste, vinegar, sugar, and mustard in a glass bowl or in the salad bowl itself. (For those who may look askance at the mention of sugar in a vinaigrette, let me assure them that the sugar does not sweeten the venerable vinaigrette, it only takes the harsh edge off the vinegar.) Stir the ingredients together.
2. Add the oil, a few drops at a time, whisking it into the mixture until you arrive at a nacreous emulsion. This emulsion has little stability and will divide easily, but it will reemulsify when the salad is tossed.
3. Stir in the pepper and check and adjust for salt.
4. Toss the greens well in the sauce and serve at once.

N O T E : Modifications are up to the individual, and vary according to regions. In the Paris area some householders leave the garlic out altogether. Some simply rub the salad bowl with garlic but do not include it in the sauce. In the Midi you are likely to encounter even more garlic in the sauce as well as a sprinkling of thyme leaves. The Nice area often adds a crushed anchovy fillet, some capers, and occasionally the yolk of a hard-boiled egg mixed to a paste with the vinegar. Finely chopped herbs are often added, parsley and tarragon being the commonest. In sum, vinaigrette is so highly adaptable that it is a fairly accurate indicator of the tastes and even the regional origins of those who prepare it. Substitute freshly squeezed lemon juice for the vinegar as a welcome change for certain greens and vegetables. Try it on steamed asparagus, boiled artichokes, or steamed broccoli.

Basic French Green Salad
LA SALADE VERTE A LA FRANÇAISE

SERVES 4 TO 5

This is the salad of salads. Time and again my American friends have asked me to entrust to them the secret that makes it so good. There is no secret. The knack is to have completely fresh, first-rate greens and excellent vinegar and oil for the vinaigrette. You must also resist the American compulsion to gild the lily. Keep it simple! After you make this salad you'll never go back to fancy, bottled dressings.

2 small heads very fresh Boston
   or Bibb lettuce
1 tablespoon coarse salt

1 small clove garlic, cut in half
¼ cup *Sauce vinaigrette*
   (page 38)

1. Pull off and discard tough and discolored or damaged leaves. Pull the other leaves apart, inspecting them carefully for dirt, grit, bugs, or slugs, and wash leaves well under cold running water. Remove and discard the dark, woody part of the stem with a stainless steel knife. Remove the core and either slice it up and put it in the salad or discard it.
2. Put the greens to soak in very cold water for 5 minutes, sprinkling the salt over them.

3. Rinse the greens again in cold running water, drain them well, and either pat them dry with paper towels or put them in a salad extractor and give them 10 turns.
4. Rub the inside of the salad bowl with the garlic halves and discard them.
5. Pour the vinaigrette into the bowl and pile the clean, dried leaves on top.
6. When you are ready to serve the salad, toss the greens in the vinaigrette. Make sure that all the leaves are completely coated with the sauce. Serve at once.

N O T E : You can vary the greens if you like. Today in the United States we have an embarrassment of riches in greens. French friends who come to visit me are astounded at the variety of greens in our supermarkets that they never see in their markets, where radicchio and arugula and many other greens we now use daily are just not known by most householders. All these new greens are fine in a mixed green salad. Another variation the French enjoy is green salad with walnut halves. Just poach the walnuts for 7 minutes in boiling salted water, rinse and scrub them in cold running water, dry them, and deposit them in the vinaigrette at the bottom of the salad bowl. Make sure they get distributed throughout the salad when it is tossed and served.

Onion Tart with Black Olives and Anchovies
LA PISSALADIERA
SERVES 8 TO 10

This pizza-like tart, called variously pissaladiera, pissaladière *or* pissaladina, *is sold all along the Côte, but the best by popular agreement is one sold in the open-air market in the old quarter of Nice. Shoppers stop to buy it to present as a first course at home and pause a moment to have a slice themselves between their errands. I enjoy preparing it at home, where I can make a somewhat fancier version for my family and friends.*

FOR THE PASTRY:

1½ cups all-purpose flour
1 package dry yeast
1 teaspoon coarse salt

1 cup warm water
1 tablespoon light olive oil

FOR THE FILLING:

4 or 5 medium-sized yellow
onions, peeled, trimmed,
and thinly sliced
3 tablespoons light olive oil
1 bay leaf
½ teaspoon dried thyme leaves

1 teaspoon coarse salt
12 to 15 flat fillets of anchovy,
drained (save the oil)
½ cup water
12 to 15 black niçois olives or
black oil-cured olives

Make the pastry:

1. Place the flour in a mound on a hard, clean working surface.
2. Dissolve the yeast and salt in the warm water and set aside for 5 minutes.
3. Make a little crater in the mound of flour, pour the yeast mixture and oil into it and, using your fingertips, combine the ingredients and knead the mass into a smooth, elastic dough, working it hard with the heel of your hand. If the dough is too wet, add flour, or if it is too dry, add water. Work the mass for a good 5 to 7 minutes to develop the gluten so the dough will stretch without tearing.
4. Roll the dough into a ball, oil it lightly, and place it in a bowl. Cover the bowl and leave it in a warm place for 1 hour.

Make the filling:

1. Place the onions, oil, bay leaf, thyme, salt, and the oil from the anchovies in a heavy kettle. Toss the onions until they are completely coated with the oil.
2. Cover the kettle and sauté the onions at low heat until they are tender and transparent. Stir them occasionally to make sure they do not stick to the bottom and scorch.
3. Add the water, stir the onions about, and continue sautéing the onions until they are almost a paste.

Assemble the pissaladiera:

1. Preheat the oven to 400°.
2. Lightly oil a cookie sheet or 11×17-inch jelly roll pan.
3. Roll out the dough very thin, making it somewhat larger than the cookie sheet or pan. Line the sheet or pan with the dough and roll

the edge toward the center all around to form a little ridge to enclose the filling.

4. Discard the bay leaf and spread the onion filling over the dough, right up to the ridges.
5. Distribute the anchovies and olives over the surface either haphazardly or in formal designs. Place them close enough together that each portion will get an anchovy and an olive.
6. Bake for about 20 minutes or until the crust is nicely browned.
7. Cut the *pissaladiera* into rectangular slices and serve it warm or cold.

N O T E : If you prefer, you may make what the French call a *pâte brisée* or plain, short pie crust instead of the raised crust. However, I advise you to knead it about 5 minutes to make it a little tough. My dear, departed mother would scream at the idea of kneading a pie crust, but in this particular case it needs to be a little tough or the juice from the onions will cause the crust to go soggy. If you decide to use the short crust, you may want to use the trimmings cut in fancy shapes to decorate the surface over the anchovies and olives. It makes this wonderfully ordinary first course a festive one, but you certainly don't need to do it. The version sold in the old quarter in Nice is pretty rough—something like a Neapolitan pizza—and that is its charm.

La Salade niçoise

SERVES 4 TO 6

Salade niçoise, *like so many other delicious French dishes that have caught on in the States, is listed on menus everywhere, and, unfortunately, most of what is served here for this genial regional dish resembles the original in name only. A proper* salade niçoise *should be made in summer when garden-fresh lettuce, scallions, sweet basil, fresh artichokes, and sun-ripened tomatoes abound. Otherwise it is a travesty of the delightful salad as it is made and served all along the Côte from June to October.*

6 to 8 fingers of French bread,
toasted and rubbed with
1 plump clove garlic,
halved

½ cup *Sauce vinaigrette*
(page 38)

6 fillets of tinned anchovies
(reserve the oil for the
vinaigrette)

1 small tin tuna, coarsely
chunked

2 small, fresh scallions, white
part only, trimmed and
finely julienned

3 or 4 red, ripe tomatoes, hard
flesh surrounding the stem
cut away and discarded, cut
in quarters

10 to 12 black niçois olives or
black oil-cured olives

2 hard-boiled eggs, quartered

2 fresh artichokes, stems, leaves,
and chokes removed and
discarded, the hearts sliced
with a stainless steel knife
and carefully rubbed with
½ fresh lemon

2 small heads very fresh Boston
or Bibb lettuce, thoroughly
washed, cleaned, and dried

1 small head romaine lettuce,
the tough outer leaves
removed and discarded, the
pale inner leaves and core
thoroughly washed, dried,
and broken into bite-size
pieces

8 to 10 tender basil leaves,
washed and dried

1. Rub a large salad bowl with the garlic left over from rubbing the toast
   fingers and put the vinaigrette sauce in the bottom. Discard the garlic.
2. Place the anchovy fillets, their remaining oil, the tuna, scallions,
   tomatoes, olives, hard-boiled eggs, and artichoke hearts in the sauce,
   then the toast fingers, with the greens piled on top.
3. Toss the salad lightly but well just before serving, making sure not to
   crush all the ingredients together.

A WORD ABOUT PAN BAGNAT

Pan bagnat, literally "soaked bread," is a sandwich version of *salade niçoise*
that is sold everywhere along the coast from Marseilles to Nice as a quick
snack. It makes a lovely light lunch in summer. Use very fresh kaiser rolls
for individual sandwiches or a large cottage loaf for a *pan bagnat* that will
serve 4 or 5. Cut the rolls or loaf in two lengthwise and remove a little
of the soft white interior to make a space for the stuffing. Dissolve 1
teaspoon of coarse salt in a cup of cold water and sprinkle the soft interior
of both halves of the rolls or loaf. Sprinkle the interior of the halves with
a little vinegar and some very good olive oil. Layer in tomato slices,

lettuce, a little sliced onion if you like it, shredded tuna, and a fillet or two of anchovy. You may add what you like. Some people like to put in some sliced radishes and some pitted black olives. Put the bread halves together and press them firmly together. Place a plate or breadboard on top with a weight of some sort to press the *pan bagnat* together for 5 or 10 minutes. It is then ready to eat. I was told by a friend who was born and brought up in Nice that this niçois specialty was often prepared by her mother for late afternoon excursions to the beach to be eaten as a picnic supper after swimming. If you make a large one from a cottage loaf, just cut it in individual wedges like a pie when the moment comes to serve it. When I make this for children, they always like it, and they request it again and again.

Bell Peppers Catalan Style
LES POIVRONS ECORCHES
A LA CATALANE

SERVES 4 OR 5

The French and Spanish Catalans love to fire-skin bell peppers and marinate them with various things. They may then be served as a first course or as an accompaniment for grilled meats or fish. I can remember spending hours fire-skinning peppers, tomatoes, and onions over a charcoal stove that had to be constantly fanned to keep the fire hot enough to blacken the peppers sufficiently. Even the Catalans don't have to do that anymore. They blacken the vegetables over a gas burner now, and it goes very quickly. A word of caution, however: Charring peppers causes lots of smoke, so turn on your air vents and open the windows or you might set off the smoke alarm. My Italian friends have suggested that baking the peppers in a hot oven is a good solution, but somehow the peppers never have the wonderful grilled taste that is proper to the Catalan style when they are simply baked. Another reason for preparing the peppers this way is that it does away with the skin, which, I'm told, is the culprit in "return ticket" syndrome. I cannot eat raw bell pepper without getting indigestion, but I have never experienced any discomfort after eating peppers prepared in this way.

If you have any of these peppers left over, try making a sandwich of them on crispy, well-buttered French bread. It's an unbelievably exquisite combination!

4 large, meaty bell peppers (mix red and green ones for a pretty effect)
½ teaspoon coarse salt
3 tablespoons freshly squeezed lemon juice
4 to 8 flat fillets of anchovy (save the oil)

3 tablespoons light olive oil
1 plump clove garlic, peeled, trimmed, and finely sliced lengthwise
12 to 15 capers
¼ teaspoon dried thyme leaves

1. With a long fork, hold each pepper over the gas flame until the pepper is charred on all sides and completely black. (In an electric oven, broil the peppers, turning them often, until they are charred all over.)
2. Place the charred peppers in a brown paper bag, roll it shut, and allow the peppers to cool.
3. Remove the peppers from the bag and put them in a colander under cold running water. Using your fingers, slip the charred skins off, bit by bit. They should come off easily. Use a stainless steel knife to scrape off any stubborn bits. Pare out and discard the core, seeds, and inner ribs.
4. Cut the peppers in ½-inch strips and blot them dry with paper towels.
5. Mix the salt, lemon juice, oil from the anchovies, and the olive oil to a light emulsion.
6. Put the peppers, layered with the garlic, into a glass dish and bathe them in the sauce. Sprinkle in the capers and thyme leaves and allow the peppers to chill completely in the refrigerator.
7. Serve the peppers cold as a first course or at room temperature as an accompaniment for grilled meats or fish.

N O T E : Traditionally, these Catalan-style peppers are often served along with baked onions in a dish called *escalibat* or *escalivada*. Baked onions are easy to make: wrap medium-sized, unpeeled onions in aluminum foil and bake them in a preheated oven at 400° for 20 to 30 minutes. Let them cool for 10 minutes, drain them, remove and discard their skins (which slip off like a glove), and they are ready to use in whatever way you wish. They may be reheated and served with meat, chilled and served with the Catalan peppers, or as the major ingredient in the Baked Onion Salad on page 59.

• • •

Catalan Fire-Roasted Peppers Stuffed with Rice Salad

LES POIVRONS FARCIS A LA CATALANE

SERVES 4

This dish will charm your guests both by its appearance and its light, appealing taste. Be sure the peppers are quite chilled before they are stuffed. Keeping them overnight in a covered glass or porcelain dish in the refrigerator enhances their taste remarkably. But don't make the mistake of refrigerating the rice salad. It tastes best at room temperature. For the maximum in taste and texture, stuff the chilled peppers with the rice salad at room temperature and serve them soon afterward.

3 tablespoons wine vinegar
1 teaspoon coarse salt
1 small scallion, white part only, trimmed and finely chopped
1½ cups plain boiled rice (see page 125)
1 tablespoon tinned tuna, finely shredded
1 small red ripe tomato, skinned, seeded, and finely chopped

1 tablespoon finely chopped flat-leaf parsley
2 tablespoons mild olive oil
4 large red bell peppers, fire-skinned (see page 44), cored and seeded but kept intact
2 tablespoons freshly squeezed lemon juice
1 hard-boiled egg yolk

1. Mix the vinegar, salt, and scallion.
2. Place the rice in a bowl with the tuna, tomato, and parsley.
3. Add the vinegar mixture and the oil and toss the ingredients together lightly but well.
4. Stuff the pepper pockets loosely with the rice salad.
5. Place each stuffed pepper on its side and spoon a little lemon juice over each.
6. Before serving, garnish each stuffed pepper with a little hard-boiled egg yolk forced through a sieve for what the cooks on the Côte d'Azur call a mimosa effect.

• • •

Tomato Salad with Scallion and Caper Sauce
LA SALADE DE TOMATES CLASSIQUE

SERVES 4

As a student in France I always wondered why this simple tomato salad tasted so incredibly good, so much better than the simple sliced tomatoes we used to eat in the United States. The secret is the tomatoes themselves. They should be sun-ripened and never larger than medium-sized for this salad. The second part of the secret, of course, is the combination of scallion and capers in the sauce.

½ teaspoon coarse salt
½ tablespoon Dijon mustard
2 tablespoons wine vinegar
2 large scallions, white part only, trimmed and very finely chopped
1 tablespoon finely chopped capers
1 tablespoon finely chopped flat-leaf parsley
1 tablespoon very light olive oil
6 small red ripe tomatoes, stem ends cut out and discarded, thinly sliced

1. Dissolve the salt and mustard in the vinegar.
2. Add the scallions, capers, and parsley and mix briefly.
3. Add the oil and stir it in well.
4. Toss the tomatoes lightly in this sauce, put them in a glass or ceramic dish, and allow them to chill completely.
5. Arrange the tomato slices on a cold serving dish and pour whatever remains of the sauce over them.
6. Serve cold. If available, a few fresh young basil leaves make a remarkably tasty garnish for this good, simple dish.

• • •

Aunt Annette's Stuffed Mushrooms
LES CHAMPIGNONS FARCIS
A LA TANTE ANNETTE

SERVES 4

These are extra special! Not your usual stuffed mushrooms. An old friend from Marseille days used to make these and always promised to give me the recipe, but she never did. She has been dead now for over twenty years, but I have succeeded in guessing what she must have done to make them so wonderful. Here is my version of Tante Annette's famous mushrooms. I sometimes think she must be giggling at me from somewhere in heaven and remarking that my recipe is a fine reconstruction but not exactly her own.

24 medium-sized very fresh white
    mushrooms, wiped clean,
    stems trimmed with a
    stainless steel knife
1 fresh lemon, halved
1 tablespoon sweet butter
1 small shallot, peeled,
    trimmed, and sliced paper
    thin
1 teaspoon finely chopped
    flat-leaf parsley
2 chicken livers, filaments,
    spots, and fat removed
3 tablespoons soft white
    breadcrumbs in
    3 tablespoons milk

1 large egg
1 cup dry white wine
¼ teaspoon dried tarragon
    leaves, finely crumbled
⅛ teaspoon finely ground salt
⅛ teaspoon freshly grated
    nutmeg
⅛ teaspoon freshly ground white
    pepper
1 tablespoon Cognac
4 slices toast
2 tablespoons heavy cream

1. Remove the stems from the mushrooms and rub the caps all over with the lemon halves. Set them aside in a glass or other noncorrosive dish.
2. Chop the mushroom stems almost to a pulp.
3. Heat a frying pan and melt the butter over gentle heat. Sauté the shallot, chopped mushroom stems, and parsley very slowly for 5 minutes.
4. Add the chicken livers and sauté them for 3 minutes on each side.
5. Remove the ingredients from the frying pan and chop or process to a paste.

6. Squeeze the milk from the breadcrumbs and discard it. Add the breadcrumbs and egg and mix thoroughly with the paste.

7. Stuff the mushroom caps loosely.

8. Deglaze the frying pan with the white wine and set the stuffed mushrooms, stuffed side up, in the liquid. Cover the frying pan, reduce the heat to very low, and simmer the mushroom caps for 10 minutes.

9. Remove the mushrooms with tongs and place them on a warm plate.

10. Add the tarragon, salt, nutmeg, pepper, and Cognac to the pan juices and increase the heat. Reduce sauce for 10 minutes with the pan uncovered.

11. Place a piece of toast on each serving dish and arrange 6 stuffed mushrooms, stuffed side down, on each piece of toast.

12. Swirl the cream into the sauce quickly and spoon some of the sauce over each serving. Serve the mushrooms at once while they are still hot.

N O T E : The sauce must be properly reduced before putting the cream in, so if it hasn't reduced to about ½ cup, continue to boil it until it does.

Poached Leeks Vinaigrette
LES POIREAUX EN VINAIGRETTE
S E R V E S 4

The French believe that cooked leeks are a sure cure for a hangover. Fortunately this good dish is not restricted to those nursing a hangover.

4 tablespoons (½ stick) sweet butter

12 to 16 medium-sized leeks, white part only, trimmed and cleaned of all grit under cold running water

3 tablespoons freshly squeezed lemon juice

1 cup broth or water

1 cup *Sauce vinaigrette* (page 38)

1. Melt the butter in a kettle over gentle heat. Add the leeks and toss them in the melted butter, coating each one well.

2. Add the lemon juice and broth or water, cover the kettle, and braise the leeks over low heat for 1 hour.
3. Drain the leeks well, place them in a glass or ceramic dish, and chill them.
4. Serve the leeks on individual serving plates or on one big platter, stacked like logs. Pass the vinaigrette in a sauceboat so that each diner may serve himself.

NOTE: Don't discard the juices. They are delicious and can be added to soup or *Béchamel* for another meal.

Assorted Raw Vegetables
LES CRUDITES
SERVES 4

Raw, grated, or julienned vegetables, delicately sauced, are often served in France as a first course. They are not merely a favorite of the weight-conscious. Properly prepared crudités are light, fresh-tasting, and healthy, and they clear the palate for whatever is to follow. Sometimes, especially in summer, an elaborate platter of crudités may be the principal dish at lunch, with a selection of cheeses and fruit as the only thing to follow. I cannot think of a wiser lunch nor a more appetizing one. The knack, of course, is to serve only vegetables that are impeccably fresh, at the peak of perfection, and deliciously sauced with light vinaigrettes, not creamy dressings.

FOR THE VEGETABLES:

2 tablespoons coarse salt
1 large cucumber, peeled, halved, seeded, and thinly sliced
1 small fresh onion, white bulb only, peeled, trimmed, and thinly sliced
4 ribs celery, coarse strings pulled out, trimmed and thinly sliced
12 to 16 cherry tomatoes, quartered

1 tablespoon finely chopped flat-leaf parsley
4 medium-sized carrots, scraped, trimmed, and coarsely grated
½ head small purple cabbage, core removed, thinly julienned
1 plump fennel bulb, trimmed, tough outer ribs removed and discarded, cut lengthwise in eighths

FOR THE DRESSINGS:

1 cup *Sauce vinaigrette* (page 38)

1 cup "lemon" vinaigrette
(follow the recipe on page 38,
but substitute 3 to 4

tablespoons freshly squeezed
lemon juice for the vinegar,
and omit the mustard and
garlic)

1. Salt the cucumber and onion and let them leach for 15 to 20 minutes, then wash them very well under very cold running water. Drain them well and pat them dry with paper towels.
2. Toss each vegetable as follows:
   * Mix the cucumber and onion and toss them in plain vinaigrette.
   * Toss the celery in plain vinaigrette.
   * Toss the tomatoes in plain vinaigrette, then sprinkle well with the chopped parsley and toss well again.
   * Toss the carrots, cabbage, and fennel separately, but all in "lemon" vinaigrette.
3. Serve all the tossed vegetables well chilled in individual bowls at the same time or arrange each vegetable in a diagonal line across a very large serving platter. In France, crudités are usually served in a special tray fitted with individual glass or porcelain dishes.
4. Place a saltcellar, a peppermill, and cruets containing olive oil and vinegar on the table for those who wish to adjust the seasonings.

N O T E : The vegetables I have suggested here are only a few of the standard vegetables that can be prepared and presented as crudités. There are all kinds of possibilities. Sometimes, too, cooked beets, boiled potatoes, and other poached vegetables are sauced lightly and included in a presentation of crudités, so don't feel you must remain dogmatically attached to the term crudité as meaning literally raw.

• • •

Celeriac in Mayonnaise
LE CELERI REMOULADE

SERVES 4 OR 5

When I was a poor, struggling student in France, céleri rémoulade *was one of the great take-out treats that could be bought in a shop and taken back to one's room for an improvised meal. It was a delicious dish I had never tasted at home in the States because celery root was an unknown vegetable where I came from. Now, of course, celery root, or celeriac, as it is properly called, is available in many supermarkets here. However, American household cooks are still a little shy about purchasing this big, often grotesquely ugly but very delicious root. Every time I buy it in the United States someone asks me how to prepare it and whether it is good. I've learned that you can rarely make a convert in a supermarket, but a guest sampling* céleri rémoulade *at my table is easily convinced. You try it. I'm sure that you, too, will be convinced that it is a vegetable that should be better known.*

1 celeriac root weighing about 1 pound
1 fresh lemon, halved
½ teaspoon coarse salt
1 egg yolk, at room temperature
1 tablespoon Dijon mustard
¼ teaspoon freshly ground white pepper
3 tablespoons wine vinegar
1 cup light vegetable oil, at room temperature

1. Peel the root with a stainless steel knife and rub it all over with one of the lemon halves, making sure that you squeeze out plenty of juice to coat the exposed surfaces.
2. Cut the celeriac in half and grate it coarsely into a glass or ceramic bowl. Squeeze the rest of the juice from the lemon halves into the bowl. Add the salt and toss the grated celeriac with a wooden implement so that the salt and lemon juice coat the grated root very well; otherwise it will turn brown.
3. Set the mixture aside to leach for 1 hour.
4. Place the egg yolk, mustard, and pepper in a small bowl and mix them well with a pestle or whisk until they make a paste.
5. Add the oil to the paste, a few drops at a time, producing a rather thick mayonnaise.
6. Squeeze the juice out of the grated celeriac with your hands and discard the juice. Return the celeriac to the glass or ceramic bowl and toss it so that it becomes light and detached.

7. Add the mayonnaise gradually, whipping the sauce into the celeriac.
8. Cover the bowl and chill the dressed celeriac. Toss the chilled celeriac again just before serving.

NOTE: If you serve the celeriac by itself as a first course, you may want to dress it up with a little finely chopped parsley, fresh dill, or mint. It would be an elaboration, however. When I bought this wonderful dish from my *traiteur* in Paris almost forty years ago it was sold, as it is today, unadorned—a heap of ivory-colored, glistening goodness!

Curly Endive with Bacon and Garlic Dressing
LA FRISEE AU LARD
SERVES 4 OR 5

For most French people, this is a down-home, nostalgia-producing salad. Until recently it was almost impossible to find it on anything but a regional restaurant menu, but now it is a standard first-course offering. Traditionally, this salad is often served with a heavy dish such as cassoulet because, despite its heavy-handed use of garlic, it has a light, stimulating effect on the digestion. I still like to serve it after the main course and pass the cheese at the same time. Cheese and frisée au lard *have a nice affinity for each other.*

One caveat: Don't try to make this salad unless you can find curly endive that has been bleached to a light yellowish white inside. The dark green, tough, and bitter curly endive sold in most supermarkets in the United States may be good for feeding rabbits, but it simply will not produce a proper frisée au lard.

2 or 3 thick rashers streaky smoked bacon, rind removed, cut in ¼-inch matchstick-like lardoons
2 plump cloves garlic, peeled, trimmed, and crushed to a paste with
    1 teaspoon coarse salt
2 tablespoons Dijon mustard
3 tablespoons wine vinegar

¼ teaspoon granulated sugar
½ teaspoon freshly ground black pepper
1 large head bleached curly endive, leaves torn apart into manageable bits, washed well in cold water, and thoroughly dried
3 tablespoons light vegetable oil

1. Sauté the lardoons until they are crisp but not dry.
2. While the fat is still hot stir in the garlic paste, mustard, vinegar, sugar, and pepper. Allow this sauce to boil up once, then immediately remove it from the heat.
3. Place the endive in a large salad bowl, pour the oil over the leaves, and toss the salad until the leaves are completely covered with the oil.
4. Add the sauce and toss the salad well, distributing the sauce and bacon bits throughout. Serve at once, while the *frisée* leaves are still crisp.

NOTE: My recipe for this salad comes from the back country along the Tarn River. I ate it there for the first time at a farm when I was on a walking trip in 1957. The old woman who made it for me was astonished that I could like something so ordinary. She was even more astonished when I asked for the recipe. I have reproduced it here very faithfully with one exception: she used 3 plump cloves of garlic in her dressing instead of 2!

Russian Salad
LA SALADE RUSSE

SERVES 4 TO 6

This is a substantial, hunger-satisfying salad. It is sometimes called macedoine de legumes en mayonnaise, *but it was taught to me as* salade russe. *As such I pass it on to you.*

2 tablespoons tinned tuna, finely shredded
3 tablespoons wine vinegar
1 teaspoon coarse salt
2 tablespoons freshly squeezed lemon juice
½ teaspoon freshly ground white pepper
1 egg yolk, at room temperature
1 cup light vegetable oil
1 cup cold boiled potatoes in ½-inch cubes

½ cup cold boiled carrots in ½-inch cubes
½ cup cold, slightly undercooked green peas
½ cup slightly undercooked green beans in ½-inch lengths
1 medium-sized scallion, white part only, trimmed and finely chopped
12 to 15 capers
2 hard-boiled eggs, finely chopped

1. In a large glass or other noncorrosive mixing bowl place the shredded tuna, vinegar, salt, lemon juice, pepper, and egg yolk and combine them well with a pestle or whisk.
2. Add the oil, a few drops at a time, whisking continuously to form an emulsion.
3. Add all the other ingredients and toss them together lightly but well. When tossing this salad, beware of breaking up the boiled vegetables. In a perfect Russian salad, all the vegetables should remain distinguishable and attractive.
4. Cover the bowl and chill the salad well.
5. Pile the salad in a large, smooth mound on an oblong platter and serve.

NOTE: If you want to garnish this dish, it is customary to cover the mound with mayonnaise and decorate it. I suggest making poinsettia-like petals from bottled pimiento. In the center deposit a mound of egg yolk mimosa (the mimosa effect is obtained by pushing hard-boiled egg yolks through a sieve) and place a few capers in it to represent the stamens of the flower.

Boiled Artichokes Vinaigrette
LES ARTICHAUTS EN VINAIGRETTE
SERVES 4

Artichokes are not a luxury in France; they are far less expensive there than in the States. They are not only delicious, they are very good for the digestion, and they contain a good amount of easily assimilated iron. This is how the French prepare them most often at home.

4 fresh globe artichokes	1 tablespoon cornstarch,
2 lemons, halved	dissolved in
2 quarts water	2 tablespoons cold water
	⅔ cup *Sauce vinaigrette* (page 38)

1. With a stainless steel knife remove and discard the stems, cutting them off flush with the head so the heads will sit up properly. Pull off and discard any small outer leaves and any discolored ones.

2. With the knife or a pair of stout kitchen shears cut about 1 inch from the top of each artichoke. This can be a job because the leaf ends are very tough.
3. Rub all the cut surfaces with lemon, and rub some of the juice on your fingers to prevent them from being discolored by the artichoke juices.
4. Put the artichokes in the 2 quarts water to simmer in a glass or enameled pan. Stir in the dissolved cornstarch and squeeze the remaining lemon juice into water. Throw in the squeezed lemons as well, and boil the artichokes for 30 minutes.
5. Remove the artichokes from the water and drain them upside down.
6. Allow them to cool and serve them on individual plates in a generous pool of vinaigrette or pass the vinaigrette in a sauceboat.

N O T E : These artichokes may be served warm with a simple sauce of clarified butter and lemon juice.

Cold Purée of Summer Vegetables
LA RATATOUILLE AIXOISE

SERVES 4

Long before ratatouille became chic and took the form of large chunks of underdone vegetables, the inhabitants of the areas of Aix and Arles knew ratatouille as a twice-cooked, almost scorched purée with a powerful, concentrated taste. Here's that version. It makes a marvelous cold spread to be eaten with drinks. It can also be served, as it traditionally was, as an accompaniment with grilled meats.

1 large eggplant, peeled, in
    ½-inch lengthwise slices,
    salted with
    1 tablespoon coarse salt
½ cup light vegetable oil
3 medium-sized zucchini,
    washed, dried, and sliced in
    ¼-inch-thick roundels
2 plump cloves garlic, peeled
    and halved
3 medium-sized red, ripe
    tomatoes, skinned, seeded,
    and coarsely chopped

1 large bell pepper, fire-skinned
    (see page 44), cored,
    seeded, and coarsely chopped
1 bouquet garni consisting of 1
    bay leaf, one 2-inch piece
    dried orange peel, 1 sprig
    thyme, and 1 sprig rosemary,
    tied up together with cotton
    string
1 tablespoon extra virgin olive
    oil

1. Rinse the eggplant slices well to remove the salt and the bitter brown water that has leached out of them. Pat them dry with paper towels.
2. Heat a large frying pan over medium heat. Add the vegetable oil. When it hazes, fry the eggplant until it is brown on both sides, and drain the slices well on paper towels.
3. Fry the zucchini until brown on both sides. Blot the fried zucchini with paper towels to remove as much oil as possible.
4. Pour off and reserve half the oil for another use.
5. Sauté the garlic briefly, but remove it before it browns.
6. Return the eggplant, zucchini, and garlic to the frying pan and add the tomato, pepper, and the bouquet garni and stir over high heat for 3 minutes.
7. Reduce the heat, cover the pan, and simmer for 40 minutes.
8. Discard the bouquet garni and pass the ratatouille through a food mill or process it a few pulses in a food processor.
9. Return the purée to the frying pan and reduce it until it is quite thick. Stir in the olive oil.
10. Serve the purée warm or cold.

  N O T E : For the most spectacular-tasting canapés, spread this purée on small pieces of toast, sprinkle heavily with grated Gruyère cheese, and grill quickly under a very hot broiler. Wait until they are cool and serve them sparingly with drinks (more than 2 apiece will spoil appetites). This purée, to use the expression uttered by my brother-in-law when he tasted it for the first time, is dynamite!

A   W O R D   A B O U T   B E E T S

Beetroot seems to be much more appreciated in France as a staple vegetable than it is in the United States. Beets figure prominently in many regional dishes in France, and most of the year beets are offered for sale already baked in their skins. When I lived in Aix-en-Provence I quickly learned to love the large, fist-size beets that were sold every market day by most of the farm women who set up shop in the Place des Prêcheurs. Those beets, baked the day before, slipped out of their skins almost without help, sweet, firm, and ruby red. Though I often ate them dressed only with salt and oil, I learned to make many dishes with them. This one is an ancient Provençal salad that the people in the region prepare. It is unique in that both the beets and the onions must be baked the day before if the salad is to taste as it should. It is one of the many dishes that the people of Provence prepare in the cool of the night to escape cooking during the noonday heat of the Provençal summer.

Provençal Beet Salad
LA SALADE DE BETTERAVES
A LA PROVENÇALE

SERVES 4 OR 5

4 small new potatoes, boiled in
   their jackets
3 large beets, baked
3 medium-sized yellow onions,
   baked (see below)
1 cup leftover boiled ham, cut
   into ¼-inch dice
¼ teaspoon dried thyme leaves
1 small clove garlic, peeled,
   trimmed, and crushed to a
   paste with
   1 teaspoon coarse salt and
   1 flat fillet of anchovy

½ tablespoon Dijon mustard
3 tablespoons wine vinegar
5 tablespoons light olive oil
1 large scallion, white part only,
   finely julienned
3 tablespoons finely chopped
   flat-leaf parsley

1. The day before you make this salad, boil the potatoes and bake the beets and onions. Preheat the oven to 400°. Leave the roots and 1 inch of the stems on the beets. Leave the onions unpeeled. Wrap the beets and onions individually in sheets of aluminum foil. Bake the onions for 1 hour, the beets for 2. Let them cool in their aluminum jackets overnight.
2. Peel the potatoes and cut them into ¼-inch roundels.
3. Peel the beets and cut them into ⅜-inch slices.
4. Pour off and discard the juice that will have accumulated around the onions. Peel them, quarter them lengthwise, and pull them apart.
5. Place the beets, onions, potatoes, and ham in a large, colorful salad bowl and sprinkle them with the thyme leaves.
6. Make the dressing:
   • Put the garlic, salt, and anchovy paste, mustard, and vinegar in a small glass jar with a cover.
   • Add the olive oil.

- Close the lid tightly and shake the ingredients for 15 seconds or until they combine.
7. Pour the dressing over the salad, add the scallion and parsley, toss lightly, and serve.

NOTE: Provide a bouquet of fresh parsley and mint for your guests to chew on afterward. The garlic in the dressing is a little aggressive.

Baked Onion Salad

LES OIGNONS ROTIS EN SALADE

SERVES 2 OR 3

Onions are transformed into a marvel of sweetness when they are baked, sauced, and served up cold. This is the Catalan way of preparing them.

3 medium-sized yellow onions, baked (see page 58) and chilled
1 large, fire-skinned bell pepper (see page 44)
3 flat anchovy fillets, chopped

½ cup *Sauce vinaigrette* (page 38)
¼ teaspoon dried fennel seed
2 tablespoons extra virgin olive oil
2 tablespoons finely chopped flat-leaf parsley

1. Drain and discard the water that has accumulated inside the aluminum foil around the baked, chilled onions. Peel and quarter the onions and pull the layers apart.
2. Cut the cleaned, cored, seeded pepper into 1-inch strips.
3. Place the onions, pepper, and anchovies in a large glass bowl and pour the vinaigrette over them. Sprinkle in the fennel seed. Toss the ingredients together thoroughly.
4. Cover the bowl with foil or plastic wrap and refrigerate for several hours.
5. Just before serving, toss the salad again, drizzle it with the olive oil, sprinkle with chopped parsley, and serve.

NOTE: This onion salad is wonderful as an accompaniment to grilled lamb chops or baked leg of lamb. I sometimes serve it with grilled tuna steaks. The grilled tuna and this dish are phenomenally compatible.

Light Summer Potato Salad
LES POMMES DE TERRE A L'HUILE
SERVES 4

Have you had it with potato salad? Well, here is a simple, light one that goes well with pickled or cream herring, or just by itself. It is an old French standard still made exactly the way I was taught to make it in the early 1950s.

½ clove garlic, peeled, trimmed, and crushed with
  ½ teaspoon coarse salt
2 tablespoons wine vinegar
12 capers
½ teaspoon freshly ground black pepper

1 flat fillet of anchovy, crushed
1 tablespoon finely chopped flat-leaf parsley
½ cup light salad oil
8 to 10 small boiled potatoes, peeled and thinly sliced

1. Mix the garlic paste, vinegar, capers, pepper, crushed anchovy, and parsley together.
2. Whip the oil into this mixture, a little at a time.
3. Toss the potatoes in this sauce and serve them at room temperature.

CHAPTER FOUR

Soup

La Soupe

Soup is greatly esteemed all over France. In many French homes the evening meal is light, but it frequently begins with soup, which is apt to be a light, fresh, vegetable broth with a handful of rice or soup pasta thrown in. Sometimes it is a light vegetable purée laced with a little milk or cream and a small lump of sweet butter. However, on occasion, the soup is heavier, more elaborate. The repertoire of household soups is very wide, even in an ordinary home. Naturally, too, every household has its own favorites.

The quality that distinguishes French household soups from those in most other countries is their fresh, generally light taste. Even if the soup served one evening contains, as is often the case, what was left over from the soup of the night before, the French home cook usually adds some fresh vegetables to revive it.

Since broths are basic to all French cooking, the French cook automatically purchases a leek or two, a carrot, an onion, and a bunch of fresh parsley when doing the daily marketing, and habitually makes a broth of them when returning home. That broth will be served as soup that evening or eventually find its way into a sauce, that day or the next. For the French cook, broth is a staple of everyday cooking, as essential as oil or butter.

Soup lore in France is vast. The term *la soupe* is generic and can be used, as I have at the head of this chapter, to designate any soup. Three hundred years ago, English-speaking people used the word *potage* to designate thick pulse or lentil soups such as the mess of pottage Jacob traded to Esau in the Bible. The old Norman term is now obsolete in English, but the French still use it to designate soups made of a light broth and vegetables and even, at times, light puréed soups.

The oldest soup in the French household's repertoire is *la bouillie*, a thick gruel made by boiling flour or meal with water, broth, milk, or wine. It is still prepared for babies, small children, the aged, and the infirm. *Le bouilli*, on the other hand, refers to an unrefined meat broth.

Le bouillon is a meat broth that has been refined by skimming, degreasing, and clarifying. *Le consommé* is bouillon that has been concentrated by boiling it down, a process known in cooking as reduction. I could go on, but the list of French soup-making terms is very long, and with the few I have presented here you will have a good, simple working vocabulary for making most French household soups.

French Home-Style Vegetable Soup
LE POTAGE MENAGERE
SERVES 4 OR 5

This soup is perhaps the best known to the greatest number of French households. Many of my French friends, having eaten it almost every evening of their childhood, have formed a nostalgic attachment to it.

2 tablespoons sweet butter
1 plump shallot, peeled, trimmed, and sliced paper-thin
2 medium-sized leeks, white part only, trimmed, split, washed free of all grit, and coarsely chopped
2 medium-sized carrots, scraped, split, and cut into 2-inch pieces
1 rib celery, cut into 2-inch pieces
1 medium-sized onion, peeled and spiked with 1 clove

1 small turnip, peeled and quartered (optional)
2 medium-sized potatoes, peeled and quartered
1 small slice peeled pumpkin (optional)
1 bouquet garni consisting of 1 bay leaf, 1 sprig parsley, 1 sprig thyme, and one 2-inch piece dried orange peel (optional), bound together with cotton string
5 cups boiling water
Salt

1. Melt the butter in a soup kettle over low heat.
2. Sauté the shallot and leeks slowly until almost melted.
3. Add all the other ingredients and bring to a boil. Reduce the heat to a simmer and allow to cook for 45 to 50 minutes.
4. Discard the bouquet garni and spiked onion. Pass the remaining solids

through a food mill or sieve and return the purée to the broth. Stir well.

5. Adjust the seasoning with salt and serve.
6. Pass around a jug of milk for those who wish to add it. It is a common practice in most French households.

N O T E : A clear vegetable broth can be made in the same way, provided the potatoes and the slice of pumpkin are left out. Strain out and discard the solids. They will already have given up most of their flavor and nutritive value to the broth. At this point it is a common practice in French households to return the broth to the kettle along with a handful of rice, soup pasta, or coarsely ground tapioca and cook it another 12 to 15 minutes.

French Leek and Potato Soup
LE POTAGE AUX POIREAUX ET AUX POMMES DE TERRE
SERVES 5 OR 6

Leek and potato soup has been a favorite in French households for at least two centuries. Just two decades ago, the great French chef Louis Diat refined this homely favorite, added heavy cream, served it chilled, and dubbed it vichyssoise. I sometimes wonder if Diat wasn't joking when he gave his version such a name. A la vichyssoise usually means that carrots are a major ingredient. Not in Diat's soup! First I give the basic, old-fashioned version, then I tell you how it can be transformed into vichyssoise, in case you want to try that much richer version.

2 tablespoons sweet butter
3 or 4 medium-sized leeks, white part only, trimmed, split, carefully washed, and finely sliced
4 cups unsalted chicken broth
3 or 4 medium-sized potatoes, peeled, quartered, and thinly sliced

1 bay leaf
1 teaspoon coarse salt
4 white peppercorns, finely crushed
1 cup whole milk, heated to the scalding point
3 tablespoons finely chopped flat-leaf parsley

1. Heat a heavy kettle over low heat and gently melt the butter.
2. Sauté the leeks very slowly, stirring them from time to time. They should become transparent and almost melt without browning. This step must be done with attention so as not to destroy the fresh, sweet taste that leeks and butter will impart to the soup.
3. Add the broth and allow the leeks and broth to simmer for 5 minutes.
4. Add the potatoes and bay leaf and allow to simmer for 1 hour or until the potatoes are very soft.
5. Discard the bay leaf and purée the soup in a food processor or by putting it through a food mill or a sieve.
6. Add the salt, peppercorns, and hot milk to the purée and heat the soup to the boiling point, but remove it from the heat right away.
7. Pour the soup into a tureen, sprinkle the surface with parsley, and serve immediately.

N O T E : To make an elegant, chilled vichyssoise, follow the same recipe through Step 6. Strain the purée through a sieve lined with 2 thicknesses of dampened cheesecloth. Refrigerate the purée, tightly covered, until very cold. (This base may be kept for as long as 3 days, tightly covered, in the refrigerator.) Just before serving, add ¾ cup well-chilled half-and-half. Vichyssoise is generally garnished with a tiny amount of finely chopped fresh chives. Very recently, it was served to me in Paris with finely chopped fresh dill weed and a tiny amount of ground cumin. It was a surprising departure from the classic vichyssoise, but clearly a wonderful variation worth trying.

• • •

Parisian Rice Soup
LA SOUPE AU RIZ A LA PARISIENNE

SERVES 4 OR 5

Part of the mythology of this soup is that it is considered by Parisians to be a surefire cure for la gueule de bois *or "wooden mouth," the French equivalent for a hangover.*

2 tablespoons sweet butter
2 or 3 medium-sized leeks, white part only, split, well washed, and finely chopped
4 cups water
1 teaspoon coarse salt
⅓ cup rice

3 medium-sized potatoes, peeled, quartered, and thinly sliced
2 tablespoons finely chopped flat-leaf parsley
18 to 20 thin slices French bread, oven-toasted
¼ pint whole milk

1. Heat a 2-quart kettle over low heat and gently melt the butter. Sauté the leeks slowly until they are transparent and soft.
2. Add the water, salt, rice, and potatoes and simmer for 25 to 30 minutes. Test the potatoes. They should be cooked, but not falling apart.
3. Add the parsley, cover the pot, and remove it from the fire, allowing the parsley to steep for 5 minutes.
4. Serve at once. Pass the milk and toast for those who wish it.

NOTE: If you have leftover boiled rice, substitute 1 cup of cooked rice for the ⅓ cup raw rice and add it only at Step 3.

• • •

Provençal Garlic Soup
LA SOUPE A L'AIL

SERVES 4

In many parts of rural France garlic soup is believed to be a better and cheaper cure for a bad cold than the steaming dark rum and lemon grog we favored as students. There are many versions of French garlic soup. Here is a particularly delicious one. I will swear to its effectiveness, too: it once helped me shake a very tenacious bronchitis. But, for heaven's sake, don't reserve this old standby for the sick; it is a fantastic strengthener for healthy folks, too.

24 plump cloves garlic, peeled, cut in half lengthwise, and any center shoots removed
3 cups broth or water
1 cup dry white wine
1 bouquet garni consisting of 1 bay leaf, 1 sprig thyme, 1 dried fennel stem, 1 sprig rosemary, and one 2-inch piece dried orange peel, bound together with cotton string

12 thin slices oven-toasted stale French bread
¼ teaspoon freshly cracked black pepper
Salt to taste
2 teaspoons light olive oil

1. Simmer the garlic with the broth or water, wine, and the bouquet garni until the garlic is completely soft. This usually takes 15 to 20 minutes.
2. Discard the bouquet garni.
3. Press the cooked garlic through a sieve and put the purée back into the soup. Reheat the soup to a boil, cover the pot, and remove it from the fire to steep.
4. Arrange the toasted bread in 4 bowls and sprinkle the toasts with cracked pepper.
5. Salt the soup to taste, reheat it to the boiling point, and pour it over the toasted bread.
6. Drizzle the toasts in each bowl with ½ teaspoon of the olive oil.
7. Serve at once while very hot.

N O T E : An egg is sometimes broken into each bowl of hot soup. Old folks from rural Provence say that the garlic should be browned in oil before simmering it, and also insist that the garlic be left in pieces and not puréed. However, I find that browning the garlic gives a bitter taste to the broth and that the browned bits are certainly harder to digest than the boiled purée. Provençal garlic soup is one of the many country soups to which old farmhands in France love to add a glass of wine.

Purée of Chick-Pea and Sage Soup
LA SOUPE AUX POIS CHICHES
SERVES 4

This substantial soup is particularly good when served with plenty of fried bread cubes that have been rubbed with a clove of garlic and sprinkled with some powdered coriander.

¼ cup light olive oil

2 plump cloves garlic, peeled, trimmed, and finely sliced

2 medium-sized leeks, white part only, well washed and finely chopped

1 medium-sized carrot, scraped, quartered lengthwise, and very thinly sliced

1 medium-sized onion, peeled, trimmed, and thinly sliced

1 quart broth or water

1 bouquet garni consisting of 1 bay leaf and 1 or 2 branches fresh sage (there should be about 10 leaves; if you have no fresh sage, substitute 1 teaspoon dry sage), bound together with cotton string (if you use dry sage, tie it up in a small piece of cheesecloth)

1 16-ounce tin cooked chick-peas, rinsed and hulled

¼ teaspoon ground cumin

½ teaspoon coarse salt

½ teaspoon freshly ground black pepper

2 teaspoons extra virgin olive oil

1. In a soup kettle, gently heat the light olive oil and slowly sauté the garlic, leeks, carrot, and onion until almost melted.
2. Add the water or broth, the bouquet garni, and the chick-peas and simmer for 30 minutes.
3. Discard the bouquet garni.

4. Purée the soup in a food processor or pass it through a food mill.
5. Add the cumin, salt, and pepper and reheat. If the soup looks too thick, add a little hot water or hot milk.
6. Serve the soup very hot in a tureen with the virgin olive oil floating on the surface.

Hearty Lentil Soup

LA SOUPE AUX LENTILLES BONNE FEMME

SERVES 5 OR 6

For thousands of years, lentils have been a major source of nutrition for many cultures. Lentils are inexpensive, they cook in less time than most of the other dried beans, peas, and pulses, and they are very nourishing.

This lentil soup is very hearty. It is difficult to believe when you taste it that only two slices of smoked bacon went into it! An entirely meatless version of the soup, called à l'ancienne, or "the way it used to be made," can be prepared by omitting the bacon and substituting light olive oil for the butter. That is the version that was eaten for centuries during the abstinence days of Lent.

2 cups brown lentils, picked over and washed well under cold running water
4 tablespoons (½ stick) sweet butter
2 thick slices smoked bacon, rind removed, cut up into ¼-inch lardoons (optional)
2 medium-sized carrots, scraped, trimmed, split twice, and thinly sliced
2 medium-sized leeks, white part only, split, carefully washed, and thinly sliced
2 plump cloves garlic, peeled, trimmed, and finely sliced

1 medium-sized onion, peeled, trimmed, and spiked with 3 cloves
1 bouquet garni consisting of 1 bay leaf, 1 sprig thyme, 1 sprig rosemary, and one 2-inch piece dried orange peel, all bound together tightly with cotton string
2 quarts water
2 cups whole milk
½ teaspoon freshly ground black pepper
Salt to taste
8 to 10 thin slices of oven-toasted stale French bread

1. Soak the lentils in enough cold water to cover them for 1 hour.
2. In a heavy skillet melt 2 tablespoons of the butter over gentle heat and sauté the bacon, carrots, leeks, and garlic until transparent but not browned.
3. Wash the soaked lentils in a sieve under cold running water.
4. Put the lentils, sautéed vegetables, spiked onion, and bouquet garni into a heavy soup kettle with the 2 quarts of cold water. (Many traditional cooks insist that 1 tablespoon of wine vinegar be added at this point, claiming that it tenderizes the lentils.) Bring the kettle to a rolling boil, skim off the froth that rises for the first 5 minutes, then reduce the heat to a low simmer and allow the lentils to cook covered for 1 hour and 45 minutes.
5. Discard the bouquet garni and the spiked onion.
6. Purée the soup in a food processor or by putting it through a food mill. Return the purée to the kettle with the milk and pepper and heat to boiling point. Remove from the heat at once. Salt to taste.
7. Pour the soup into a tureen, swirl in the remaining 2 tablespoons butter, and serve immediately, passing the toasts for those who wish to add them.

Spring Vegetable Soup with Pistou
LA SOUPE AU PISTOU

SERVES 4 OR 5

In early summer, as soon as the sweet basil plants are in leaf, it is time to make and consume gallons of la soupe au pistou *in Provence and all along the Côte d'Azur. The perfume of this magic dish invades the streets from Marseille to Nice, making everyone crazy to have it. I know of no other cooking smell that is quite as evocative or nostalgic. For anyone who has spent the summer along the Côte d'Azur, that light, steamy odor of basil leaves and vegetable broth will bring back the vision of summer noondays along that incomparable coast.*

1 cup Great Northern navy
  beans, well picked over,
  washed, and soaked
  overnight in
    1 quart cold water to which
    has been added
    1 teaspoon baking soda
6 cups cold water
1 bouquet garni consisting of 1
  bay leaf, 1 sprig thyme, and
  1 sprig fresh parsley, bound
  together with cotton string
½ pound fresh green beans,
  tailed and snapped into
  2-inch lengths
2 medium-sized carrots, scraped,
  trimmed, and cut into ½-inch
  roundels
2 medium-sized potatoes,
  peeled, quartered, and cut
  into thin slices
3 medium-sized leeks, white
  part only, trimmed, split,
  carefully washed, and finely
  chopped

3 small zucchini, washed,
  trimmed, halved, and cut
  into ¼-inch slices
2 medium-sized ripe tomatoes,
  skinned, seeded, and coarsely
  chopped
½ cup elbow macaroni or
  vermicelli broken into 3-inch
  lengths
4 plump cloves garlic, peeled,
  trimmed, and coarsely
  chopped
1 teaspoon coarse salt
10 to 12 fresh basil leaves, well
  washed, stems removed, and
  blotted dry with paper
  towels
2 blanched almonds (optional)
¼ cup freshly grated Parmesan
  cheese
¼ cup freshly grated soft Edam
  or Gouda cheese
½ cup extra virgin olive oil

Make the soup:

1. Rinse the soaked beans well under cold running water, place them in a heavy soup kettle with the water and the bouquet garni, and bring to a rolling boil.
2. Reduce the heat and simmer for 1 hour.
3. Add the green beans, carrots, potatoes, leeks, and zucchini, and continue to cook for another 15 to 20 minutes.
4. Discard the bouquet garni.
5. Add the tomatoes and pasta and increase the heat, allowing the soup to cook for another 12 to 15 minutes, occasionally skimming off and discarding any froth that rises as the ingredients cook.

Make the pistou:

1. Grind and pound the garlic, salt, and basil leaves together to a coarse purée. (I prefer a stone mortar and a wooden pestle for this, but it can also be done very efficiently in a food processor.)
2. Add the almonds and continue to grind the ingredients together.

3. Add the cheeses and continue to grind the ingredients into a thick paste. Use a little of the olive oil to facilitate the process.
4. When all the ingredients have been combined to a thick mass, add 2 or 3 tablespoons of hot broth from the soup and grind them into the *pistou.*

Add the *pistou* to the boiling soup, stirring it quickly so that the *pistou* mixes well into the hot soup. Serve at once. Let each guest add olive oil as he chooses.

N O T E : To my mind, *soupe au pistou* is best when the dried beans are omitted and the soup is made only with a wealth of fresh garden vegetables. That version, which I have eaten most often in Aix and Marseille, is quicker to prepare and certainly much easier to digest! In the summer this hot soup brings out the beads of perspiration on your face as you eat it, but it doesn't matter, since this marvelous dish seems to feed both the body and the soul.

Burgundian Onion Soup
LA SOUPE A L'OIGNON GRATINEE
SERVES 4

Almost everyone knows some version of French onion soup. Although it is served in many restaurants, you are not likely to find it served in French households outside the Burgundian and Lyonnais areas, where it is said to have originated. In those regions it is pretty generally considered modest country fare for a cold winter evening.

3 large, sweet onions, peeled, cores removed, sliced very thin
3 tablespoons sweet butter
3 tablespoons light oil
3 tablespoons flour
1½ teaspoons coarse salt
6 cups hot stock or water
1 bay leaf

2 cups dry white wine
10 to 12 slices of French bread, ½ inch thick
1 plump clove garlic, cut in half
2 tablespoons light olive oil
¾ cup freshly grated Gruyère cheese

1. In a heavy soup kettle sauté the onions in the butter and 3 tablespoons light oil over a low flame. The onions should sauté very slowly, never browning, until they melt. Take plenty of time for this. The success of the soup depends upon it.
2. Sprinkle the flour and salt over the sautéed onions and stir well so that no lumps form.
3. Add the stock or water, bay leaf, and wine and simmer over the lowest heat for at least 45 minutes.
4. Toast the bread slowly in the oven. It should be crisp but not browned.
5. Rub the surfaces of the toasted bread with the garlic halves and brush both sides with a little olive oil.
6. Choose a good-sized earthenware, ovenproof bowl for each guest and rub the inside of each bowl well with the rest of the garlic halves. Ladle the soup into the bowls, filling them ¾ full, and float pieces of toast on each, making sure that the surface of the soup is generously covered.
7. When the bread has swollen with the soup, sprinkle the surface liberally with the grated cheese.
8. Place the bowls under a very hot broiler and allow the cheese to melt and brown.
9. Serve the soup while it is still bubbling.

N O T E : Warn your guests about trying to eat the soup too quickly; melting Gruyère is like dealing with napalm! When the weather is very cold in Burgundy, it is the custom to add a shot of country brandy to this soup while it is still sizzling. A good substitute for country brandy (*marc du pays*, which is hard to find in the States) is half a jigger of port or dry sherry.

• • •

Provençal Fish Soup
LA BOURRIDE

SERVES 4 OR 5

Like all typical, regional, family-style dishes, this simple fish soup is the subject of endless arguments and disagreements. Every household cook thinks the version he or she uses is the correct one. Even as I set down this recipe for you, I am unsure of how many of my old friends will disagree with it. Nevertheless, here it is adapted to fish that you can easily find in the United States.

½ pound monkfish
½ pound ocean perch
½ pound scrod or cod
4 to 6 whole, medium-sized shrimp
1 medium-sized onion, peeled, cored, and finely chopped
2 bay leaves
1 branch thyme
1 or 2 dried fennel stalks, 4 to 6 inches long
1 branch fresh parsley
One 2-inch piece dried orange peel
12 saffron threads, toasted and crumbled

½ teaspoon coarse salt
½ teaspoon freshly ground black pepper
¼ teaspoon ground cayenne pepper
6 cups hot water
8 to 10 slices of French bread ¼ inch thick, oven-toasted
½ cup light olive oil at room temperature
4 egg yolks at room temperature
4 plump garlic cloves, peeled and crushed to a paste with 1 teaspoon coarse salt

1. Cut the fish into 2-inch pieces.
2. Pull the shrimp in two, dividing the head and thorax from the tail, and clip down the back of the tails with a pair of kitchen shears, cutting through the shell and just to the dark vein running down the tail. Rinse out the dark vein under cold running water.
3. Put the fish, the upper parts of the shrimp, onion, bay leaves, herbs, orange peel, saffron, salt, and black and cayenne pepper in a heavy soup kettle with the hot water and simmer for 15 minutes.
4. Add the shrimp tails and cook for another 3 minutes.
5. Remove the fish and shrimp tails and reserve them.
6. Increase the heat and let the soup boil for another 10 minutes.
7. Strain the soup and discard everything that does not pass through the

sieve. Return the strained soup to the kettle and allow it to continue boiling while you prepare the garlic sauce.

8. In a mortar, mix the oil, egg yolks, and garlic paste into a simple mayonnaise.

9. Remove the soup from the fire so that it is no longer boiling and add 3 or 4 tablespoons of the hot liquid to the garlic sauce, stirring the mixture well.

10. Choose a wide soup bowl for each guest and place some of the toasted bread in each bowl. Ladle a little of the hot soup over the toasts just to moisten them.

11. Using a wooden spatula, stir the garlic sauce into the soup and return the kettle to the burner, lowering the heat to the very faintest point. Stir the soup, scraping up the bottom constantly to keep it from hardening. The soup is ready when it coats the spatula.

12. Add reserved pieces of fish and shrimp tails to the individual bowls and ladle the hot soup over the bread and fish. Serve while soup is still steaming.

Versions of this fine soup are served in all the elegant restaurants along the Côte d'Azur. Some are very sumptuous indeed, often a costly concoction of rockfish reduced to a fragrant, strong purée. The garlic sauce is passed separately, or a *rouille* (page 77) is offered instead. The version I have given you is very simple. It closely resembles the one Reboul gives in his household standby, *La Cuisine Provençale.*

If you are purchasing your fish from a fishmonger, ask him for some fish heads and spines. If you remove the gills from the heads, the heads and spines can add flavor and richness to your soup.

•   •   •

Provençal Hot Sauce for Fish Soup
LA ROUILLE

MAKES ABOUT ⅔ CUP

Old-timers along the Côte d'Azur insist on stirring a generous spoonful of a pale, rusty-tinted sauce they call rouin into their fish soup. The custom has caught on in restaurants all along the coast. You will see the sauce listed on menus as la rouille. *The sauce adds an authentic, peppery richness to the soup, but beware: a little goes a long way.*

2 plump garlic cloves, peeled and trimmed
½ teaspoon coarse salt
½ teaspoon ground cayenne pepper
2 almonds, blanched and roasted

1 slice white bread, crust removed
½ cup milk
4 tablespoons light olive oil
½ cup hot broth from the soup rouille is to be served with

1. Crush the garlic, salt, cayenne and almonds to a fine paste in a mortar.
2. Soak the bread in the milk. Squeeze out and discard the milk. Add the moist bread to the mortar and grind it into the paste.
3. A drop at a time, grind in the oil.
4. Add the hot broth, grinding it in, a spoonful at a time, to produce a creamy emulsion.
5. Pass the sauce in a bowl when the soup is served, allowing the guests to add it as they like.

N O T E : If you have a food processor, you can make this sauce in 30 seconds. Process all the ingredients except the broth for 15 seconds, then add the broth a little at a time, continuing to process the sauce for another 15 seconds.

• • •

Purée of Green Pea Soup
LE POTAGE ST. GERMAIN

SERVES 4 OR 5

This rich, creamy purée of fresh green garden peas is a great favorite in every region in France where green peas are plentiful. (I have never seen it served in any household in the arid Midi.) The knack in making a really successful potage St. Germain *is to use only the freshest green peas you can find and not to stint on the sweet butter. Frozen peas make a very acceptable substitute, though they don't quite come up to the mark of the real thing. It is hard to find truly garden-fresh, tender, young green peas in the United States unless you grow them yourself in your own garden.*

¼ pound (1 stick) sweet butter	1 teaspoon coarse salt
2 pounds fresh green peas	¼ teaspoon freshly ground white
2 cups lettuce, finely chopped	pepper
(use only a stainless steel	1 teaspoon granulated sugar
knife)	Croûtons
3 cups water	

1. Heat a heavy soup kettle and very gently melt the butter.
2. Sauté the peas and the lettuce in the butter very slowly for 15 to 20 minutes, stirring them from time to time with a wooden spatula.
3. Add the water and allow the ingredients to simmer for 45 minutes.
4. Purée the soup in a food processor or pass it through a food mill.
5. Return the purée to the kettle. Add the salt, pepper, and sugar and reheat the soup to the boiling point.
6. Serve the soup at once with a good supply of oven-dried croûtons. It isn't necessary to fry the croûtons; the soup already contains plenty of butter.

   N O T E : Some of your guests may want to add some milk to this lovely soup. The French do. It might be wise to have a jug of milk on the table.

• • •

Basque-Style Fried Bread and Garlic Soup

LA PANADE A LA BASQUAISE

SERVES 4 OR 5

Fifty years ago not a crumb of bread was wasted in French households. Stale bread was toasted for breakfast, fried for supper, pulverized to thicken soups or to "bread" fried foods. Bread soups are perhaps the very oldest way of making stale bread palatable. Every region in France has a panade *or bread soup. Here is one that is still eaten a great deal in the Pyrenees.*

One ½-inch-thick slice streaky salt pork
½ cup light olive oil
18 to 20 plump cloves garlic, peeled, trimmed, and thinly sliced lengthwise
24 thin slices day-old French bread

1 bouquet garni consisting of 1 bay leaf, 1 sprig thyme, 1 sprig rosemary, and 1 small, dried, hot red pepper pod, tied together with cotton string
6 cups broth or water
4 or 5 poached eggs

1. Remove and discard the rind from the salt pork and cut the slice into ¼-inch lardoons.
2. In a heavy soup kettle, gently heat the oil and sauté the lardoons until they are very lightly browned on the edges.
3. Remove the lardoons and reserve them.
4. Add the garlic to the kettle and sauté quickly, removing the pieces before they have a chance to brown. Reserve them with the sautéed lardoons.
5. Brown half the bread slices in the fat and set them aside. Break the rest of the bread slices into small pieces and put them in the kettle.
6. Add the lardoons, half the sautéed garlic, the bouquet garni, and the broth or water to the kettle and simmer the soup for 45 minutes, stirring it often with a wooden spatula so that it doesn't stick to the bottom.
7. Discard the bouquet garni and salt the soup to your taste.
8. Place a poached egg in each soup plate.
9. Ladle the soup into the plates around the poached eggs, garnish each serving with the rest of the sautéed garlic and the fried bread, and serve the soup hot.

N O T E : In Basque country this soup sometimes contains several roundels of the local peppery garlic sausage, which the Basques put in so many of their regional dishes. Served up with sausage, this soup becomes the entire evening meal for many Basque farmers. Should you find the garnish of sautéed garlic offensive, I suggest you lighten the soup by garnishing it with chopped parsley instead.

Sweated Beef Broth
L'ESSENCE DE BOEUF

SERVES 1

When I arrived in France in 1950, I was pleasantly surprised to discover that many French grandmothers, like my own, made sweated beef broth for their grandchildren when they were sick in bed or in poor health. Sweated beef is a household panacea that serves the same purpose as chicken soup. I can vouch for the almost miraculous strengthening power of this rich, entirely greaseless broth.

1 pound lean top round beef
1 small onion, peeled and thinly
  sliced
3 or 4 drops freshly squeezed
  lemon juice

1 teaspoon dry sherry (optional)
Salt to taste

1. Trim away and discard all visible fat from the meat.
2. With a very sharp chef's knife or a lunette, hand chop the beef as if you were preparing a Tartar steak. (A lunette or *hachoir* is a crescent-shaped blade mounted between two handles so that the blade may be rocked from one side to the other. It is an ancient and wonderful tool.)
3. Scald a quart fruit jar, drain it, and put the beef and onion inside. Seal the lid of the jar and put it in a large kettle ¾ full of water.
4. Simmer the kettle slowly for 3½ to 4 hours, replenishing the water as it evaporates. If the jar dances about, place a weight on top of it so the jar won't hit the sides of the pot and crack. My own great-grandmother used to keep a well-washed brick handy for this purpose.
5. Strain the contents of the jar through a fine sieve lined with 2 layers of dampened cheesecloth.
6. Add the lemon juice, sherry, and salt, and serve to the invalid.

NOTE: Never one to waste food, my great-grandmother would always brown what was left of the chopped beef and onion after sweating it and use it in a kind of gratinée or *hachis Parmentier* (page 213).

Leafy Endive and Rice Soup
LA SOUPE A L'ESCAROLE ET AU RIZ
SERVES 4

This delicate soup is a delight. It is well known to households in the southeastern part of France, but perhaps came originally from Piedmont, just across the border, since the Italians make a soup that is very similar. It is light and lovely and deserves to be more widely known.

2 tablespoons light olive oil
2 tablespoons sweet butter
1 thin slice smoked bacon, rind removed and discarded, the bacon cut into ¼-inch matchstick-like lardoons
1 large head leafy endive, well washed, cored, and coarsely chopped
1 medium-sized scallion, white part only, trimmed, split, and finely chopped
1 quart broth or water
¼ cup rice
Salt to taste
Freshly grated Parmesan or Gruyère cheese

1. Heat a heavy soup kettle and gently warm the oil and butter together.
2. Slowly sauté the bacon until just transparent.
3. Add the endive and scallion and toss with a wooden spatula until they are well coated with the sautéing fat.
4. Add the broth or water and simmer for 30 minutes.
5. Add the rice and continue to simmer for 15 minutes. Salt to taste.
6. Serve hot and pass freshly grated Parmesan or Gruyère cheese to sprinkle in the soup.

NOTE: Leafy endive is often called by its French name, escarole, in the United States. It must not be confused with feathery endive or *frisée*, which is excellent as a salad but not satisfactory for this recipe.

Norman-Style Potato, Bean, and Cabbage Soup

LA SOUPE NORMANDE

SERVES 5 OR 6

This is the great soup of the north in France. To make it properly, you must begin by making the graisse *normande, a mixture of beef suet and pork fat flavored with herbs and vegetables and processed very slowly for hours. You could make a kind of reasonable facsimile without going to the trouble of making the famous* graisse, *but I suggest you do it right the first time. You will discover that the* graisse *does indeed impart a very different taste to the soup. Why not make a project of it and invite some friends with healthy appetites to celebrate the* Soupe normande *on a cold winter evening.*

¼ pound beef suet, preferably from around the kidney, in ¼-inch cubes

¼ pound fat, fresh pork cut up into ½-inch cubes

1 small onion, peeled and finely chopped

1 small carrot, scraped, quartered lengthwise, and finely sliced

¼ teaspoon crumbled marjoram

6 rosemary leaves

1½ cups cooked dried lima beans

2 cups potatoes, peeled and cut into ½-inch cubes

3 ribs celery, strings pulled off, cut in 1-inch pieces

1 small head cabbage, cored and shredded

3 medium-sized leeks, white part only, trimmed, split, well washed, and cut into ½-inch pieces

1 cup green beans, tailed and snapped in 2-inch pieces

2 quarts hot water

1 teaspoon coarse salt

½ teaspoon freshly ground black pepper

Make the flavored grease the day before:

1. In a heavy iron skillet gently render the suet and pork, stirring often.
2. Add the onion, carrot, marjoram, and rosemary and sauté the mixture very gently for 30 minutes, taking care that it does not brown.
3. Cover the skillet and bake the mixture in a 300° oven for 1 to 2 hours, taking care not to allow it to carbonize.
4. Strain the grease through 2 thicknesses of cheesecloth, discarding the residue.
5. Keep the grease refrigerated in a closed jar.

Make the soup:
1. Put the cooked beans, potatoes, celery, cabbage, leeks, and green beans in a soup kettle with the water, salt, and pepper and simmer uncovered for 40 minutes.
2. Add 4 tablespoons of the prepared grease to the soup and simmer, covered, for 20 minutes.
3. Ladle the soup into a large tureen and serve at once.

Purée of Navy Bean Soup
LE POTAGE AUX HARICOTS BLANCS
SERVES 4 OR 5

If you like Yankee bean soup, you will probably love this soup. It is a little more refined and takes a bit more time to make, but it is well worth the effort.

1 cup Great Northern navy beans, carefully picked over

1 bouquet garni consisting of 1 bay leaf, 1 sprig dried thyme, 1 sprig dried rosemary, and 1 sprig fresh parsley, all tied together with cotton string

1 medium-sized onion, peeled and spiked with 2 cloves

2 plump cloves garlic, peeled, trimmed, and halved lengthwise

4 tablespoons (½ stick) sweet butter

3 medium-sized leeks, white part only, split, well washed, and coarsely chopped

3 ribs celery, coarser strings removed, leaves removed and discarded, coarsely chopped

3 ripe, red tomatoes, skinned, seeded, and coarsely chopped

Coarse salt to taste

½ teaspoon freshly ground white pepper

¼ teaspoon freshly grated nutmeg

3 egg yolks

Toasted croûtons

1. Wash the beans well in a colander under cold running water. Put them in a heavy soup kettle with enough cold water to cover them and heat them gently to a boil.
2. Remove the kettle from the fire at once and allow the beans to cool completely.
3. Drain the swollen beans in a colander and rinse well again under cold running water.

4. Return the beans to the kettle and cover them with plenty of freshly boiling water. Add the bouquet garni, the spiked onion, and the garlic and simmer for at least 1 hour, or until the beans are cooked through and tender.
5. Warm a sautéing pan over low heat. Melt half the butter (2 tablespoons) and gently sauté the leeks and celery until they are transparent.
6. Add the tomatoes and simmer the ingredients for 40 minutes.
7. Remove from the beans and discard the bouquet garni and the spiked onion. Add the sautéed vegetables to the beans and purée the soup by putting it through a food mill or by pulsing it 5 to 7 times in a food processor.
8. Return the purée to the kettle and heat it to the boiling point. Add the salt, pepper, and nutmeg and stir them in well.
9. Beat the egg yolks until they are light and lemon-colored, then beat 3 or 4 tablespoons of the hot purée into them. Add the egg mixture to the soup and stir it in quickly. Do not allow the soup to boil after adding the egg mixture or the yolks will curdle.
10. Swirl in the rest of the butter and serve the soup at once with plenty of toasted croûtons.

N O T E : This is another of the soups to which the French *en famille* often add milk, so you might want to pass a jug of milk around at table. I like to garnish this soup with finely chopped flat-leaf parsley. It not only looks beautiful with the warm ivory color of the soup, it also adds a great, fresh taste.

Chilled Cucumber Soup
LA SOUPE FROIDE AU CONCOMBRE
SERVES 4 OR 5

This is the lightest summer soup that I know of. I have never encountered it anywhere in France except in Paris, unless I made it myself. Its lightness and fresh taste recommend it for summer dining, and I feel that it should be much better known. Let me say from the outset that those who suffer from indigestion when they eat cucumbers need harbor no reservations about this soup. Not only are the seeds and peelings—the usual sources of indigestion—removed, the flesh of the cucumber is purged with salt and boiling water. I recommend this soup as a piquant starter for a summer luncheon.

3 medium-sized cucumbers
2 tablespoons coarse salt
Boiling water
4 cups unsalted, degreased
   chicken broth
½ cup dry white wine
3 tablespoons freshly squeezed
   lemon juice

1 teaspoon granulated sugar
1 slim scallion, white part only,
   trimmed, split, and finely
   chopped
5 tablespoons heavy cream
2 teaspoons finely chopped fresh
   mint leaves

1. Peel the cucumbers and cut them in two lengthwise. Run a tablespoon down the center of each half, removing the core and the seeds. Discard whatever you remove.
2. Place the halves cut side down and slice them paper-thin. Sprinkle the slices well with the coarse salt, tossing them with your fingers so that all surfaces are touched by salt. Put the salted slices in a colander and allow them to leach for 20 to 30 minutes.
3. Pour the boiling water over the cucumber slices in the colander. Immediately rinse the slices well under cold running water and pat them dry with paper towels.
4. In a large, noncorrosive saucepan heat the broth, white wine, lemon juice, and sugar to the boiling point, stirring well to dissolve the sugar.
5. Add the cucumber slices and the chopped scallion and simmer for 3 to 5 minutes.
6. Pour the soup into a glass bowl, seal it well with plastic wrap, and refrigerate it for at least 6 hours.
7. Serve the soup in chilled bowls. Garnish the surface with a dollop of cream and a sprinkling of chopped mint leaves.

N O T E : Some cooks like to reduce the cucumber slices to a pulp by pulsing them in the food processor. I think the crunchy quality of the slices adds to the exquisite piquancy of this soup. If you like fresh dill weed, you may prefer to substitute finely chopped fresh dill weed for the mint.

Vegetables

Les Légumes

France is blessed by nature with abundant fresh groundwater and frequent rainfall. The soil in most of its regions has been rich and fertile
since time immemorial. In those few regions where the soil is less fertile,
industrious local populations have devoted more than a millennium to
enriching it. As a result, the produce grown all over France is among the
best in the world. Thanks to this tradition of excellence, French household cooks grow up knowing how to judge produce with an uncompromising eye. They see fine produce every day and can recognize the signs
of its freshness. They refer to food shopping as carrying out *commissions*,
an expression that suggests responsibility! They not only learn to be
shrewd in their buying, but how to preserve the best qualities of their
purchases in preparing them for table.

French household cooks are usually full of traditional wisdom about
the produce that is raised locally, and they are also knowledgeable about
the fruit and vegetables they have adopted from other regions of France
and from other countries as part of their standard diet. Having adopted
them, they seem to excel in producing them. I always marvel at how
superior in flavor are the potatoes, tomatoes, bell peppers, and eggplants
I purchase and prepare in France compared to those available in supermarkets in the United States, though all of those vegetables came originally from the Americas. My French friends usually attribute this
superiority in flavor to the use of natural fertilizers, immediate marketing,
and sagacious preparation. Be that as it may, French householders out
shopping are generally much more demanding in their dealings with
shopkeepers and greengrocers than their American counterparts. French
shopkeepers and greengrocers wouldn't dare try to foist off on their
customers the withered, bruised, or dried-out produce I often see this
side of the Atlantic. Were we as aggressively demanding as the French
food shopper, I believe we would quickly see a decided change in the
attitudes of our own retailers.

In France, devotion to good food is something of a national phenomenon, a devotion almost universally shared, so that not only the cooks who shop but the very shopkeepers and greengrocers themselves are devoted to good food. That is a cardinal difference between our two cultures. However, in my own lifetime I have seen such a growth in interest in good food in the States that perhaps we will one day force our suppliers to do a better job. Meanwhile, we should learn what we can from those who have something to teach us about produce, its purchase, and its preparation, and the French household cook has plenty to teach us, if we are wise enough to learn it. Here are a few of the many recipes and some of the lore about vegetables that I have come to know through living in French households. Both the recipes and the lore have brought me a lot of pleasure. I hope they will do the same for you.

French-Style Smothered Green Peas
LES PETITS POIS A LA FRANÇAISE
SERVES 4

The quality and taste of the green peas in France are legendary. They grow so well in the rich soil of la belle France that I wonder why and how they ever got the name of English peas. Also, the French have learned that peas, pearl onions, baby lettuce, and sweet butter are extremely compatible, as this recipe demonstrates. Each time I prepare green peas in this fashion there are always exclamations of bewilderment as to why they taste so uniquely right. Most Americans find cooked lettuce strange indeed, but once they have sampled the little miracle that young lettuce performs in this simple dish, they are ready to accede that braised lettuce can be wonderful.

3 tablespoons sweet butter
2 cups shelled, very fresh, young green peas
12 to 15 pearl onions, or half the quantity very small white onions, peeled, root pared out, well washed
1 small head Boston or Bibb lettuce, well washed and coarsely chopped with a stainless steel blade

1 scant teaspoon granulated sugar
Coarse salt and freshly ground white pepper to taste
1 teaspoon finely chopped chervil or an equal quantity of finely chopped fresh mint leaves

1. Heat the butter gently in a heavy-bottomed stew pan over the lowest heat. Add the peas, onions, and lettuce and toss them well in the butter until they are all well coated.
2. Instead of its proper cover, place a soup plate over the pan as a cover and half fill the plate with water.
3. Smother the peas, onions and lettuce for 50 minutes, replenishing the water in the soup plate if necessary.
4. Test the peas for tenderness and at the right point of doneness, remove the pan from the fire, add the sugar, salt, pepper, and chopped chervil or mint, toss and serve at once.

N O T E : The knack of covering the pot with a plate of water dates from centuries ago when stew pots were all ceramic and the tops were recessed to hold water. When I was a young man, the old *daube* pots used on Provençal farms had just such tops. If the heat is ever so faint and constant, the vegetables will sweat instead of boiling, and their juices will be retained rather than evaporated and drawn off in steam through the top. When the peas are perfectly cooked this way, they will still be plump and not wrinkled and overcooked. I am confident that you will find this method of cooking green peas, even frozen ones, much the best way.

A WORD ABOUT GARLIC, ONIONS, SHALLOTS, AND LEEKS

French household cooking would be unthinkable without those aromatic members of the lily family: garlic, onions, shallots, and leeks. They are all used to varying degrees in the cooking of each region. In some regions, such as most of the south of France and Provence in particular, garlic is used much more than any of the others. In the north, east, west, and center of France, garlic is used with much more restraint, while onions, shallots, and leeks are commonly employed. However, all four of these aromatic bulbs find their way into the repertoire of every region, so it is important to be on familiar terms with them. Though they belong to the same family, each is very different from the others, and within each of these four categories there are many varieties, each with its distinct qualities. A good cook thinks in specifics and will choose as nearly as possible the variety of garlic, onion, shallot, and, though to a lesser degree, the kind of leek that the projected dish requires. The cook must know that a plump white garlic clove will usually be milder in flavor than a small purple one, though each has its proper use. The sweet yellow onion will usually make a better onion tart than the white one, and so forth. Naturally, no household cook knows everything about these splendid bulbs in the beginning. The main thing is to give your recipe close consideration before shopping. Fifteen minutes spent looking at your proposed menu and thinking of specifics before setting out to do the shopping will save you both time and frustration.

Here are a few notes that should help you in shopping for garlic, onions, shallots, and leeks.

GARLIC: Have a good look at the heads to see that they are neither sprouting nor dried up. Sometimes a head of garlic seems to be firm but proves, when broken open, to be completely dry and powdery. A first-rate head of garlic is firm, plump, and hefty. If it is light, it is sure to be dry or shriveled inside. Shriveled or wrinkled cloves of garlic should be discarded. They have already lost the strong, fresh, aromatic juice that makes them valuable, and withered, blighted garlic will impart a peculiar taste to the dish if used.

It is better to buy a head or two of garlic at a time than to purchase whole garlands. Unless you use inordinate amounts of garlic each day, a garland or ring of plaited garlic hung in a warm kitchen, though lovely to see, will usually spoil. If there is much humidity in your kitchen, the moisture will "wake up" the slumbering heads and cause them to sprout. If you buy a whole garland, do as the Provençals do: hang it in a cellar or dark storeroom and clip off a few heads at a time for the kitchen.

To open a fresh head of garlic, place it on its side on a hard surface and strike it a sharp blow with the side of your fist. If it is first-rate, it will break open and the hard center stem will detach itself, letting a number of the tightly wrapped cloves drop loose. A few minutes in warm water will make the job of peeling the cloves much easier.

If you discover that a garlic clove you have peeled has sprouted, slit it lengthwise and remove the sprout with the point of your paring knife. If you leave it in, the sprout will not purée properly and it will sometimes impart a bitter taste.

ONIONS: When shopping for winter onions, try to buy only those that have been properly cured. Onions are cured by hanging them or spreading them in a dark, well-ventilated place so that their outer skins dry. The dried, paperlike skins help preserve the flavor and juice of the onions. Beware of winter onions that have no such paperlike outer skins, especially if they seem damp or yielding when you squeeze them. A damp, bare, somewhat shriveled outer skin on a winter onion indicates that the onion has been stored in a humid place and is already beginning to decompose.

Don't buy sprouted onions unless you intend to plant them. Sprouting causes the onion to disintegrate in an effort to nourish the sprout. If onions you have already bought begin to sprout, you can use the sprouts as you would scallion or green onion, but I do not advise using the bulb.

SHALLOTS: Shallots are prized for the subtle flavor they impart to sautéed dishes. When preparing them, remove the hard root stem found at the bottom of the bulb. If you plan to sauté them, slice them very thin and sauté them very gently. If you sauté them slowly enough, the shallots will "melt" and leave only their pleasant flavor.

Shallots are very expensive in the United States. Make sure they are neither dried up nor sprouted when you purchase them. A first-rate shallot bulb should be plump, the outer skin should be shiny—not wrinkled or tough—and the bulb should show no signs of sprouting. A sprouted shallot is useless. In the States shallots are usually sold in little plastic baskets. Inspect them well before buying that quantity.

LEEKS: Leeks are so expensive in the United States that I think twice before buying enough of them to serve as a dish; however, I usually buy one bunch regardless of their price because they have an incomparable taste. French vegetable or potato soup without leek just isn't the same, and the difference can be detected at once. First-rate leeks have resilient roots and leaves. The white stalk should be waxy in appearance, shiny and white. The leaves should be firm and crisp and break when bent. A slightly withered leek can sometimes be salvaged if you have allowed it to wither after purchasing it. Just peel away the withered outside layers until you get down to the firm part, which you can then use.

Although many French household cooks use the green leaves of the leek in making broths, it is traditional to use only the white stem of the leek. Cut off and discard the green leaves; then, with a sharp paring knife, make a 2-inch split down the stem from where you cut off the leaves. That way you can peel back the sides and wash the grit out of the layers. Leeks pick up grit in their growth, and you want to be sure you get all of it out. There are few things worse than finding grit in a mouthful of food.

Glazed Pearl Onions
LES PETITS OIGNONS GLACES
SERVES 4 AS SIDE DISH

The special way the French have with vegetables is no mystery. The vegetables must be garden-fresh and their natural taste must be carefully preserved in preparation, and, when necessary, carefully accentuated. Here is a very good example of that set of simple principles.

1 pound pearl onions, carefully peeled, derooted, and washed
4 tablespoons (½ stick) sweet butter

1 cup cold water or broth
¼ cup dry white wine
2 tablespoons granulated sugar
¼ teaspoon coarse salt

1. Place the onions, butter, water, and wine in a heavy-bottomed stew pan and bring them to a boil. The pan should be stainless steel, enameled, or coated. If you use aluminum, the onions will discolor.
2. Add the sugar and salt and gently shake the pan about until these ingredients are completely dissolved.
3. Reduce the heat to very low and gently simmer for about 20 minutes, until all the liquid has evaporated and the onions are covered with a shining, buttery coating.
4. Serve as a garnish or as a side dish.

N O T E : These exquisitely flavored onions have many uses. Add a few to garnish a grilled chop or a slice of roast. I sometimes toss them with plain boiled rice, a little finely chopped flat-leaf parsley, and freshly grated Gruyère cheese instead of taking the time to do a risotto. With a tiny grilled chop or a couple of thick rashers of grilled, well-drained bacon you can make a simple, distinguished lunch. (Tiny new turnips and baby carrots can also be glazed the same way.)

• • •

Provençal-Style Sautéed Zucchini
LES COURGETTES SAUTEES
A LA PROVENÇALE

SERVES 4 OR 5

*This is a very common and quite delicious way to prepare zucchini. The knack is to brown the zucchini without overcooking it. Old cooks of the Midi swear that zucchini must be slightly scorched (*carbonisée, *they say, or* charred!*) before they become assertive enough to be properly called* à la provençale.

4 very fresh medium-sized zucchini
1 tablespoon coarse salt
2 tablespoons vegetable oil
1 medium-sized yellow onion, peeled, halved, and thickly sliced
1 plump clove garlic, peeled and finely chopped

1 medium-sized ripe red tomato, skinned, seeded, and finely chopped
1 bay leaf
¼ teaspoon dried thyme leaves
6 rosemary leaves, crumbled
¼ teaspoon freshly cracked black pepper
Salt to taste

1. Wipe the zucchini well, trim them on each end, and split them lengthwise. Slice them ¼-inch thick.
2. Salt the zucchini and let them leach in a colander for 30 minutes. The salt will draw moisture to the surface.
3. Rinse the zucchini and pat them dry with paper towels.
4. Heat the oil in a heavy frying pan and quickly fry the zucchini until they are quite brown on both sides.
5. Add the onion and toss lightly, reducing the heat to a simmer.
6. When the onion is transparent, add all the other ingredients except the salt and simmer for 20 minutes.
7. Salt to taste and serve hot or cold.

N O T E : You can change this fine dish slightly by adding a few black oil-cured olives, a tablespoonful of capers, a couple of chopped anchovy fillets, and a handful of fresh basil leaves. Nothing could be more typically Provençal summer fare.

A variation once served to me took the form of a flat omelet that the cook called *fritouille.* Since then I have made *fritouille* quite often. (My

Italian friends call it *frittata*.) If you'd like to try it, after Step 7 beat 3 large eggs with 2 teaspoons of water and mix them well with the cool sautéed zucchini. Heat a medium-sized frying pan and add 3 tablespoons of vegetable oil. When the oil is hot, but not smoking, turn the mixture into it, smooth it down, and allow it to cook gently for about 7 minutes. Invert a plate over the skillet and turn out the *fritouille* done side up. Slip it back into the frying pan, uncooked side down, and cook it until that side is nicely browned. Turn it out and serve it in wedges. That's one more dish from the Midi to grace your table when you're looking for a good, simple item for lunch.

Grilled Zucchini
LES COURGETTES GRILLEES
SERVES 4

Here is a quick, perfect garnish for grilled chops, steaks, or chicken thighs.

4 medium-sized, very fresh zucchini, wiped, trimmed, and split lengthwise
1 tablespoon coarse salt
¼ teaspoon dried thyme leaves
¼ teaspoon freshly cracked black pepper
1 tablespoon light olive oil

1. Sprinkle the cut sides of the zucchini with salt and allow them to leach for 15 minutes. (Water will be drawn to the surface.)
2. Wipe the cut sides dry (do not wash), and sprinkle them with thyme and pepper.
3. Heat a deeply grooved, cast-iron grill. When the grill is quite hot, grill the zucchini halves for 3 minutes on each side, starting with the green, uncut sides.
4. Sprinkle the grilled, cut sides with olive oil and serve hot.

• • •

Fried Zucchini Slices
LES COURGETTES FRITES

SERVES 4

4 very fresh, medium-sized
  zucchini
1 tablespoon coarse salt

1 cup milk
1 cup flour
¼ cup vegetable oil

1. Wipe the zucchini well and trim off the ends. Slice the zucchini lengthwise in ⅛-inch slices.
2. Sprinkle the slices on both sides with salt and allow them to leach for 15 minutes, then rinse them in ice water and drain them well on paper towels.
3. Dip the slices quickly in milk, then dredge them carefully in flour, making sure that they are completely covered with the flour.
4. Lay the floured slices on wax paper and refrigerate them for 15 to 30 minutes. This helps the flour to adhere.
5. Heat a large frying pan over medium heat. Add the oil and when it hazes fry the floured slices, allowing them to brown nicely on each side.
6. Drain the sliced zucchini on paper towels and serve them very hot.

NOTE: These fried slices are fine as they are, but my family likes them even better sprinkled with a little grated Parmesan cheese and a light dusting of dried thyme leaves.

• • •

Provençal-Style Stuffed Zucchini
LES COURGETTES FARCIES
A LA PROVENÇALE
SERVES 4 OR 5

All along the Côte d'Azur, households are fond of stuffed vegetables served either hot or cold. They are a frequent item in summer fare, made early in the morning or the night before to escape cooking during the hottest part of the summer days. Years ago, when very few homes boasted an oven, great baking tins of these stuffed vegetables were carried to the neighborhood bakery to be put in the oven when the bread was taken out. There they would stay, baking slowly as the oven cooled. At noon, some member of the family went to fetch them for the noon meal.

This recipe will serve equally well for medium-sized, hollowed-out tomatoes, peppers, or small eggplant. An old friend of mine from Toulon even includes a few peeled, hollowed-out, partially boiled onions and potatoes. All of those stuffed vegetables served up together make a very attractive lunch to be eaten at home or on a picnic.

6 very fresh, medium-sized
  zucchini
3 tablespoons vegetable oil
1 rasher streaky salt pork, rind
  removed, finely chopped
1 small onion, peeled, trimmed,
  and coarsely chopped
2 slices white bread, crusts
  removed and discarded,
  soaked in
    ½ cup milk
3 tablespoons finely chopped
  beef or lamb (leftover boiled
  beef may also be used)

1 small clove garlic, peeled,
  crushed, and teased to a paste
  with
    1 teaspoon coarse salt
2 tablespoons finely chopped
  flat-leaf parsley
⅛ teaspoon fennel seed
½ teaspoon freshly ground black
  pepper
1 teaspoon thyme leaves
3 tablespoons cooked rice
1 egg, lightly beaten
2 tablespoons freshly grated
  Parmesan cheese
2 or 3 tablespoons water

1. Wipe the zucchini well with a damp towel and slice off the ends. With a potato peeler make 3 or 4 striations the entire length of the zucchini, removing ¼-inch strips of green while leaving a good deal of the green skin. This creates a nice striped effect, but it also helps the zucchini to cook through evenly while retaining their shape.

2. Cut the zucchini into 2-inch lengths. With a melon baller or apple corer carefully hollow out the centers, leaving ¼ inch of zucchini flesh all around the hole.

3. Plunge the zucchini sections into boiling water for 3 minutes. Drain them and run cold water over them. Pat the sections dry and put them aside.

4. Preheat the oven to 350°.

5. Heat a heavy frying pan over medium heat. Add the oil. When it hazes, sauté the bacon and onion until they are transparent.

6. Squeeze out the bread and add it, along with the meat, garlic paste, parsley, fennel seed, pepper, thyme, and rice, to the frying pan and toss lightly, allowing everything to sauté for 5 minutes, stirring so that the ingredients do not stick.

7. Remove the pan from the fire and quickly stir in the beaten egg.

8. When the stuffing is cool enough, stuff the zucchini lightly. Arrange them close together in a greased baking dish and bake them for 30 minutes.

9. Sprinkle the grated cheese over the zucchini and place them under the broiler for 5 minutes or until they are golden.

10. Remove the pan from the oven. So that the zucchini will be tender and succulent, add the 2 or 3 tablespoons of water to the pan and allow the zucchini to cool for 10 to 15 minutes before serving or chilling.

NOTE: I sometimes strew 1 cup of skinned, seeded, coarsely chopped tomatoes over the zucchini just before putting them into the oven. I like the taste, and it usually creates enough sauce so that no water need be added.

• • •

Provençal-Style Grilled Tomatoes
LES TOMATES A LA PROVENÇALE
SERVES 6

Sometimes—too often, in fact—a half-baked tomato is served up along with a main course in the United States and billed as tomate à la provençale, *which it isn't. Tomatoes are used almost as often in regional Provençal cooking as garlic is, and the cooks of Provence certainly have a way with tomatoes. In the case of this common favorite, the tomatoes are gently grilled until they collapse, and are frequently served cold. It is a joy to see a whole baking dish of these grilled tomatoes served up chilled in summer, sprinkled, often enough, with fresh basil leaves.*

6 firm, red, ripe, medium-sized
    tomatoes
1 cup dry white bread fragments
2 plump cloves garlic, peeled
    and crushed to a pulp in
      1 teaspoon coarse salt

½ teaspoon freshly cracked black
    pepper
1 teaspoon thyme leaves
3 tablespoons finely chopped
    flat-leaf parsley
3 tablespoons light olive oil

1. Wash the tomatoes and pare out the stem ends. Cut a thin slice from the other end of each one so that they will sit up properly when cut in half and arranged on the baking dish.
2. Cut the tomatoes in half horizontally. With your thumb, gently press out most of the seeds in the sections and turn the halves upside down in a plate to drain.
3. Pound the bread fragments into pea-size bits. Put these in a mixing bowl with the juice that has drained out of the tomatoes, the garlic paste, pepper, thyme, and parsley and toss lightly.
4. Oil a shallow porcelain or glass baking dish. It should have straight sides so that the collapsing tomatoes are maintained in place. Calculate the size of the dish for the number of the tomatoes so that the tomatoes fit snugly.
5. Preheat the oven to 375°.
6. Stuff the tomato halves loosely, pressing the bread mixture into the seed cavities. Arrange the tomatoes, stuffed side up, in the baking dish and sprinkle the olive oil over them. (The 12 halves present a much better appearance and they bake more evenly when they are a little crowded in the dish.)

7. Bake the tomatoes for 15 minutes, then grill them under very intense heat until nicely browned and a little blackened along the edges nearest the heat. They should grill in 3 to 5 minutes.
8. Serve the tomatoes slightly warm. (When served at once these tomatoes are amazingly hot, so let them cool!) Alternatively, they may be chilled overnight in the refrigerator, where they will improve in taste.

Braised Belgian Endives
LES ENDIVES BELGES BRAISEES
SERVES 4 OR 5

In the United States, Belgian endives are generally used in salad. They are unreasonably expensive here and we rarely see them cooked. In French households, on the contrary, they are more often served braised than raw. They are delicious when properly braised. I always prepare an extra head or two because inevitably someone asks for seconds. If not, they are delicious to eat cold the next day with a sandwich. This is how the French braise these wonderful vegetables.

5 or 6 large heads of Belgian endive (choose only those that are very white and crisp)
2 tablespoons freshly squeezed lemon juice

4 tablespoons (½ stick) sweet butter
½ teaspoon coarse salt
1½ cups water

1. With a stainless steel knife trim off and discard the brownish root from each head. Remove and discard any of the outer leaves that are discolored. Rub all the cut surfaces immediately with lemon juice to prevent them from darkening.
2. Put the endives in a stainless steel or enameled braising pan with all the other ingredients and bring the water to a quick boil.
3. Reduce the heat to the faintest simmer, cover the pan, and allow the endives to cook for 35 to 40 minutes.
4. Serve the endives as they are or drain them well, flour them lightly, and brown them in sweet butter over gentle heat.

NOTE: There are a number of interesting and delicious ways to present braised endives. They may be sprinkled liberally with grated Gruyère cheese and grilled until the cheese melts and turns golden. In my house we like them wrapped in a thin slice of boiled ham, arranged in orderly rows in a well-buttered shallow baking dish, covered well with a rich *Béchamel* sauce (page 25), sprinkled with fresh breadcrumbs and grated Gruyère, and baked until nicely brown. Prepared in this fashion they make a light but perfectly satisfying main course. Still another way to serve braised endives is simply to drain them well and serve them with roast fowl or veal, spooning a little of the natural cooking juices over them.

A WORD ABOUT POTATOES

Ever since more than two hundred years ago, when Parmentier recommended potatoes to the French as a source of delicious nutrition, the potato has been a major staple in French households. The French raise very tasty potatoes with natural, not industrially produced, fertilizers. French householders also know how to shop for good potatoes. Here are a few of their observations:

- Never buy a wrinkled potato, or one that yields when it is squeezed. Such potatoes are either older than they should be or suffering from faulty storage.
- Never buy a potato that has a greenish hue. Such potatoes have been exposed for a long time to light and their skins are slightly toxic.
- Buy rough-skinned potatoes for baking and deep-frying.
- Buy shiny-skinned potatoes for boiling and sautéing.

• • •

Crispy Fried Potatoes
LES POMMES FRITES

SERVES 4

Certainly not all French household cooks prepare frites—*the common expression in France for french fries—in this fashion, but it was a French home cook who taught me this method long ago. Over the years I have often prepared them this way and they have always pleased the people I have served them to.* Frites *made this way are apt to keep their crispness a little longer.*

4 large white potatoes, peeled, cut in long ¼-inch strips, well washed in running water, and well dried with paper towels	1 cup flour 1 cup vegetable oil 1 teaspoon coarse salt

1. Dredge the strips well in flour, making certain they are completely covered with flour. Lay them out, carefully separated from each other, on paper towels.
2. Heat the oil in a deep frying pan until a tiny bit of potato bubbles when thrown into the oil.
3. Toss the strips into the hot oil, a handful at a time. Allow them to just cook through, and remove them with a skimmer before they begin to brown. Drain on paper towels.
4. Seven minutes before serving them, reheat the oil and fry the potatoes until they are golden brown and very crisp.
5. Drain them briefly on paper towels. Salt and serve them as soon as possible.

   N O T E : It is amazing how much better these dredged, twice-fried potatoes are than the usual fries. Nor is this way of preparing fries a secret. A friend who grew up on a farm in Burgundy informs me that the cook in his house often prepared them in this fashion.

• • •

Parsleyed New Potatoes
LES POMMES NOUVELLES A L'ANGLAISE

SERVES 4

To be perfectly correct, potatoes should be called pommes de terre *or earth apples; however, by and large, they are commonly called* pommes, *or apples, for short, so this recipe has to do with new potatoes, not apples. Calling them "new potatoes done as the English do them" is a bit satiric, as there is a widespread belief among the French that English cooks only know how to boil vegetables. I never think of these little boiled new potatoes with their slathering of sweet butter and chopped parsley as anything but typically French. They are excellent by themselves or as an accompaniment for fish, fowl, or meat.*

16 to 20 tiny new potatoes, well scrubbed

1 tablespoon coarse salt

½ cup (1 stick) sweet butter at room temperature

¼ teaspoon freshly ground black pepper

2 tablespoons finely chopped flat-leaf parsley

1. With the point of a very sharp paring knife, make a tiny incision around the middle of each potato, just piercing the skin. This will prevent the skins from bursting during boiling.
2. Put the potatoes in a large enameled or Pyrex pan and cover them with cold water. Add half the salt to the water and boil the potatoes over high heat for 25 minutes.
3. Drain and peel the potatoes and put them back in the pan.
4. Add the butter and shake the pan gently to coat the potatoes well. Sprinkle the rest of the salt, the pepper, and chopped parsley over the potatoes and shake the pan again so that the potatoes get a good coating.
5. Place the potatoes in a warm serving dish, pour over them whatever butter is still in the bottom of the pan, and serve at once.

• • •

Marthe's Sautéed Potatoes
LES POMMES SAUTEES A LA MARTHE

SERVES 4

Almost half a century ago when I was a child in Texas, a huge old farm woman named Marthe used to make sautéed potatoes for us when we visited her. I do not know who taught her to make them so perfectly, but many years later, when I lived in France, I was pleasantly surprised to see that Marthe's recipe was indeed the classic for perfectly sautéed potatoes. They are still my favorite way to prepare potatoes. Make plenty of them. Your guests will demand seconds.

²/₃ cup vegetable oil
  6 to 8 medium-sized potatoes,
    peeled and quartered
  3 tablespoons sweet butter

2 tablespoons finely chopped
    flat-leaf parsley
Salt and pepper to taste

1. Heat a large frying pan and add the oil. When the oil hazes, reduce the heat and sauté the potatoes slowly, turning them to see that they brown evenly all over. This will take 20 to 30 minutes.
2. Drain off the oil and save it for another purpose.
3. Add the butter to the pan, and when it melts shake the potatoes about in the melted butter so they are evenly coated.
4. Cover the frying pan and allow the potatoes to crisp very slowly in the butter, taking care that they do not burn. The heat must be very low.
5. Remove the potatoes to a hot serving dish and pour the butter from the crisping over them. Sprinkle the potatoes with the parsley and salt and pepper to taste and serve them immediately.

N O T E : The perfect sautéed potato must be at least 1 inch thick. It is crisp on the outside and dry and light on the inside. The knack is to seal the potatoes in hot oil, then cook them gently, finishing them with butter. If you do it correctly, the potatoes will never be soggy or oil-laden. The French household cooks of the southwest swear by duck and goose fat for sautéing potatoes. I have eaten them and find them delicious but probably disastrous for the arteries. A good, light vegetable oil was the choice of my Provençal neighbors. That is what I use.

• • •

Scalloped Potatoes Dauphiné Style
LE GRATIN DAUPHINOIS
SERVES 5 OR 6

Le Dauphiné is a rough, mountainous area that lies to the north of Provence and along the eastern border of France. There is a gastronomic joke that in that region, the menu can only vary from potato and cheese to cheese and potato. If it was ever true, it certainly isn't now, but it is undeniable that dauphinois *cooks know their potatoes. They invented this dish, to my mind the great triumph of potato cookery. It is universally liked. We know rather bad imitations of it in the United States called au gratin potatoes or Lyonnaise potatoes. Neither of those sticky, Cheddar-cheese-sauced casseroles comes anywhere near the perfection of the perfectly made* gratin dauphinois *with its layered velvetiness. There are many recipes for this great dish. Some cooks insist that it should contain some egg and cheese. Other cooks add a little bacon or ham. Here is the recipe as it was handed on to me.*

4 large baking potatoes
2 plump cloves garlic
1 cup whole milk
1 tablespoon sweet butter
2 tablespoons scallion, white
　　part only, finely sliced

1 teaspoon coarse salt
½ teaspoon freshly ground white
　　pepper
⅛ teaspoon freshly grated
　　nutmeg (optional)
1 cup heavy cream

1. Peel the potatoes, wash and dry them, and halve them lengthwise. Lay them cut side down and cut them into ⅛-inch slices.
2. Rinse the slices well under cold running water and blot them dry with paper towels.
3. Peel one of the cloves of garlic and chop it fine.
4. Put the potatoes in a large frying pan and add the chopped garlic and the milk. Bring the milk to the scalding point, turning the potato slices so that each one is well coated with the hot milk. Simmer the potatoes in the milk very slowly for 15 minutes.
5. Preheat the oven to 300°.
6. Select a baking dish with a cover. It should be large enough to accommodate all the potatoes in 5 or 6 layers. Cut the other clove of garlic in half and rub the interior of the baking dish with the cut edges. Discard the garlic. Butter the baking dish.
7. Layer in the potatoes, covering each layer with a sprinkling of scal-

lion, salt, pepper, nutmeg, and some cream. Pour whatever is left of the cream over the top.

8. Cover the dish and place it in a shallow pan or another, larger baking dish containing 1 inch of water. Place the setup in the center of the oven and bake the potatoes for 1½ to 2 hours, or until the cream is absorbed.

9. Remove the cover and brown under the broiler for a few minutes until the surface is dark and crusty.

10. Let the gratin cool for a few minutes before serving it

N O T E : A perfectly made *gratin dauphinois* has an extraordinary texture. The cream and potatoes combine perfectly, yet the layering remains beautifully precise, resembling that Central European pastry known as a *Baumkuchen.* The knack is never to stir the gratin once it is ready to go into the oven.

Gratin dauphinois may be served by itself or as an accompaniment to ham or boiled beef. If by chance there is any left over, it can be reheated perfectly if you put the baking dish back in a low oven, again in a 1-inch-deep water bath. The gratin is also good cold (it slices like a pâté), and with a green salad it makes a good light lunch.

A   W O R D   A B O U T   E G G P L A N T

When choosing eggplant, make sure that the skin is glossy, firm, and unblemished. Eggplant has the kind of affinity for oil that a sponge has for water, so cooks around the Mediterranean, where eggplant is a great favorite, have learned a knack for preventing it from absorbing too much oil. When the eggplant is sliced or cubed, they sprinkle it liberally with coarse salt. This not only causes the eggplant to render a dark, bitter fluid, it actually inhibits its ability to absorb oil. Just rinse the salted pieces well in cold running water to remove all the fluid and the salt, then squeeze out the eggplant as if you were gently wringing out pieces of cloth. Pat the slices back into shape and you are ready to proceed with the recipe.

Some present-day cooks are disdainful of this ancient way of dealing with eggplant, but if you are doubtful about its efficacy, I invite you to make a simple experiment: take 2 slices from the same eggplant. Salt 1 and let it leach for 20 minutes. Rinse, squeeze, and pat it back into shape. Dust both slices with flour and fry them in hot vegetable oil until they are golden brown. Sample them. The leached slice will be light and sweet. The other slice will have taken on a great deal of oil and will be sodden and perhaps bitter. Leached eggplant slices take about ¼ the amount of oil that unleached ones require to fry. That used to be an economic consideration in thrifty French households. It is now primarily one of saving yourself and your family from indigestion!

Aunt Annette's Fried Eggplant
LES AUBERGINES A LA TANTE ANNETTE
SERVES 4

This recipe was given to me by a charming old lady from Marseille whom everyone called la tante Annette. *Annette passed on long ago, but every time I make this winning little recipe, I bless her memory. The recipe should be made in high summer when sweet basil and fresh, sun-ripened tomatoes are at their best. The freshness of the dish recommends it highly for the central offering in a summer lunch out of doors.*

2 medium-sized eggplants
1 tablespoon coarse salt
1 cup flour
¼ cup vegetable oil
½ cup freshly grated Gruyère cheese
2 medium-sized, firm, sun-ripened tomatoes, stem cores trimmed out, cut in paper-thin slices

1 tablespoon virgin olive oil
1 teaspoon freshly ground black pepper
¼ teaspoon thyme leaves
¼ teaspoon crumbled oregano
12 to 16 fresh basil leaves, washed and patted dry with paper towels

1. Stem and peel the eggplants. Cut them lengthwise into ¼-inch slices, sprinkle the slices on both sides with salt, and put them in a colander to leach for 20 minutes.
2. Rinse the slices well under cold running water. Squeeze them out gently and pat them dry with paper towels.
3. Dredge the slices well with flour, dusting off the excess.

4. Heat a large frying pan over medium heat and add the vegetable oil. When the oil hazes, fry the slices quickly until they are golden brown on both sides.
5. Drain the slices well, pressing them gently between paper towels.
6. Arrange the slices on a large, attractive platter. Cover the eggplant with a generous sprinkling of grated cheese, add a layer of tomato slices, and sprinkle the tomatoes with olive oil, pepper, thyme leaves, and oregano.
7. Arrange the basil leaves all over the tomatoes and serve the dish at once.

Breaded Eggplant with Tomato Sauce
LES TRANCHES D'AUBERGINE PANEES, SAUCE TOMATE

SERVES 4

In the Midi, the generic designation for the southeastern part of France, breaded eggplant is often served by itself or in a combination of other vegetables such as zucchini, green onions, sliced green tomatoes, and even slices of Gruyère cheese, all breaded in exactly the same way, much like the mixed fry of northern Italy.

2 medium-sized eggplants	¼ cup vegetable oil
1 tablespoon coarse salt	1½ cups Light Tomato Sauce
1 cup flour	(page 290)
2 eggs	3 tablespoons finely chopped
1 teaspoon water	flat-leaf parsley
1 cup fine dry breadcrumbs	

1. Prepare the eggplant, following the first 3 steps for the recipe for Aunt Annette's Fried Eggplant, above.
2. Beat the eggs and water together well and carefully dip each floured slice of eggplant in the egg and water mixture, taking care to see that the slices are completely coated.
3. Roll the slices in breadcrumbs. Once again, see that the slices are completely covered, this time with the breadcrumbs.
4. Carefully stack the slices on top of each other on a plate, separating

the layers with wax paper, and let them chill. This step may be skipped, but the eggplant will be lighter and less oily if you let the slices set. (It is also good to know that this dish may be prepared up to this point hours ahead, provided you cover the stack of breaded slices to prevent them from drying out, and refrigerate them.)

5. Heat a large frying pan. Add the oil. When the oil hazes, fry the slices until golden brown on each side and drain them quickly on paper towels.
6. Heat the tomato sauce and pour it into a heated serving platter.
7. Arrange the slices in the sauce, sprinkle them with parsley, and serve at once.

N O T E : You may prefer serving the slices plain, passing the sauce in a sauceboat.

Braised Eggplant Arles Style
LES AUBERGINES BRAISEES
A L'ARLESIENNE

SERVES 4

I have found versions of this wonderful recipe in Italy and Greece. This one, from the region around Arles in Provence, is a bit lighter and less oily than others.

2 medium-sized eggplants	One 8-ounce tin tomato sauce
1 tablespoon coarse salt	½ teaspoon freshly cracked black
¼ cup olive oil	pepper
2 medium-sized onions, peeled, cored, and coarsely chopped	½ teaspoon granulated sugar
	½ cup dry red wine
3 plump cloves garlic	½ cup freshly grated Parmesan
4 flat anchovy fillets	cheese
3 medium-sized red, ripe tomatoes, skinned, seeded, and coarsely chopped	½ teaspoon thyme leaves
	2 tablespoons finely chopped flat-leaf parsley

1. Trim off and discard the stems and hard area surrounding them from the eggplants. Cut the eggplants in half lengthwise. Trim off and

discard a thin slice from the curved side of each eggplant half so that the halves will sit up straight. Score the flesh on the flat sides of the halves in ½-inch crisscross and rub salt into the incisions.

2. Place the eggplant halves, crisscross sides down, between 2 large inverted plates. Place something such as canned goods, weighing 1 to 2 pounds, on the top plate and let the eggplant halves leach for 30 minutes.
3. Gently heat 1 tablespoon of the oil in a frying pan and slowly sauté the onions until they are translucent.
4. Peel and crush the garlic with the anchovy fillets, add them to the onions, and sauté them for 3 minutes, stirring frequently.
5. Add the tomatoes and continue sautéing the mixture for 5 minutes, stirring and pressing the ingredients against the bottom of the frying pan with a wooden spatula.
6. Add the tomato sauce, pepper, sugar, and wine and simmer for 20 minutes.
7. Rinse the eggplant halves under plenty of cold running water, squeezing the halves well. Pat them dry with paper towels.
8. Gently heat the rest of the oil in another frying pan that will accommodate all 4 of the halves, cut side down, and sauté the eggplant for 5 to 7 minutes.
9. Pour the sauce over the halves, just as they are, face down, and braise the eggplant, covered, for 30 minutes at the lowest heat.
10. Serve the eggplant halves face up in their sauce, sprinkled with cheese, thyme, and parsley.

N O T E : If you like, you may grill the eggplant briefly under a very hot broiler until the grated Parmesan cheese begins to color; however, I find these braised eggplants far more tasty when completely chilled. If you decide to serve them chilled, put them in a covered glass dish in the refrigerator and don't add the cheese, thyme, and parsley until you are ready to serve them. Chilled, they are marvelous with Provençal Rice Salad (page 128).

A W O R D A B O U T A S P A R A G U S

Thirty years ago asparagus was considered a great luxury both in France and in the United States. At that time the spears, or *branches*, as they are called in France, were inevitably as thick as your thumb, about 5 inches long, and they were ground-bleached to an ivory or mauvish white color. Today asparagus is very plentiful in season, reasonably priced, and rarely ground-bleached. The French ground-bleach such vegetables as endive and asparagus and some types of celery. The vegetables are literally buried by heaping the earth over them in the field and are left there to lose their chlorophyll. Ground-bleaching not only whitens the vegetables, it also sweetens them, or—more correctly—removes a great deal of their natural bitterness. It is still possible to purchase the old-fashioned bleached spears of asparagus, but they are astronomically priced. Today asparagus is available in every size from tiny, thin shoots, which are prized for omelets, to ½-inch-thick giant spears.

When asparagus is fresh, it has a unique flavor, at once distinct and delicate. Green asparagus has a fresher taste than the bleached variety, but that delicate, fresh taste begins to dissipate almost as soon as the spear is cut, so it is important to buy asparagus that is very fresh. When examining asparagus spears for freshness, the French use the following signs:

- The leaves at the top of the spear must be tightly pressed against the sides of the spear and not "bloomed out" and loose.
- The cut ends must be moist, not dry and woody.
- The surface of the stem should be smooth, firm, and unwrinkled.

Many French cooks do not peel asparagus. Unless the spears are tiny and tender, I always do. It makes an appreciable difference in texture and appearance. An expensive tool is sold for that purpose, but I suggest you peel the spears with a potato peeler that swivels. Just hold the spear point toward you, cut end away, and starting about 2 inches from the top, peel away the thin outer layer in tiny ribbons, turning the spear as you go. This, I find, preserves much more of the flesh of the spear than the traditional asparagus peeler does. Rinse each spear under cold running water and rub it all over with half a lemon. When you have peeled all the spears, trim them to equal lengths and bind them in bundles with cotton string.

The usual way to serve asparagus is poached or steamed, cold or hot, with vinaigrette or melted butter as sauce. To poach the bundles, if you haven't an upright poacher or steamer, choose an enameled or glass receptacle that will accommodate them and see that they are completely covered with water. To help preserve the beautiful chartreuse color of the peeled spears, I suggest you poach them *au blanc*, and you'll see how easy that is: just add 1 tablespoon cornstarch dissolved in 3 tablespoons cold water and the juice of 1 lemon to the poaching water. The trick works like a charm on almost all green vegetables.

Asparagus should never be overcooked; in fact, it is more delicious a little underdone and crunchy. Usually asparagus spears should be poached only 3 to 6 minutes, depending upon their size. (It is a good idea to test one of the spears first.) When you remove the bundles from the poaching liquid, rinse them quickly under cold running water. If you plan to serve the spears hot, you can plunge them for a few seconds before serving into boiling, acidulated water, that is, boiling water to which a few drops of lemon juice or vinegar have been added. It is a good idea to leave the bundles tied until just before serving the asparagus so the spears will keep their shape.

Place a saltcellar and a peppermill near at hand for those who wish to salt and pepper their asparagus.

Poached Asparagus Spears with Butter Sauce

LES BRANCHES D'ASPERGES AU BEURRE

SERVES 4

16 to 20 fresh asparagus spears,
  ½ inch thick
4 to 6 tablespoons clarified
  sweet butter (see below)

3 tablespoons freshly squeezed
  lemon juice

1. Prepare the asparagus spears as described on page 112.
2. Gently heat the clarified butter and whisk the lemon juice into the hot butter.
3. If you have precooked the asparagus and the spears are cool, plunge them again for no more than 1 minute into boiling water to which you have added a little lemon juice. Remove the bundle, cut the strings away, and arrange the asparagus on a warm serving dish.
4. Serve the asparagus at once and pass the butter sauce in a warm sauceboat.

To clarify butter:

At 250°F the nonfat ingredients in fresh butter burn and turn black, making raw butter alone a very chancy, unreliable fat for frying. Some cooks reduce this hazard by using half raw butter and half vegetable oil. Clarified butter, on the other hand, can be heated to 349°F without danger of scorching. Clarified butter has another advantage: when it is well solidified, carefully rinsed in cold water, patted dry with paper towels, sealed in a jar, and kept in a cool place, it will keep for many weeks. Use the following instructions for converting any amount of sweet butter to clarified butter:

1. Cut the butter up into pat-sized pieces, or smaller.
2. Place the pieces of butter in a cup-like Pyrex vessel so that you can oberve and control the result.
3. Place the vessel on a cookie sheet in the middle of the oven and light the oven at its lowest indication. It should not be hotter than 200°.
4. Allow the butter to melt slowly without stirring it. It takes about 45 minutes to melt a stick of butter in this way.
5. Remove the vessel from the oven and allow it to cool. Through the Pyrex you will see that there are three layers: a layer of foam at the top, a thicker layer of golden milk-fat, and a thinner layer of milk and milk-solids at the bottom.
6. Cover the vessel with foil and set it in the refrigerator until the milk-fat solidifies. Don't put it in the freezer compartment or the three layers will freeze together.
7. When the fat has solidified, remove it from the vessel, wipe away the foam with paper towels, rinse the fat quickly in cold water, and pat it dry with paper towels. This is the clarified butter.
8. Discard whatever remains in the vessel.
9. If you do not plan to use the clarified butter at once, put it in a clean, tightly closed jar and refrigerate it until you are ready to use it. It keeps well for at least a month.

N O T E : French cooks who use a great deal of butter for frying and sautéing habitually make up a pot of clarified butter from time to time to keep on hand in the refrigerator. It is one of those great resources of French cooking which takes time to prepare; however, having a supply of clarified butter on hand can save a great deal of time for the cook later.

• • •

Cold Poached Asparagus Spears Vinaigrette

LES BRANCHES D'ASPERGES A LA VINAIGRETTE

SERVES 4

16 to 20 fresh asparagus spears,   ½ cup *Sauce vinaigrette* (page 38)
each ½ inch thick

1. Prepare the asparagus spears according to instructions on page 112.
2. After you have rinsed the bundle of poached spears, drain and blot the bundle dry with paper towels and wrap it in plastic wrap, then in a layer of aluminum foil, and chill it for 3 hours or overnight in the refrigerator.
3. Pour a pool of vinaigrette into each of 4 serving dishes.
4. Unpack the chilled spears, snip away and discard the string, and arrange an equal number of spears on each plate.
5. Serve the asparagus cold.

N O T E : There is a strong popular belief that cold asparagus in vinaigrette sauce destroys the bouquet of a fine wine. If you are planning to serve a fine wine when this dish is on the menu, then hold off: Serve the wine with the following course.

A WORD ABOUT MUSHROOMS

Mushrooms, both wild and cultivated, are eaten with great relish in every region of France. In the wooded areas the inhabitants hunt the wild ones with elaborate secrecy and do not welcome poachers. I once went mushrooming with an acquaintance from Grasse in the Verdon area of Upper Provence. We brought back a great number of luscious wild mushrooms, some of them as big as your fist. The local innkeeper's wife informed us ruefully that we had certainly raided one of the areas that she considered her own. She was as much a poacher as we, but a cardinal difference between us was that she was from the region. Needless to say we never repeated the exploit.

A chance harvest of wild mushrooms is the joy of almost every French home. It is also rare. But every household consumes kilos of the handsome, cream-colored, domestic mushrooms called *champignons de couche* or *champignons de Paris.* These cultivated mushrooms have so much less flavor than chanterelles, cèpes, and almost any of the other wild mushrooms that the famous writer, Colette, refused to have them in her kitchen. Fortunately, most French cooks do not share her animosity for "tamed" mushrooms. In fact, I really like their delicate flavor, and I use them often.

Here are some French household criteria for judging domestic mushrooms:

- They should be uniformly cream white in color.
- Brown spots indicate staleness or rough handling.
- An opening between the cap and the stem indicates that the mushroom is a little too ripe to be first-class. "Bloomed" mushrooms may still be used, but they are not as good in flavor or appearance.

Here are some rules about cooking domestic mushrooms:

- Mushrooms darken easily in cooking. Lemon will usually prevent darkening. Cut them with a stainless steel knife, and cook them in an enameled or noncorrosive pan. Contact with aluminum is particularly counterindicated.
- Mushrooms, like onions, usually produce quite a lot of liquid in cooking. If you are adding them to an omelet or a sauce whose consistency is crucial, you should sauté them gently until most of the liquid has evaporated.

A final "don't" about mushrooms:

- Domestic mushrooms are raised in sterile soil, so they do not need to be washed. Simply wipe them clean with a damp cloth or paper towel. They already contain a lot of water. Washing them only waterlogs them.

• • •

Mushrooms Poached in White Wine
LES CHAMPIGNONS AU VIN BLANC

SERVES 4

28 to 32 small, very fresh
  domestic mushrooms
2 tablespoons freshly squeezed
  lemon juice
2 tablespoons sweet butter
1 plump shallot, peeled,
  trimmed, and cut paper-thin
¼ teaspoon dried tarragon
  leaves, crumbled

½ teaspoon freshly ground
  white pepper
⅓ teaspoon dried chervil,
  crumbled
½ cup dry white wine
1 tablespoon finely chopped
  flat-leaf parsley
Salt to taste

1. Wipe the mushrooms clean with a soft, damp cloth. With a stainless steel knife trim off the woody ends of the stems and discard them.
2. Place the mushrooms in a glass bowl. Sprinkle the lemon juice over them and shake them about until they are well coated.
3. Heat a heavy enameled pan and melt the butter over medium heat. Sauté the shallot very slowly in the butter until it is transparent.
4. Add the tarragon, pepper, chervil, and the mushrooms and toss the ingredients together in the pan with a wooden spoon or spatula. Sauté for 10 minutes, tossing gently from time to time.
5. Add the white wine, cover the pan, and allow the ingredients to steam-poach for 5 minutes.
6. Add the parsley, toss quickly, adjust for salt, and remove from the fire immediately.
7. Serve the mushrooms hot or cold as an accompaniment or as a snack with drinks.

• • •

Mushrooms Grilled with Garlic and Parsley

LES CHAMPIGNONS GRILLES A LA FLORENTINE

SERVES 4

This is a very beguiling dish that can take the place of a meat course. I like to serve these mushrooms in a bed of vermicelli or risotto and follow them with a simple green salad. With some good, tart apples and some 5-year-old Gouda or a good Pont l'Evêque cheese to end the meal, you have a lunch to elicit raves.

8 to 12 very large, fresh, domestic mushrooms or 4 large shiitake mushrooms
2 plump cloves garlic, peeled, trimmed, and cut lengthwise into tiny, pointed spikes
3 tablespoons light olive oil

1 jigger Cognac
½ teaspoon leaf thyme
2 tablespoons finely chopped flat-leaf parsley
Freshly ground black pepper and salt to taste

1. Wipe the mushrooms clean with a soft, damp cloth and carefully pare away the stem ends with a stainless steel knife. If you have the good fortune to be using verified, edible wild mushrooms, brush away any dirt or foreign matter with a soft brush.
2. Drive the point of the stainless steel paring knife into the caps several times and push the garlic spikes into the incisions.
3. Brush the mushrooms all over with oil.
4. Line a baking tin with aluminum foil, set the mushrooms on it, and grill them under a very hot broiler.
5. Turn the mushrooms once, sprinkle the Cognac over them, and return them to the broiler. The Cognac will flame, so beware.
6. Remove the mushrooms to a warm dish and sprinkle them with the thyme and parsley.
7. Serve them as they are or with pasta or risotto, providing a saltcellar and a peppermill for those who wish to heighten the taste.

N O T E : If we were in Savoy or Dauphiné the recipe would read "1 jigger *marc du pays*" or country brandy instead of Cognac. However, French country brandy is hard to come by in the States, so Cognac or vodka are suggested as good alternatives. I can find the Italian equivalent, grappa, occasionally in United States liquor stores. It is the closest thing to the genuine article.

Sautéed Leaf Spinach
LES EPINARDS AU BEURRE
SERVES 4

This is the easiest and most delicious way to serve spinach. More often than not, the French householder will continue this recipe and make a purée of it, but my family and I prefer the spinach left en branche, *or with the leaves intact.*

1½ pounds well-washed leaf
   spinach, the larger stems
   removed and discarded
1 plump clove garlic, peeled
   and thinly sliced crosswise

2 tablespoons sweet butter
½ teaspoon freshly ground
   white pepper
½ teaspoon coarse salt

1. Choose a large enameled kettle and scatter the sliced garlic over the bottom.
2. Put the still wet spinach in the kettle, cover the kettle, and put it over medium heat. Leave the covered kettle on the fire for 5 to 7 minutes, or until the spinach leaves have wilted and collapsed. Then turn off the heat.
3. Add the butter, salt, and pepper and toss the spinach lightly. Cover the kettle and leave it for 2 minutes.
4. Serve the spinach hot.

   N O T E : Some cooks like to squeeze out the spinach before buttering it. You may do as you like. It certainly will sweeten the spinach considerably. There is a variation on this recipe that I like very much and often serve in summer: squeeze out the spinach after Step 2 and chill it. Serve it as a side dish with oil and vinegar or a *Sauce vinaigrette* (page 38).

• • •

Spinach Sautéed with Raisins and Pine Nuts

LES EPINARDS A LA CATALANE

SERVES 4

This is a recipe from the area of Perpignan. It can also be made with côtes de blettes, *or Swiss chard.*

1 pound fresh, well-washed leaf spinach, larger stems removed and discarded	2 tablespoons light olive oil
	⅓ cup pine nuts
	½ cup white raisins, rinsed in hot water and drained
1 scallion, trimmed, split, and coarsely chopped	½ teaspoon coarse salt

1. In a large enameled pot with a cover, place the spinach and scallion. Cover the pot and heat over medium heat for about 7 minutes or until the spinach has wilted and collapsed.
2. Turn the spinach out into a colander and rinse it under cold running water. Squeeze it well, getting rid of the juice, and put it on a chopping board.
3. Chop the spinach coarsely.
4. Heat a heavy frying pan over medium heat. Add the oil and the pine nuts. As soon as the nuts begin to take on a little color, immediately throw in the spinach, the raisins, and the salt, and toss the ingredients quickly until they are all coated with the oil and heated through.
5. Remove from the frying pan and serve at once.

NOTE: Should you want to try this recipe with Swiss chard, cut the green part off the chard and discard it. Cut the ribs up into pieces about 2 inches long and ½ inch wide and parboil them for 30 minutes in salted water. Drain them well, rinse them under cold running water, dry them with paper towels, and proceed from Step 4.

Les Produits Alimentaires Sccs de Base

There arc many famous dishes in the French household cook's repertoire that are prepared from dry staples. Nevertheless, if you could peek into the pantry of most contemporary French homes you would not find a large store of dried provisions. You might find a handful of rice, a little soup pasta, some dried noodles, and a bouillon cube or two—barely enough dried provisions to make a quick soup in an emergency.

The diet of most French households usually includes dishes made from rice, dried beans, lentils, and, often enough, couscous and chick-peas. Like us, the contemporary French householder recalls with nostalgia the elaborate, time-consuming dishes that used to be prepared almost daily in most homes from dry food staples. Today in France, just as in the United States, everyone seems to be in a greater hurry and to have less time for preparing meals. Consequently, a pot of white beans simmered for half a day "at a murmur," as they still are in the back country of the Navarre, or a casserole of lentils slowly braised with salt pork, sausage, onion, and fresh mint, as one's grandmother used to make them, are more appreciated now than they were years ago. But such dishes are no longer prepared as frequently as thcy were forty years ago when I was a student in France. Gone are the hordes of dried provisions that most French householders used to keep in the pantry and cellar. Today they usually buy only enough dry staples for their immediate needs, and dried beans, lentils, and chick-peas are often purchased partially cooked from the neighborhood *traiteur*. That is an enormous help to the harried French cook who wants to prepare a *navarin* or old-fashioned braised lentils but is pressed for time.

I have included some of the old-time, much loved, time-consuming household recipes in this chapter so that you can have the joy of preparing them from scratch when you have the time. However, not all of the recipes I have chosen for this section require long preparations. Many can be done in an hour, some in twenty minutes. I have arranged the recipes according to the dry food staples they employ, so that I can give you a few of the observations I have gleaned over the years about each staple and its role in the French household diet. Setting each recipe off with a little food lore or a personal remembrance is like saucing or garnishing a dish: It heightens the cook's enjoyment, which in turn is bound to enhance the pleasure of the diners.

Rice

LE RIZ

Next to white bread and potatoes, rice is the most frequently used dry staple in French households. It was not always so. In fact, during the 1870 siege of Paris when there was a terrible shortage of bread, the city warehouses were stockpiled with rice. It went uneaten. The grain was unfamiliar to the Parisian populace, and they had no idea how to prepare it. In less than a hundred years rice became a mainstay in France and the basis for many dishes that are great favorites in French homes.

Many varieties of rice are available to the French homemaker, but most of the household cooks I know in France prefer the short-grain rice of the Camargue, the Rhône delta area south of Arles. Like other short-grain varieties, the *camarguais* rice easily sheds its coat of starch in cooking, making it ideal for the creamy rice puddings and risottos that appear so often on French family menus.

You can find a short-grain rice similar to the *camarguais* rice in United States supermarkets. It is usually packaged in 1-, 2- and 5-pound cellophane bags. The brand names to look for are Goya and Vitarroz.

Today in the United States, most household cooks prefer converted and "minute" rice of the long-grain variety. It is quick, easy to prepare, it doesn't stick together, and is therefore a boon to busy cooks. However, I encourage you to master cooking natural, unprocessed rice—both the short- and long-grain varieties—from scratch so that you can appreciate their very different qualities. Both are available in United States supermarkets. Converted rice doesn't ever stick together, but its flavor is flat and paperlike, and you cannot make a creamy rice pudding or a proper risotto with it. Cooking raw white rice from scratch takes only 14 to 18 minutes, depending upon the relative hardness of the rice. The little expenditure of a few more minutes pays off in superior flavor and texture.

THE THREE CLASSIC WAYS OF PREPARING RICE IN A FRENCH HOUSEHOLD

THE BOILED RICE METHOD. Choose either short- or long-grain rice. Spread the rice on a flat surface and pick out and discard any foreign matter. Put the rice in a fine sieve or colander and wash it well under cold running water. (Rice processors instruct us not to wash rice, since they often enrich it with vitamin powder, but rice picks up lots of dust in warehousing, so I always wash it well.) Calculate the amount of rice you need by allowing ⅓ cup dry rice for each serving and boil it in 4 to 6 times its volume of water. When the water is boiling, throw in the washed rice and let it cook at a rolling boil for 14 to 18 minutes. Test it when it has been cooking for 13 minutes. The proper degree of doneness is referred to as "al dente," the Italian term for slightly resistant to the teeth. Drain the rice quickly by pouring it into a sieve or colander. Shake it a time or two and immediately return it to the hot kettle in which it was boiled. Add a small lump of sweet butter or a tablespoon of light oil and shake the pot a few times so that the rice is lightly coated with the butter or oil. This prevents the grains from sticking to each other as they cool. Cover the kettle and let the rice sit and puff up for a few minutes. The boiled rice is now ready to serve. Plain boiled rice is the perfect accompaniment for richly sauced dishes. It can be eaten as is or with milk, it can be added to soup, or it can be sauced with vinaigrette and served as a salad.

THE PILAF METHOD: The pilaf method of preparing rice originated in the Middle East and was probably introduced to French household cooking in the early twentieth century. In any case, it now belongs to the household repetoire. Pilaf can be made with short-grain rice, but it is traditionally made with the long-grain variety. In a perfectly made pilaf the individual grains of rice should be plump, cooked just to the al dente stage; the grains must never stick together. Allow ⅓ to ½ cup of dry rice per serving. Spread the rice out, pick it over, and wash it just as if you were going to make boiled rice. Dry the cleaned rice well on a tea towel and let it sit for a moment while you sauté a tablespoon of minced or grated onion in a little sweet butter or oil. When the onion is transparent, throw in the rice and sauté it with the onion, stirring it with a wooden spatula. As soon as the rice begins to turn white, add 1 cup of water or broth for each ⅓ to ½ cup dry rice and turn the fire down to a simmer. The rice should be cooked uncovered, and not be stirred while it is cooking. It should absorb all the liquid that does not evaporate. After 13 minutes, test the rice for doneness. If it seems too hard, add a little more water and allow it to cook another minute or so, but watch it carefully so that it does not overcook. Empty the pilaf into a serving dish and serve it at once. Pilaf is a perfect accompaniment for grilled meats, fowl, and fish. It is often served with meatballs. Pilafs may be flavored with cumin, saffron, and tomato, but French household cooks usually prefer making them as I have explained above, saucing them instead.

THE RISOTTO METHOD: A true risotto has the individual grains of rice cooked al dente and bathed in a creamy, thick sauce formed in cooking by the starchy outer layer of the rice, white wine, broth, and grated cheese. The perfect rice for a risotto is a fat short-grain variety. I use the short-grain rice sold under the Goya and Vitarroz labels. Long-grain rice, converted, or "minute" rice will not make a good risotto. If all the ingredients are ready, a perfect risotto takes only 20 minutes to make. Master the simple method and your reputation as a great cook is launched. Allow ⅓ to ½ cup dry rice for each serving, and clean, wash, and towel-dry the rice just as if you were making a pilaf. In a heavy saucepan, sauté 3 tablespoons grated onion in 3 tablespoons sweet butter. Before the onion begins to brown, throw in the rice and stir until it is well coated. Pour in 1 glass of dry white wine and allow it to be absorbed. Continue to cook the rice over a hot flame, adding successively 1 cup of boiling chicken broth for each ⅓ to ½ cup dry rice, stirring the rice as it cooks, and adding the broth only as each addition is absorbed. When the rice is al dente, and the broth has become a thick, rich coating for the rice, add 15 to 20 crumbled saffron threads, 2 tablespoons sweet butter, and 2 tablespoons freshly ground Parmesan cheese. Stir all these ingredients in well. Your risotto is now ready to serve.

Risotto is the richest of the three styles of rice preparation. It may be served alone as a separate course, or as an accompaniment. Provide more freshly grated Parmesan so that those who wish may add it.

Naturally, not all French households use all three rice preparation techniques. But all are widely used in France and throughout the rice-eating world. There are thousands of variations, but you now know how to recognize and distinguish basic boiled rice from pilaf or risotto. Let us now apply these techniques to specific recipes so that you can see how they work and master them. Some of the recipes I have chosen may seem like literal repetitions of the techniques themselves as I have described them above. However, they are given with more exact measurements, more explicit instructions, and in some instances specific variations.

Perfect Buttered Rice
LE RIZ AU BEURRE
SERVES 4 OR 5

This is classic boiled rice, the perfect and simplest way to prepare rice to accompany a main course. The rice is buttered to prevent the grains from sticking together. (The butter seems to enhance the natural taste of the rice.) This boiled rice will take on the taste of whatever you serve with it, so it is particularly good when sauced with the juice and drippings from roasts or grilled chops.

1½ cups short- or long-grain rice	3 tablespoons sweet butter (3
4 to 6 cups fresh water	tablespoons light olive oil
1 tablespoon coarse salt	may be substituted)

1. Spread the rice on a flat surface and pick out and discard any impurities or foreign matter.
2. Put the rice in a large sieve or finely pierced colander and wash it well under cold running water.
3. Bring the water and salt to a rolling boil in a large, heavy kettle. Add the rice and cook it at a rolling boil for 14 to 18 minutes. After 13 minutes, test a grain. It should be just slightly underdone—al dente, or slightly resistant to the bite at the very center. Rices vary in hardness, so it is difficult to predict just how many minutes a rice will take. Keep on testing it.
4. When the rice is properly cooked, pour the contents of the kettle through the colander. Shake the colander a couple of times to get rid of the water, then dump the rice back into the hot kettle in which it cooked, add the butter or oil, and shake the rice about in the kettle to coat the grains.

5. Cover the kettle tightly and let the rice sit for about 3 minutes. This puffs the rice slightly.
6. Serve the rice at once or, if you must hold it, put the covered kettle in a 250° oven until you are ready.

NOTE: French householders often cook more rice than will be eaten at a meal. Leftover rice can be added to a soup, an omelet, or a salad.

Provençal Rice Salad
LA SALADE DE RIZ A LA PROVENÇALE
SERVES 4

This simple dish from Provence is so good that you wonder why it isn't as well known as the salade niçoise. *Understandably, cooks in the Midi are reluctant to light the kitchen stove in the middle of the day during the scorching heat of summer, when even the shutters are closed to keep out the heat. Cooking is often done after dark or in the very early morning, and this dish is one that Provençal cooks can prepare early in the morning and set aside to serve hours later. The rice is cold and delicious when it has been allowed to sit and take on all the flavors of the fish, herbs, and dressing. Rice salad is a great summer favorite in Provence. This version is wonderful for a picnic.*

2 tablespoons tinned tuna or 4 flat anchovy fillets
1 plump clove garlic, peeled and crushed
1 teaspoon coarse salt
10 to 12 capers
4 fresh tarragon leaves, finely chopped, or ¼ teaspoon dried tarragon leaves, crumbled
1 tablespoon Dijon mustard
3 tablespoons wine vinegar
1 large hard-boiled egg, peeled and finely chopped

1 medium-sized Belgian endive
2 to 2½ cups cold, boiled rice
2 large, red, ripe tomatoes, skinned, seeded, and coarsely chopped
6 to 8 black oil-cured or niçois olives, pitted
¼ teaspoon fresh or dried thyme leaves
½ teaspoon freshly ground white pepper
3 tablespoons extra virgin olive oil

1. Pound the tuna or anchovy fillets, garlic, salt, capers, tarragon, and mustard in a mortar or pulse them 5 times in a food processor.
2. Place this paste in the bottom of a glass salad bowl and stir the vinegar and chopped egg into it.
3. With a stainless steel knife, trim away and discard the hard root end of the endive. Cut the endive crosswise into ½-inch slices.
4. Add the rice, tomatoes, olives, and endive to the salad bowl and toss all of the ingredients together.
5. Sprinkle the thyme leaves and pepper over the salad and drizzle the olive oil over the surface. Toss the salad lightly again to make sure the thyme, pepper, and oil are spread through the rice.
6. Cover the bowl and place it in a cool—but not frigid—place to meld for at least half an hour.
7. Serve as first course or as one of several hors d'oeuvre.

NOTE: Most of the cooks I know in Provence who make this salad add various things such as thinly sliced baby zucchini, flame-roasted bell peppers, and sometimes cucumber. You may add whatever seems right to you, but remember that an authentic Provençal rice salad must have that faint flavor of tuna or anchovy and thyme, and the main ingredient of the salad must be rice. A "vinaigrette" made with freshly squeezed lemon juice instead of vinegar makes a wonderfully light dressing for this salad. For those who have not learned to love the strong taste of extra virgin olive oil, I recommend any of the lighter oils.

• • •

Rice Pilaf with Tomato Sauce
LE RIZ PILAF A LA GRECQUE
SERVES 4 TO 6

This is the classic pilaf. In France it is sometimes called Greek, sometimes Turkish, sometimes Russian. Though a good pilaf can be made with short-grain rice, long-grain rice is usually preferred.

3 tablespoons sweet butter, light oil, or a mixture of both

1 medium-sized onion, peeled and finely chopped or grated

2 cups rice, picked over, well washed, and dried

3 cups broth or water

½ teaspoon salt

¼ teaspoon freshly ground white pepper

10 to 15 threads of saffron, crumbled

1. Heat the butter or oil over low heat in a heavy-bottomed pot and slowly sauté the onion, stirring it with a wooden spatula until it is just golden.
2. Add the rice and stir it well with the onion so that all the grains are coated with the hot fat.
3. When the rice begins to whiten, add the broth or water immediately, along with the salt, pepper, and saffron.
4. Cook the rice at a simmer for 14 minutes without stirring and begin to test it for doneness. Depending on the hardness of the rice, it may take as much as 20 minutes. All the liquid should be absorbed and bubbles no longer appear in the little holes that have formed while the rice was cooking.
5. Serve the pilaf in a mound with Light Tomato Sauce (page 290).

NOTE: Pilaf is an excellent accompaniment for grilled chops, steaks, and fish. It is traditionally served with lamb. For a "slim" lunch, forget the tomato sauce and serve the pilaf with plain yogurt sprinkled with chopped parsley and scallion.

• • •

Martinique-Style Rice

LE RIZ A LA MARTINIQUAISE

SERVES 4

Back in the days before Vatican II, when Lent meant meatless meals several times a week, this good, economical dish was often served in French households and student restaurants as a principal dish. Now it sometimes appears as a first course in France. It is a good choice for a light summer lunch. Followed by a simple green salad and a plate of cheeses, and accompanied by a bottle of Cabernet Sauvignon, Martinique-style rice makes a distinguished, satisfying, and unpretentious lunch. Your main concern in serving such a lunch is that the sauce be light and fluffy, the rice exactly al dente, and the egg perfectly fried.

3 scallions, trimmed, both white and green parts finely chopped

2 cloves garlic, peeled, trimmed, and finely chopped

1 bay leaf

½ teaspoon dried oregano leaves, crumbled

¼ teaspoon ground coriander

¼ teaspoon nutmeg

¼ teaspoon ground cinnamon

½ teaspoon freshly cracked black pepper

⅛ teaspoon ground cayenne pepper (optional)

2 tablespoons vegetable oil

2 medium-sized red, ripe tomatoes, skinned, seeded, and coarsely chopped

1 cup broth or water

½ teaspoon coarse salt

1 teaspoon dark rum

¼ teaspoon granulated sugar

4 medium-sized fresh eggs, at room temperature

2 cups freshly boiled rice

1 tablespoon finely chopped flat-leaf parsley

Make the sauce:

1. In a heavy frying pan, gently sauté the chopped scallions, garlic, bay leaf, all the herbs and spices, and pepper in 1 tablespoon of the oil, stirring often with a wooden spoon until the scallions and garlic are soft.

2. Add the tomatoes and increase the heat. Stir the mixture together as it fries, pressing it against the bottom of the frying pan with a wooden spatula so that the juice fries away.

3. Add the broth or water, salt, rum, and sugar and allow the sauce to reduce to half its volume. Don't overcook. The sauce should be light and fluffy. Discard the bay leaf. Remove the sauce from the fire and set it aside while you do the other steps.

4. In the other 1 tablespoon of oil, fry the eggs perfectly.

Assemble the dish:

1. Choose 4 colorful, concave dishes. Eight-inch soup plates are fine for this.
2. Place one cup of warm, boiled rice in each plate and make a crater in the center of each mound of rice.
3. Heat the sauce and ladle ¼ of the sauce into each crater. Sprinkle chopped parsley on each.
4. Place a fried egg on top of each crater of sauce and serve immediately.

N O T E : If you like, you may garnish this dish with some slices of flame-roasted bell pepper (see page 44) and fried bananas or plantains, in true Martinique style.

Rice Milanese Style
LE RISOTTO A LA MILANNAISE
SERVES 4 OR 5

No one seems to know exactly when the northern Italian way of preparing rice was generally adopted by the French. Even today it is only in the larger cities and the areas along the Italian border that risotto (actually the Italian term for a dish whose principal ingredient is rice) is commonly found on household menus. I've often eaten wonderful risottos in the homes of friends in the Aix-Marseille area. Of course, risottos are standard fare in restaurants throughout France. There is a widespread belief in France that risotto is difficult to make. It isn't! Making risotto just takes patience. If you know how, you can turn one out in 20 minutes. Here's the standard recipe.

¾ stick (6 tablespoons) sweet butter
1 medium-sized onion, peeled, hard parts pared out and discarded, finely chopped
2 cups short-grain rice, well washed, picked over, and towel-dried
½ cup dry white wine

10 to 15 saffron threads
3 cups broth or water, heated to a boil
5 tablespoons freshly grated Parmesan cheese
1 teaspoon coarse salt
½ teaspoon freshly ground white pepper

1. In a heavy saucepan, warm 4 of the 6 tablespoons of butter at medium heat and slowly sauté the onion until it is translucent, stirring it continuously with a wooden spatula.
2. Add the rice and stir well. Continue to sauté the mixture for 4 to 5 minutes, taking care that it does not brown.
3. Add the wine and stir vigorously until it is completely absorbed.
4. Crumble the saffron threads and add them to the hot broth or water.
5. Add the very hot broth or water ½ cup at a time, stirring continuously. Do not add more liquid until each ½ cup has been absorbed. The rice will release a good deal of starch, producing a thick, sticky sauce, so scrape the bottom of the saucepan often to prevent the risotto from scorching. Test the rice from time to time for doneness. It should be al dente. The whole operation of incorporating the hot liquid should take no more than 14 minutes. If the rice reaches the al dente stage sooner than expected, remove the saucepan from the heat.
6. Quickly stir in the grated cheese, the remaining 2 tablespoons butter, and the salt and pepper.
7. Serve the risotto at once or keep it warm until you are ready to serve it by setting the saucepan in hot water.

N O T E : Risotto may be served as a first course or, when garnished, does very well as a main course. It often appears as a special accompaniment for braised veal, fish, shellfish, roasts, cutlets, or chops. Risotto molds beautifully, so I sometimes serve it as individual timbales. It can be made very impressive by packing it into a Turk's head mold, unmolding it on a large platter and surrounding it with sautéed vegetables or seafood or whatever is appropriate. When risotto is to be served with fish or seafood, substitute a strong, reduced *fumet* or fish broth for the broth or water in the recipe.

Leftover risotto need never go begging. It makes a good cold snack. It can also be used to thicken soups and to make delicious croquettes (page 136).

· · ·

Green Risotto with Sautéed Chicken Livers

LE RISOTTO VERT AUX FOIES DE VOLAILLE

SERVES 4 OR 5

Chicken livers are plentiful in the United States and less expensive than they are in France. If your family and friends are fond of them, try this elegant combination. I have known professed liver-haters to eat it with pleasure and ask for seconds. The risotto, a bright green from the parsley, is lovely to look at surrounded by the sautéed livers in their richly aromatic brown sauce, but the harmony of both subtle and explosive tastes is even lovelier. I can never think of this dish without my mouth beginning to water. I hope it becomes one of your favorites.

Prepare Risotto Milanese Style with these differences:

- In a small piece of cheesecloth wrap 4 sage leaves, 4 tarragon leaves, and one 4-inch piece of fresh or dried orange peel, and tie the cheesecloth closed with a piece of cotton string.
- Put this *sachet* into the boiling broth and allow it to seethe there for 5 minutes, then remove and discard it.
- Add ½ cup dry sherry or Madeira to the broth before starting to combine it with the rice.
- For the Parmesan cheese, substitute ¼ cup finely chopped, fresh flat-leaf parsley.
- Keep the risotto warm by setting the pan in another pan of hot water until you are ready to assemble the dish.

FOR THE CHICKEN LIVERS:

1 pound fresh chicken livers	1 large onion, peeled, cored, and thinly sliced
1 jigger Cognac	
1 scallion, trimmed and finely minced	½ teaspoon thyme leaves
	6 to 8 rosemary leaves
½ teaspoon cracked black pepper	⅛ teaspoon finely crumbled sage leaves
3 tablespoons sweet butter	
1 thick rasher smoked slab bacon, in fine dice	½ teaspoon coarse salt
	1 cup light, dry red wine
½ cup flour	½ cup water

1. With a pair of kitchen shears, cut away and discard the fat and string-like adhesions from the livers. Then rinse the livers in cold water and blot them dry with paper towels.
2. Marinate the livers in a glass dish for 30 minutes with the Cognac, scallion, and black pepper.
3. Heat the butter gently in a frying pan and slowly fry the bacon cubes until they begin to crisp.
4. Remove the livers from the marinade, reserving the marinade. Pat them dry and dredge them lightly in flour,
5. Add the livers to the bacon and fry them 2 minutes on each side. Remove the livers and bacon bits and reserve.
6. Put the onion, all the herbs, and the salt into the frying pan and sauté, stirring so that they sauté evenly. When the onion is transparent, put in the reserved marinade and the wine. Reduce the heat and cover the frying pan tightly, allowing the onions to cook for 10 minutes.
7. Add the water and deglaze, scraping the bottom of the pan with a wooden spatula.
8. Return the bacon and livers to the pan and allow them to heat through. Stir them about to coat the livers in the sauce and remove immediately from the heat.
9. Pack the warm risotto into a Turk's head mold or a small, deep bowl. Unmold the risotto onto a platter and carefully arrange the livers and their sauce around the rice. Serve at once.

Rice Croquettes

LES CROQUETTES DE RISOTTO

SERVES 4

Croquettes are an attractive way to use up leftover risotto. They are so good, in fact, that I always make more risotto than will be eaten at one meal so that I can have an excuse to make croquettes. In France these rice croquettes are usually the size and shape of a wine bottle cork. About 3 of them in a pool of light tomato sauce constitute a good first course. The Sauce financière *on page 290 is very good for the croquettes, but I make a special Croquette Sauce for them. The recipe yields one cup of sauce.*

FOR THE SAUCE

One 8-ounce tin tomato sauce
(not purée)
½ cup dry white wine
½ teaspoon wine vinegar
¼ teaspoon coarse salt
¼ teaspoon granulated sugar
1 bay leaf

1 tablespoon finely chopped
fresh basil leaves
8 to 10 small fresh basil leaves,
carefully washed and blotted
dry
½ teaspoon freshly squeezed
lemon juice

FOR THE CROQUETTES

1½ to 2 cups leftover risotto
2 large eggs, well beaten
¼ cup cooked breast of chicken
or one 3½-ounce tin tuna,
finely pounded, or 3
tablespoons anchovy paste

1 cup flour
1 egg
1 teaspoon water
1 cup fine breadcrumbs
1 cup vegetable oil

Make the sauce:

1. Heat the tomato sauce, wine, vinegar, salt, sugar, bay leaf, and chopped basil leaves over medium heat until the sauce has reduced to half its volume. The sauce will froth at first; watch it to be sure it doesn't boil over. If it seems on the point of doing so, stir quickly until it subsides.
2. Strain the sauce through a fine sieve, pressing on the basil leaves with a wooden spoon to get as much sauce through the sieve as possible. Discard what is left in the sieve.
3. Add the lemon juice and mix it in well. Set the sauce aside while you prepare the croquettes.

Make the croquettes:

1. Mix the risotto with the eggs and the pounded chicken, tuna, or anchovy paste.
2. Sprinkle the flour liberally on a flat surface. Wetting your fingers with water, roll the risotto mixture over the floured surface into several long rolls the size of breadsticks, coating them well with the flour.
3. Using a sharp knife dipped in water, cut the rolls into 2½-inch pieces. If the rolls do not cut well, allow them to chill for 30 minutes.
4. Beat the egg and the water together, and dip the croquettes in the mixture, making sure they are coated all over.
5. Roll the croquettes in breadcrumbs. Examine each croquette to see

that it is completely covered and sealed with the egg and crumb coating.

6. Cover a plate with wax paper and arrange the croquettes on it. They should not touch each other. (If you make 2 layers, put another piece of wax paper between the layers.) Cover the croquettes with wax paper and put them in the refrigerator to chill for 2 hours.

7. Heat the oil in a 10-inch frying pan and fry the croquettes at medium heat for 5 minutes, turning them once, so that they are uniformly golden all over. Drain the croquettes on paper towels. (If you must delay serving them, keep them hot in the oven on paper towels. Croquettes, as the name in French implies, should be crunchy.)

8. To serve, ladle a little sauce into the bottom of each serving plate, place 2 or 3 croquettes in the center of the sauce, and float 2 basil leaves on the sauce alongside the croquettes. Serve at once.

Pasta

LES PATES ALIMENTAIRES

Pasta is sure to appear once or twice a week on French household menus, usually in the form of *nouilles* (noodles), which are about as popular with the French as boiled rice. I use the Italian word pasta in this book about French household cooking because it is the word we use in the United States to designate all the forms from tiny stars and orzo to the giant shells and lasagnes. The French have adopted many of the Italian terms, just as we have. The French equivalent of pasta, however, is *les pâtes*, or, more properly, *les pâtes alimentaires.* While the French are delighted to eat many of the forms of pasta in Italian restaurants and pizzerias, French household cooks usually confine themselves to some of the tiny soup pasta (which they often add to broths), spaghetti, and macaroni, which they sometimes serve as a first course or as accompaniments for main courses. The all-time favorite in French homes is noodles.

Pasta has a legal definition in France. *Les pâtes alimentaires* are defined as "cut and dried products made by kneading unleavened semolina with drinkable water." If pasta is labeled "made with egg," by French law that pasta must contain 3 eggs for each kilo (a little over 2 pounds) of semolina.

Packaged, dried pasta is available everywhere in France. The quality is uniformly excellent. In recent years fresh pasta, once difficult to find in stores except along the southern coast, along the Italian border, and in large towns, has caught on and can now be bought by the gram throughout France. In general, most French cooks know how to prepare pasta well. The rules are much like those for making perfect boiled rice. Here they are applied to the preparation of buttered noodles, a favorite in all regions of France, but the rules will serve for preparing almost any kind of pasta.

Buttered Noodles
LES NOUILLES AU BEURRE

This is a model recipe like the ones I have given for preparing rice. It will serve as a paradigm for preparing most of the forms of pasta.

1. Allow 2 to 2½ ounces of dry pasta for each serving.
2. Use a large kettle and plenty of lightly salted, fresh water. The proportion should be 3 to 4 quarts of cold water to ½ pound of pasta. Add 1 tablespoon of coarse salt to the kettle of water.
3. The water should reach a rolling boil before you add the pasta, and it should be kept at a rolling boil during the entire time you are cooking the pasta. Do not cover the kettle at any time.
4. Using a wooden spoon or spatula, stir the pasta when you add it to the boiling water to see that none of it sticks to the bottom of the kettle. Once it is loose and boiling, leave it alone!
5. Test the doneness of the pasta after 5 minutes by retrieving a piece and biting it. It should be al dente, or a little resistant to the bite. The cooking time will vary according to the shape and thickness of the pasta. Noodles usually cook in less time than spaghetti or macaroni, and fresh pasta always cooks far more quickly than dried pasta.
6. Just before the pasta reaches the exact stage of doneness you desire,

remove the kettle from the fire, place a colander in the sink, and pour the contents of the kettle into it immediately. Shake the colander once or twice.

7. Return the pasta to the hot kettle and toss in either a knob of sweet butter or a couple of tablespoons of olive oil. Shake the kettle about gently to coat the pasta. This will prevent it from sticking together. It will also help it to puff slightly.

8. When you are ready to serve the pasta add 2 more tablespoons sweet butter and 3 tablespoons finely grated Gruyère cheese. Toss the noodles quickly and lightly with a wooden implement and serve at once.

N O T E : Fresh, undried pasta requires very little cooking time. Despite the protests of purists that a little oil added to the water makes the pasta sauce-resistant, you will be wise to add a little vegetable oil to the boiling water before adding fresh pasta. Fresh pasta generally is sold coated with a little flour or cornmeal to prevent it from sticking together. This will sometimes cause the water to boil over, and the oil should prevent that from happening. Start testing fresh pasta for doneness after 2 minutes of rapid boiling. Once it has passed the desired stage of doneness it begins to puff up and take on water.

Macaroni with Bacon and Tomato Sauce
LES MACARONI A LA PIAULE

SERVES 4

Strictly speaking, this is not a French household recipe. It is a French student recipe and I have a strong sentimental attachment to it. La piaule *is French student slang for one's pad or room. On Sundays, when the university restaurant was closed, the students were left to fend for themselves. We were forbidden to cook in our rooms, but everyone had a tiny alcohol burner hidden away, and we all produced improvised meals* en cachette. *Aix had two wonderful open-air markets; plenty of* traiteurs *who were famous for their pâtés, quenelles, and fresh* pâtes; *splendid bakeries; butcher shops; and a Monoprix where everything from cheese and sausage and ham to dark rum, wine, and the alcohol burner itself could be bought. In those days many students practically subsisted on pasta, so they became expert at its preparation. We made this recipe often. It was years before I discovered that the Italians in the Sabine hills around Rome make a similar pasta dish called* all'amatriciana.

12 ounces dry macaroni	1 sprig fresh or dried sage
2 thick rashers slab bacon, rind removed and discarded, cut into ¼-inch matchstick-like lardoons	½ cup water or dry white wine
	¼ teaspoon freshly ground black pepper
	½ teaspoon salt
2 plump shallots, peeled, sliced paper-thin	3 scallions, white part only, split and cut into very fine 4-inch strips
5 medium-sized red, ripe, sauce tomatoes, skinned, seeded, and coarsely chopped	1 tablespoon light olive oil
	½ cup finely grated Gruyère cheese
3 large branches basil	
2 branches flat-leaf parsley	

1. Prepare the macaroni according to the instructions for buttered noodles on page 138.
2. Fry the bacon lardoons over medium heat. When they begin to sizzle, add the shallots. Stir them until they are well coated in the bacon fat and allow them to sauté gently until they are completely soft but not browned.
3. Add the tomatoes and allow them to fry for 5 minutes, stirring often.
4. Tie the basil, parsley, and sage together with cotton string into a neat bouquet garni.
5. Add the water or wine, the bouquet garni, and the pepper and salt. Increase the heat, cover the pan, and allow to cook for 5 minutes. Then uncover the pan and allow the sauce to reduce to ⅔ its original volume.
6. Discard the bouquet garni. Empty the sauce into the pot of drained macaroni, add the scallions and the olive oil, toss, and heat covered for 1 minute.
7. Serve at once. Pass the grated cheese so that the diners may help themselves.

N O T E : Some of my American friends find it hard to believe that we prepared this marvelous dish in our rooms when we were students.

We prepared many more! As one of my old student *copines* used to say: "I am practically *sans sous* [penniless], but that's no reason to eat badly!"

Macaroni with Anchovy and Fennel Sauce

LES MACARONI AUX ANCHOIS

SERVES 4

Salted anchovies are an important ingredient in the distinctive flavor of old-time Provençal food. They belong there along with garlic, tomatoes, and thyme. Salted anchovies are plumper than their more refined cousins, the flat, tinned fillets of anchovy we all know. The old-fashioned anchovies are packed in casks and are heavily layered with coarse sea salt. They keep well for a very long time, so a cask of them was usually laid in once a year on faraway farms and distant mas in Provence during the eighteenth and nineteenth centuries to provide ready protein when meat was scarce. If you discover a supplier, do try them. To prepare them you simply rinse them well in cold water and pull the flesh away from the head and down each side of the spine. Discard the head and spine and rinse the 2 fillets in more cold water and a little vinegar. They are ready to use. Many people eat them as they are with a little lemon juice or vinegar and oil. If you cannot find them, then use the tinned, flat fillets of anchovies, by all means. Their taste is milder but very good.

Traditionally macaroni with anchovy and fennel sauce is called Christmas Eve macaroni in Provence. Christmas Eve is a vigil and as such is a meatless day for Catholics. This robust, highly flavored dish was invented to eat before the Provençal family set off for midnight mass. It is a dish that brings back sentimental memories of old folks and children dressed in their regional costumes, the familiar Saboly Christmas carols, the church aglow with candles, and the icy Mistral howling outside. But don't wait for Christmas Eve to enjoy this luscious dish. You can make it any time!

1 cup coarsely chopped fennel
   bulb (save the tops)
1 branch dried thyme
1 branch dried rosemary
1 branch fennel
1 bay leaf
8 ounces dry macaroni, or an
   equal amount of noodles or
   spaghetti
2 plump cloves garlic, peeled
   and crushed
3 tablespoons finely chopped
   flat-leaf parsley
6 anchovy fillets

2 tablespoons light olive oil
½ teaspoon fennel seeds
½ teaspoon freshly ground black
   pepper
2 tablespoons tomato purée
½ cup dry red wine
1½ cups water
½ cup soft breadcrumbs
1 clove garlic, peeled and
   crushed in
   ½ teaspoon coarse salt
10 to 12 oil-cured black olives,
   pitted

1. Prepare 2 bouquets garnis:
   • Bind together all of the fennel tops from the fennel bulb with a
     piece of cotton string. If you found a supplier for dried fennel
     stems, use the dried ones instead to make the bouquet.
   • Bind the branches of dried thyme, rosemary, and fennel and the
     bay leaf together with cotton string.
2. Prepare the macaroni according to the instructions for buttered noodles on page 138 with this exception:
   • Place the bouquet garni of fennel tops or stems in the boiling
     water while you are cooking the macaroni.
   • Discard the bouquet of fennel when the macaroni has finished
     cooking.
3. In a heavy frying pan, gently sauté the 2 cloves of crushed garlic,
   parsley, and anchovy fillets in 1 tablespoon of the olive oil. As they
   sauté, press the ingredients against the bottom of the frying pan so that
   the anchovy disintegrates into a paste with the other ingredients.
4. Add the fennel seeds and pepper and fry for another 2 minutes.
5. Add the tomato purée, wine, and water and stir well before adding
   the bouquet garni of thyme, rosemary, fennel, and bay leaf, and the
   chopped fennel bulb. Increase the heat and reduce the liquid to ⅔
   its volume. Discard the bouquet of herbs. Add the olives and heat
   them just enough to warm them.
6. Using your fingers, rub the breadcrumbs, the other crushed garlic,
   and the rest of the olive oil together thoroughly. Put the oily crumbs
   in a small frying pan and heat them gently, stirring them with a
   wooden spatula until they are crisp but not brown.

7. Pour the sauce over the pasta, toss well, sprinkle with the toasted crumbs, and serve at once.

N O T E : The fennel used in Provençal cooking should really be the wild variety that grows in the arid *garrigues* of the Midi. It is stronger and tougher than the domestic type we now find in the produce sections of large United States supermarkets and in shops in Italian neighborhoods. In adapting this recipe, I have included a chopped bulb of domestic fennel. This is a change from the traditional recipe, but it will help boost the taste of fennel in the sauce. Wild fennel is much stronger, and if you had it, there would be no need to add the cup of chopped domestic fennel. Packets of fennel stems are sometimes sold in gourmet shops for grilling fish. If you can find them, use them to make the bouquets garnis in the recipe. Look for fennel seeds in the spice section of your supermarket.

Baked Macaroni Forest Warden Style
LES MACARONI A LA FORESTIERE

SERVES 4 OR 5

This baked macaroni, I am told, is much like the macaroni pie of which Lord Nelson was very fond. Friends have given me various explanations for the name. One is that the dish is usually made with the giant, wild mushrooms that grow in the dense conifer forests of Northern Provence and Savoy, where the forest wardens find them in troves and bring them down to the local villages for sale. The other explanation is that this substantial dish can be cut into thick wedges and carried along in the warden's backpack instead of a sandwich. The original recipe contains many eggs, lots of Gruyère cheese, and heavy cream. This version is much lighter, but baked macaroni forest warden style is still a substantial dish. It is preferable to serve your guests a couple of thin slices rather than a thick wedge. The dish contains a considerable amount of Béchamel *sauce to prevent it from drying out during the baking; however, I find that it needs a good helping of sauce* forestière *when served. (Sauce forestière is also very good with grilled skirt steak or lightly sautéed liver.) The recipe yields one cup of sauce.*

FOR THE SAUCE FORESTIÈRE:

4 large white mushrooms,
   wiped clean, stems trimmed,
   finely chopped
2 large shallots, peeled and
   finely chopped
1 slice boiled ham, finely
   chopped
1 tablespoon finely chopped
   flat-leaf parsley
2 tablespoons vegetable oil
5 crushed juniper berries (look
   for these in the spice section
   of the supermarket)

1 bay leaf
½ teaspoon freshly cracked
   black pepper
One 8-ounce tin tomato sauce
1½ cups bouillon or broth
1 teaspoon arrowroot powder
   (look for this item in the
   spice section; if you don't
   find it, use cornstarch)
3 tablespoons water
1 tablespoon Cognac
½ teaspoon granulated sugar
1 tablespoon sweet butter

FOR THE MACARONI:

5 tablespoons sweet butter
2 rashers smoked bacon, rind
   removed and discarded, in
   ¼-inch dice
6 large white mushrooms,
   wiped clean, stems removed
   and discarded, heads thinly
   sliced
1 leek, white part only, split,
   carefully washed, dried, and
   finely chopped
¼ teaspoon freshly grated
   nutmeg
½ teaspoon freshly cracked
   black pepper
6 chicken livers, adhesions, fat,
   and bile spots removed

3 tablespoons dry white wine
2 tablespoons flour
2 cups bouillon or broth
1 cup grated farmer cheese
½ teaspoon coarse salt
2 tablespoons heavy cream
½ cup soft breadcrumbs
6 ounces dry elbow macaroni,
   cooked al dente according to
   directions on page 138,
   drained, shaken with a little
   sweet butter, and set aside
10 to 12 fresh spinach leaves,
   well washed, large stems
   discarded, boiled for 3
   minutes, rinsed, squeezed,
   and coarsely chopped

Make the sauce:

1. Sauté the mushrooms, shallots, ham, and parsley in the oil at moderate heat, stirring constantly for 7 minutes.
2. Add the crushed juniper berries, bay leaf, and pepper and continue cooking for 3 minutes.
3. Add the tomato sauce and broth and stir well. Allow the liquid to reduce to ⅔ its volume.
4. Mix the arrowroot powder and the water and add it, the Cognac, and the sugar to the sauce, stirring them in well. Simmer for 5

minutes. Swirl in the butter and keep sauce warm until ready to serve.

Prepare the baked macaroni:
1. Heat 1 tablespoon of the butter in a heavy frying pan and gently sauté the bacon, mushrooms, and leek with the nutmeg and cracked pepper until the liquid from the mushrooms has disappeared.
2. Add the chicken livers and sauté for 4 minutes.
3. Add the wine, and as it cooks, deglaze the bottom of the pan with a wooden spatula. Allow the wine to evaporate completely. Set the sauté aside.
4. Make a *Béchamel* sauce by melting 3 tablespoons of the sweet butter in a heavy saucepan, stirring in the flour while the butter is sizzling. Before it begins to take on color, add the bouillon or broth and stir until smooth. Let the *Béchamel* continue to simmer for 5 minutes. Then add the farmer cheese, a little at a time, to the *Béchamel*, and stir until all the lumps have disappeared. Stir in the salt and remove from the fire. Swirl in the cream.
5. Butter a large soufflé dish with what remains of the butter, empty the breadcrumbs into the buttered dish, and roll the dish about until the interior is covered with the crumbs. Turn the dish over to empty out the loose crumbs onto wax paper and save them.
6. Toss the cooked macaroni with half the *Béchamel* and pack the tossed macaroni into the soufflé dish in layers with the chicken liver mixture, the spinach, a little *Béchamel*, more tossed macaroni, and top off the dish with what is left of the *Béchamel.* Sprinkle the top with the remaining breadcrumbs.
7. Preheat the oven to 375°.
8. Place the soufflé dish in a pan containing 2 inches of water and bake the macaroni for 50 minutes.
9. Remove the macaroni from the oven and let it sit for 5 minutes. Run a sharp knife around the edge of the soufflé dish to loosen the macaroni. Invert a serving dish over soufflé dish and holding the two together, turn them upside down, lift off the soufflé dish, and leave the unmolded macaroni on the serving dish. Garnish with *Sauce forestière* and serve.

N O T E : You will need a sharp knife to cut the baked macaroni into servings, and you will need a pie trowel to serve it neatly. Spoon some of the sauce over each serving.

Country-Style Meatless Macaroni
LES PATES MAIGRES A LA CAMPAGNARDE

SERVES 4

This is a meatless pasta dish for Lent, but its full-bodied flavor seems to suggest that the diners couldn't have felt that they were suffering any self-abnegation!

8 ounces dry macaroni (penne or rigatoni are good substitutes)
6 large white mushrooms, wiped clean, stems trimmed, cut top to bottom in ¼-inch slices
1 large bell pepper, flame-roasted, cleaned, cored, seeded, and cut into ½-inch strips (see page 44)
1 small white onion, peeled, halved, and thinly sliced
1 plump clove garlic, peeled and thinly sliced, top to bottom

½ teaspoon coarsely cracked black pepper
¼ teaspoon thyme leaves
1 bay leaf
2 tablespoons vegetable oil
½ teaspoon coarse salt
½ cup white vermouth
½ cup water
½ cup freshly grated Parmesan cheese

1. Prepare the macaroni according to the instructions for buttered noodles on page 138 and set aside.
2. Sauté the mushrooms, pepper, onion, garlic, cracked pepper, thyme, and bay leaf very gently in the oil until the vegetables are wilted and the juice from the mushrooms has evaporated.
3. Add the salt, vermouth, and water and cover the pan. Increase the heat and cook for 5 minutes. Uncover the pan and allow the liquid to reduce to half its volume. There should be about ½ cup of liquid. If there is less, add a little water.
4. Discard the bay leaf and empty the contents of the pan into the macaroni kettle. Toss the vegetables and sauce with the macaroni.
5. Cover the pot and heat up for exactly 1 minute.
6. Turn out on a warm platter, sprinkle liberally with the grated cheese, and serve. More grated cheese may be passed.

N O T E : This recipe is equally successful, equally delicious if you substitute boiled rice for the boiled macaroni.

If you should have the very good luck to fall heir to some fresh morels or cèpes—wonderfully tasty wild mushrooms—they are a fabulous substitute for the tame white mushrooms specified in the recipe. Just clean them thoroughly by letting them soak briefly in salted water. I know that purists would rant at the thought of wetting them, but they are often full of sand—a dreadful thing to encounter in food—and sometimes little bugs have made their home among them, so it is a good idea to soak them briefly in salt water, which usually rids them of such things. I find that they can be dried to perfection in a salad drier of the centrifugal sort. Once dried, use them in the recipe. Old-time Provençal farmers would sprinkle the dish with plenty of chopped garlic and parsley to finish it off, swearing that wild mushrooms must be served up with a great deal of both. However, unless you are willing to chew a handful of parsley afterward or spend the next twelve hours alone, I don't advise adding the garlic!

CANNELONI

Canneloni—literally cannons—are 3- to 4-inch squares of pasta dough which, when cooked, are stuffed and rolled up into little cylinders. They are then lined up in a baking dish, sauced, and baked. For me the word *canneloni* evokes warm memories of feast days, Christmas, Kings' Day, and Easter dinners *en famille.* They were always considered special, even in those long gone days, since their preparation was elaborate and required many hours of devoted work. For that reason, they were prepared only on very special occasions. In this era of fast food, canneloni have almost disappeared from the household diet. To my mind and taste, canneloni, when they are well prepared, far outshine lasagne and manicotti, which they vaguely resemble. If you have never experienced first-rate canneloni, made at home, you can scarcely imagine the excitement their appearance occasioned when I was a young man!

I learned very early on not to order canneloni in cheap restaurants, where they were always a way of dressing up a hash of leftovers. Proper canneloni are an accomplishment. I have eaten exquisite ones from Barcelona to Nice, but the best, by far, were prepared for me by my beloved Catalan friend, the late Antonieta Draper. I asked her repeatedly to write down the recipe for me. She explained it to me many times, but like so many wonderful household cooks I have known, she was appalled at exact measurements and she resisted writing down the recipe until it was too late. This is my version of her creation as she explained it to me. It does take time and patience. I warn you: don't make it! If you do you will be beset with requests to repeat the performance.

In France packaged canneloni skins are available in little boxes at one's neighborhood grocery. Your best bet for finding them in the United States is an Italian grocery or a gourmet shop. I have, in a pinch, used wonton skins, though they contain no egg. You can, of course, make the canneloni skins yourself, as I often do. Make them a day ahead and refrigerate them or dry them for future use.

Canneloni Skins
BASIC PASTA DOUGH

16 4-INCH SQUARES AND ENOUGH TRIMMINGS FOR A NOODLE SOUP

This is a handy, useful recipe for pasta dough. I use it for homemade noodles and many kinds of stuffed pasta and dumplings as well as canneloni. You can make it in just a few minutes with a food processor or pasta machine, but I love making it by hand. It literally puts me in touch with food in a way that always restores me and reminds me that I love the process of cooking almost as much as I love to eat.

1 cup all-purpose flour	2 large eggs
1 cup semolina flour (look for this in a gourmet shop or an Italian grocery)	1 tablespoon light olive oil
	Water

1. Blend the flours well. In a mixing bowl or on a marble slab, heap the flour in a mound and make a crater in the middle.
2. Beat the eggs and the oil together slightly and pour them into the crater.
3. With your fingertips combine the eggs and oil with the flour by running your fingertips around the inner edge of the crater, picking up a little flour with each circular motion until the flour, eggs, and oil are completely mixed and form a ball of dough that easily detaches itself from your fingertips. If it is sticky, add a little flour. If

it is too dry to form a ball, add a few drops of water. The dough should be dense, soft, and satiny.

4. Knead the dough on a hard, clean surface with the heel of your hand for 10 minutes.

5. Wrap the ball in plastic wrap and refrigerate for 15 minutes.

6. Cut the ball of dough in half. Wrap one half to keep it from drying out and roll out the other half very carefully on a lightly floured surface. Use plenty of pressure so that the dough is rolled uniformly thin.

7. Using a yardstick and a pizza cutter or a sharp knife, cut the dough you have rolled out into eight 4-inch squares. Wrap the scraps and set them aside.

8. Repeat Steps 6 and 7 with the other half of the ball of dough.

9. Wipe all excess flour from the squares. In a large kettle heat 3 to 4 quarts of lightly salted water. When the water is boiling vigorously, poach the skins, 8 at a time, for 3 to 5 minutes, remove them immediately with a skimmer, and allow them to drain in a colander. Then spread them on a towel.

10. Stuff and roll the skins at once according to the recipe you are using.

11. Reshape the scraps for another use and refrigerate them, or simply wrap them tightly in plastic wrap as they are and refrigerate. These scraps should be used within 48 hours. They make good noodles and tiny soup dumplings.

NOTE: You can make the canneloni skins ahead of time. There are at least these 3 possibilities:

- Dust the squares lightly with flour, wrap them well in plastic, and refrigerate them up to 48 hours.
- Follow the same procedure and freeze the skins up to 60 days.
- Dry the skins by draping them over a dowel or clean broomstick set up between 2 chair backs in a well-ventilated place. When they are completely dry, pack them in tightly closed cannisters and store them in a cool, dry place for up to 3 months.

• • •

Antonieta's Canneloni
LES CANNELONI FARCIS
A L'ANTONIETA

SERVES 8 AS FIRST COURSE,
4 AS MAIN COURSE

Antonieta's canneloni always produce ooh's and ah's when brought to the table. The dish is a bouquet of smells that can awaken the most jaded appetite. You need a knife, a pie server, and a spoon to serve the dish properly. You loosen the crusty cheese top from the dish with the knife, lift the canneloni out, two or three together, according to the size of the serving, and use the spoon to add any extra sauce. Enjoy, and feel grateful to Antonieta.

16 to 20 canneloni squares, poached, drained,
   and laid out carefully on towels

FOR THE STUFFING:

½ cup ground pork loin or
   sausage meat
1 slice boiled ham, finely
   chopped
1 tablespoon vegetable oil
1 tablespoon sweet butter
3 tablespoons finely chopped
   flat-leaf parsley
1 tablespoon finely chopped
   white of scallion
½ teaspoon finely ground white
   pepper
½ teaspoon freshly ground
   nutmeg

1 fresh chicken liver, filaments,
   fat, and bile stains removed,
   the liver chopped to a pulp
¼ cup dry white wine
1½ cups fresh white
   breadcrumbs moistened in
   ½ cup milk
½ cup *Béchamel* of the 4 cups
   you will prepare below
1 large egg white (use the yolk
   for the *Béchamel*)
1 tablespoon freshly grated
   Parmesan cheese

FOR THE BECHAMEL AND TOPPING:

5 tablespoons sweet butter
5 tablespoons flour
2 cups milk
1 cup unsalted chicken broth

1 small onion, peeled and
   spiked with
   1 clove
¼ teaspoon nutmeg
1 cup grated Gruyère cheese
1 large egg yolk

Make the stuffing:

1. In a large, heavy frying pan sauté the ground pork and ham in the oil and butter at medium heat until lightly browned.
2. Add the parsley, scallion, pepper, nutmeg, and chicken liver. Sauté for 5 minutes, stirring and pressing the mixture against the bottom of the frying pan.
3. Deglaze the pan with the white wine.
4. Add the milk-moistened breadcrumbs and stir the mixture furiously until the wine is absorbed and the mixture is a thick paste (*panade*). Remove from the fire, set aside, and prepare the *Béchamel*.

Make the Béchamel:

1. In a heavy-bottomed 2-quart saucepan, heat the butter over medium heat. When the butter is bubbling add the flour and stir with a wooden spatula until the butter and flour are completely combined.
2. Heat the milk to the boiling point and add it to the flour and butter paste (roux) one half at a time, stirring constantly. Keep scraping the spatula across the bottom so that the mixture does not stick and no lumps form.
3. Heat the broth and add it, a little at a time, stirring all the time.
4. Add the onion and nutmeg and reduce the heat to a simmer. The *Béchamel* should cook 25 to 30 minutes. Keep your eye on it and stir it from time to time. It sticks to the bottom very easily.
5. Remove and discard the onion.
6. Strain the *Béchamel*. Wash and scrub the saucepan and return the *Béchamel* to it. Bring the sauce to the simmering point and remove from the fire.
7. Add ½ cup of the Gruyère and stir until it is completely melted and combined with the sauce. Beat the egg yolk with a few drops of water and stir it in. Set the sauce aside.

Finish the stuffing:

1. Add ½ cup of the *Béchamel* to the *panade*, stir it into the mixture until it disappears. Return the frying pan to the fire. Stirring it rapidly, dry the *panade* over high heat for 5 minutes. Remove from the fire.
2. Beat the egg white until stiff. Carefully fold it and the Parmesan into the *panade*. Do not stir. The egg white serves to lighten the mixture as it bakes.

Stuffing the canneloni:

1. Preheat the over to 400°. Choose an attractive, shallow baking dish at least 8 inches long and 2 to 3 inches deep. Butter it well.
2. Place 2 tablespoons of the stuffing on each of the squares and roll the square up so that the loose end is underneath. Place the canneloni in neat rows in the baking dish, two across and close together.
3. Cover the canneloni completely with the *Béchamel.* Sprinkle evenly with the remaining ½ cup grated Gruyère cheese and bake for 40 to 50 minutes. The top should be beautifully browned and sizzling.
4. Do not serve at once. Let the baking dish sit outside the oven for at least 10 minutes before serving. This will permit the canneloni to set and the many tastes to "ripen."

N O T E : Canneloni can be filled with many things. You may want to substitute finely shredded, freshly poached chicken breast for the ground pork and ham, or poached fish, such as orange roughy or sole. Crabmeat makes a fine canneloni filling. If you substitute fish, it is preferable to be consistent and use a reduced fish broth *(fumet)* instead of the chicken broth when making the *Béchamel.*

• • •

Couscous

LE COUSCOUS

Couscous is just beginning to be known in the United States. It is the cereal staple of North Africa and is as popular with the continental French as curry is with the English or as enchiladas, tamales, and tacos are with North Americans. The term *couscous* designates the tiny, dry pellets of durum wheat; it is also the generic name for the steamed pellets and all the components that are served with it: broth, boiled meats or fish, sausages at times, and a full complement of boiled vegetables, beans or chick-peas, as a sort of North African pot-au-feu. Couscous can also designate other steamed grains served up in a similar manner, but ask for couscous in France and you will be served steamed pellets of durum wheat and an assortment of boiled vegetables and meats and their broth.

Couscous, I feel, will certainly become popular one day in the States, and you need to know how to prepare an authentic one. Except for Paula Wolfert's excellent book on the subject, there is precious little information available in English on the preparation of couscous. After reading about it here I hope you will be intrigued enough to make it yourself. The preparation is a little elaborate, but it is not difficult. Just follow the steps and remember that as it becomes familiar to you, it won't seem tricky at all. I know cooks in France who make it several times a week for their families.

As we have seen, a perfectly prepared pasta usually requires 3 to 4 quarts of boiling water to 8 ounces of dry pasta or the starch released by the cooking pasta will cause it to stick together. We have to admire the ingenuity of the North African household cooks who prepare couscous with very little water and it never sticks together! The *truc* or knack is to make the tiny pellets swell and take on moisture until they are two or three times their original size by dampening them several times, oiling them, and steaming them so that they are neither too wet nor too dry.

Couscous is sold in three different sizes of grains. The very large ones, as large as dried peas, require a great deal of skill and time, so I rarely buy them. The very tiny pellets are mainly used for sweet dishes. The intermediate-sized pellets are the ones most cooks use. You will find them in Middle Eastern, North African, and gourmet groceries. (You will also find the fast, precooked couscous along with tabouli and ready-seasoned pilafs in most supermarkets, but I do not recommend any of them.) Most health food stores sell the genuine article in bulk. Like a pot-au-feu, a

couscous can be as simple or as elaborate as you like. A complete couscous, with all the trimmings, takes about 2½ hours to prepare from
beginning to serving, but it is a complete and very outstanding meal.

HOW TO STEAM COUSCOUS

1. Put the couscous grains in a large shallow plate or baking dish. Alongside place a vessel containing cold salted water. The usual ratio is 3
   cups of water to 1 pound of couscous. Dissolve 1 teaspoon coarse salt
   in the water. With your fingers sprinkle water on the grains, a little
   at a time, rubbing the grains gently between your fingers so that all
   of the grains are touched by the dampness and no lumps remain. The
   pellets will begin to swell until they are the size of birdshot. This will
   take about 10 minutes, but it should not be rushed. If you have a
   coarse sieve, shake the pellets through it, a little at a time. The classic
   process is to dampen and dry alternately so that the grains swell
   without ever becoming saturated.

2. If you haven't a proper *couscoussière*—a lightweight, bulbous kettle
   with a close-fitting steam chamber on top—you can improvise one.
   Choose a deep kettle, preferably one with bulging sides that curve in
   toward the top, but you can also use one with straight sides. If you
   have a kettle with a metal vegetable steamer on top, it will be just the
   ticket. If not, choose a large strainer or colander that will fit snugly
   on top of the kettle you've chosen. Put water in the kettle, but not
   enough to touch the bottom of the steamer compartment you have
   improvised. Rinse out a piece of cheesecloth, wring it out, and place
   it in the bottom of the sieve. Dump the dampened couscous into it in
   a mound. Cover the sieve with plenty of aluminum foil, pressing it
   into the crack where the sieve or colander meets the kettle so that the
   steam will not escape. It should be forced to find its way through the
   pellets. Puncture a dozen good-sized holes in the top of the foil so that
   the vapor will not condense underneath and soak the pellets. If you
   are lucky enough to be using an honest-to-God *couscoussière*, take a
   strip of clean muslin or cheesecloth, dampen it and flour it, and seal
   the seam between the bottom and the top. Steam the grains for 5
   minutes.

3. Break the seal and turn the grains out again into the vessel you used
   to dampen them and repeat the process, rubbing the grains gently
   through your fingers. Pick them up and let them fall in detached

grains. Oil your hands and rub the grains gently, coating them lightly with the oil. Continue to work your fingers through the grains, raking out all the lumps and aerating the pellets.

4. Put the pellets back in the strainer, seal up the kettle and the steamer as you did before, and steam the pellets for 20 minutes.

5. Again, break the seal and work the pellets with a little water. Take your time. Aerate the pellets well and return them to steam for a third time, sealed up as before. After 20 more minutes of steaming, your pellets are ready to seal up with the *marga* instead of water. Turn the pellets out. Toss them and put them aside covered with a dampened cloth.

NOTE: This is the classic process for all couscous. Master the steps and you will see that it isn't really difficult, especially if you purchase a beautiful *couscoussière*. To the specialists in fast meals, this patient, stepped process may seem an exorbitant investment in time. Why not buy the precooked variety and be done with it? Because the difference is enormous. "Quick" rice never has the texture or taste of natural rice. Tinned spaghetti is a travesty of spaghetti prepared from scratch and served al dente! So it is with couscous: the genuine article requires time, devotion to details, and love of process. Believe me, it pays off.

Gisèle's Couscous

SERVES 6 TO 8

I was introduced to couscous thirty-five years ago by Gisèle, a Tunisian student friend who, like myself, lived at Madame Mathieu's pension in Aix-en-Provence. Gisèle and I shared one passion—good food. On Sundays, when the student restaurant was closed, we used to improvise feasts in our rooms. I remember her vividly: When one of our improvised dishes turned out well, she would try it, close her eyes and say: "Mmmmmm! Dieu existe!" ("Wow! God exists!") Coming from her, that was anything but blasphemy. It was Gisèle who explained to me the steps in preparing couscous and how if one skipped steps or got in a hurry, the couscous would turn out dry as dust and would punish whoever ate it with a burning thirst. I have lost track of Gisèle, but every time I taste a great couscous I think of her. This is my version of the Tunisian couscous she taught me to make.

FOR THE COUSCOUS:

1 pound medium-sized
  couscous grains
3 cups cold water
1 teaspoon coarse salt

2½ quarts boiling water
1 tablespoon light olive oil
2 tablespoons sweet butter

FOR THE *MARGA* (STEW):

2½ quarts cold water
One 2½- to 3-pound chicken
  with its neck and giblets
2 pounds lean breast and
  shoulder of lamb, fat
  carefully removed and
  discarded, cut into serving
  portions
3 ripe tomatoes, skinned,
  seeded, and coarsely
  chopped
3 medium-sized onions, 2
  peeled, quartered top to
  root, 1 unpeeled and spiked
  with
    2 cloves
3 large carrots, scraped, halved,
  and cut in 2-inch pieces
¼ teaspoon each ground
  cayenne pepper, black
  pepper, cumin, cinnamon,
  and ginger
1 large bunch flat-leaf parsley
3 branches fresh mint
1 tablespoon strong honey

2 large potatoes, peeled and
  cut in large chunks
3 large artichokes, trimmed to
  the heart, chokes removed,
  hearts quartered, rubbed all
  over with juice of
    1 lemon
3 large bell peppers, cored,
  seeded, ribs removed,
  quartered
3 medium-sized turnips, peeled
  and quartered
1 small head cabbage,
  quartered
½ cup white raisins
½ teaspoon crumbled saffron
  threads
3 medium-sized zucchini,
  wiped, trimmed, and cut
  into 1-inch-thick pieces
One 1-pound tin chick-peas
Harissa (a fiery concentrated
  paste of red peppers, cumin,
  garlic, salt, and a little oil,
  sold in tubes in Middle
  Eastern groceries)

Make the couscous:

1. Prepare the grains as explained on page 153.

Make the marga:

1. If you have a *couscoussière*, prepare the couscous from beginning to end
   in the two compartments simultaneously, but as this recipe is adapted
   for beginners, I advise preparing the pellets and the stew apart and
   sealing them up together at the last step. So in a separate kettle start
   heating the water for the *marga* or stew.
2. Truss the chicken securely with cotton string. Tie a piece of string to
   the chicken and attach one end to the handle of the kettle so that you

can take the chicken out easily when you want. Put the trussed, "leashed" chicken in the kettle of water. Add the neck and giblets, the lamb, tomatoes, onions, carrots, the ground spices and the parsley and the mint tied up together with cotton string. Let all this come to a rolling boil, and cook for 10 minutes. Keep skimming off the froth that rises to the surface and reduce the heat to a "murmur." Continue cooking for 30 minutes.

3. Preheat the oven to 375°.
4. Remove the chicken from the kettle, drain it, detach the anchor string from it, and brush it all over with the honey. Place it in an uncovered baking dish and bake it for 30 minutes or until it is nicely browned all over. Turn off the oven, cover the chicken, and leave it in the oven for the moment.
5. To the broth add the potatoes, artichokes, peppers, turnips, cabbage, raisins, and the crumbled saffron threads. Simmer for 30 minutes.
6. Discard the bundle of herbs. Empty the water out of the kettle you used for steaming the grains and put all the stew into it, along with the zucchini and chick-peas. Seal the steaming compartment with the steamed grains in it to the top of the kettle again so that in the final steaming, the grains become permeated with the aromatics from the broth. Continue to simmer the stew for another 30 minutes.
7. Carve the chicken into 8 pieces.

Assemble the couscous:
1. Choose a large circular platter and warm it.
2. Break the seal on the steamer and add the sweet butter to the grains in little knobs, tossing the grains lightly with a fork so that the butter coats them. Empty the grains into the platter and form them into a big mound. In the middle of the mound make a large crater. Place the stew and the carved chicken in the crater.
3. With a wad of absorbent paper towel remove as much fat from the broth as you can, then strain the broth into a tureen. Provide a serving ladle.
4. Put the *harissa* in a small bowl on a plate with a little spoon alongside.
5. Sprinkle a little broth over the couscous and serve it.

N O T E : Provide serving spoons and tongs for dealing with the pellets, the vegetables, and the meats. Make sure each guest has a good-sized soup plate and a soup spoon in addition to the usual flatware.

This is the customary way to serve couscous in the French homes where I have eaten it: The guests serve themselves, first putting a portion of the steamed grains on their plates. They then pile the *marga* (meat, vegetables, and so on) on top. Taking a ladleful of broth, they drop in as much *harissa* as they wish and stir it with a small spoon. (Some people like the broth very hot and spicy, some like it without *harissa*; so do as you prefer.) The broth is then poured over the entire heap of *marga* and couscous. The dish is usually attacked with a soup spoon and a fork.

For us, this is a sumptuous meal. North Africans usually think of it as a final course among many others. We haven't the capacity or the appetite for such fabulous quantities of food. For the usual North American appetite, this couscous will prove more than ample. In fact, I suggest that you give your guests and yourself a little recovery time after the meal. Better still, serve everyone a little hot mint tea and let them take a siesta.

White Beans Navarre Style
LES HARICOTS BLANCS
A LA NAVARRAISE

SERVES 4 OR 5

White beans are very much appreciated all over France. In many regions they are the base for celebrated regional specialties such as cassoulet. Although we cannot find pochas, *the white bean so much esteemed in the Pyrenees, in the United States, the Great Northern navy bean is a very acceptable substitute when making this famous recipe from the Navarre.*

2 cups Great Northern navy
    beans
2 quarts cold water
½ teaspoon baking soda
1 tablespoon vegetable oil
1 slice salami, finely chopped
One ⅛-inch slice salt pork,
    blanched, rinsed, dried, and
    finely chopped
1 small onion, peeled and
    coarsely chopped
1 clove garlic, peeled and finely
    chopped

1 medium carrot, scraped,
    trimmed, and finely chopped
1 tablespoon flat-leaf parsley,
    finely chopped
1 bay leaf
¼ teaspoon freshly cracked black
    pepper
1 medium-sized ripe tomato,
    skinned, seeded, and coarsely
    chopped
1 tablespoon virgin olive oil

1. Spread the beans on a clean surface and remove all the pebbles and the imperfect or discolored beans. Wash the beans well in a fine colander under cold running water. Put them in a heavy kettle with the water and the baking soda and bring them to a rolling boil. Take them off the fire and let them cool and plump for 1 hour.
2. Heat the vegetable oil in a small skillet and make a *soffritto* as follows: fry the salami and the salt pork until golden. Then add the onion, garlic, carrot, parsley, bay leaf, and pepper. Stirring frequently, fry the vegetables until soft but do not brown them. Add the tomato and stir well with a wooden spoon. Reduce the mixture to a thick purée. Your *soffritto* is made.
3. Rinse the beans in cold water and put them on the fire again with 2 quarts of fresh water. Add the *soffritto* and heat the kettle very gently. In the Navarre, one hears old cooks counseling: "Never allow a bubble to break the surface of the water. It should threaten but never boil." Why such attention? The perfectly cooked bean must be creamy inside but with its skin unbroken by the long cooking. Never mind! If the skins on your Great Northerns should split, the beans will still be delicious.
4. Cook the beans for 2 to 2½ hours or until they are done. Do not stir them, or they will surely break up. Just before serving them, pour the virgin olive oil gently over the surface.

N O T E : It is advisable not to salt the beans during the time they are cooking. Salt induces the skins to break and the interior of the beans to cook unevenly. However, the taste of the beans is greatly enhanced by salt, so provide a saltcellar of good, coarse sea salt or a saltmill so that the guests may salt the beans to their liking.

Lentils

LES LENTILLES

Lentils are the oldest known cultivated pulse. They have been eaten constantly by the inhabitants of Central Asia since prehistoric times. At present they are eaten all over the world, and no wonder! They contain more protein and more calories per ounce than any other pea except soy.

The lentil's edge over the soy bean is that it cooks more quickly and has a delicious, meaty flavor, making it a favorite staple with the thrifty French householder. The French serve them as soup, as purée, as stew and *en vinaigrette* as a salad.

One word of warning: lentils germinate and start to sprout within a few hours. Germinating lentils exude a bitterness that is unpleasant to the taste, and they may prove troublesome to the digestion, so it is inadvisable to soak them overnight. Soak them for an hour, if you must. Even that is unnecessary. After picking over them to remove any pebbles or foreign matter, rinse them well and begin to cook them at once. Lentils are the base for a number of perennial favorites in the French household repertoire. I have chosen two of them to present to you here.

Lentils Stewed with Salt Pork
LES LENTILLES AU PETIT SALE
SERVES 4 TO 6

This dish is usually done in two stages. Don't be confused by my dividing the ingredients into those proper to the stewing of the lentils and those that have to do with finishing the famous dish.

FOR STEWING THE LENTILS:

1 fennel stem
1 branch thyme
1 branch rosemary
1 bay leaf
1 pound brown lentils
4 quarts cold water

1 medium-sized onion, peeled
   and spiked with
   2 cloves
1 large carrot, scraped, trimmed,
   and cut in ¼-inch roundels
2 plump cloves garlic, unpeeled

FOR FINISHING THE LENTILS:

1 tablespoon vegetable oil
2 thick rashers streaky salt
   pork (about 4 ounces),
   blanched in boiling water,
   rinsed, dried, and cut in
   ¼-inch dice
1 tablespoon flour
1½ cups cooking liquid from the
   lentils

¼ teaspoon freshly grated
   nutmeg
Coarse salt to taste
1 tablespoon wine vinegar
1 tablespoon light olive oil
¼ teaspoon freshly ground
   black pepper

1. Make the bouquet garni by tying the fennel, thyme, rosemary, and bay leaf together with cotton string. If you cannot find these herbs in branch form, prepare a *sachet* instead by tying up ¼ teaspoon of dried fennel seeds, dried thyme leaves, and rosemary with the bay leaf in a small square of cheesecloth.
2. Spread the lentils out on a clean, flat surface and carefully remove any pebbles or foreign matter. Wash the lentils in a large sieve under cold running water.
3. Put the washed lentils in a heavy kettle with 2 quarts of water and bring them to a rolling boil. Remove the kettle from the fire. Discard the boiling water and once more rinse the lentils under cold running water.
4. Return the lentils to the kettle with 2 fresh quarts of water, add the bouquet garni, the spiked onion, the carrot, and garlic, and simmer them for 1 hour. Test the lentils by taking one between the thumb and forefinger and pressing it. The lentils are done when you can easily crush the lentil in this fashion. Lentils vary in hardness, so their cooking time can vary from 1 to 2 hours. Test them often, otherwise you may cook them to a purée.
5. Discard the bouquet garni, the onion, and the garlic.
6. In a heavy frying pan heat the vegetable oil and fry the salt pork cubes. When they begin to take on a little color, add the flour and stir well so that the flour is completely absorbed into the hot fat.
7. Before the flour has a chance to scorch, add 1½ cups of liquid from the cooked lentils and stir carefully until a smooth sauce has formed. Add the thickening to the kettle of lentils, stir it in well, and allow to cook for 5 minutes.
8. Add the nutmeg, salt, vinegar, olive oil, and pepper and stir them into the lentils. It is customary to stir in a glass of dry white wine at this point, but it is optional. Serve hot.

• • •

Cold Lentil Salad
LES LENTILLES EN VINAIGRETTE
SERVES 4 OR 5

Cold lentil salad is often served in French homes as a first course. It often appears, as well, on an hors d'oeuvre tray along with several other selections. It makes an appealing accompaniment for grilled or roast lamb. Speaking of roast lamb: lentil salad and cold, sliced leftover roast lamb make a delicious and unusual lunch—one that can be prepared well ahead of time. The knack is to double the onion vinaigrette recipe and use half of it to sauce the cold lamb. Lighten up the plate with a few leaves of mixed greens and you have a winner. Cold lamb is often a little greasy. The onion vinaigrette will control the greasiness far better than the usual mayonnaise.

3 tablespoons wine vinegar
1 teaspoon coarse salt
1 tablespoon Dijon mustard
¼ cup light olive oil, at room temperature
1 medium-sized onion, peeled, trimmed, coarsely chopped, and "killed" (see Note)
2 cups cooked lentils, rinsed and drained according to the instructions on page 161

3 tablespoons freshly squeezed lemon juice
½ teaspoon dried thyme leaves
2 tablespoons finely chopped flat-leaf parsley
2 tablespoons finely chopped fresh mint
½ cup very thinly sliced celery
2 scallions, white part only, cut lengthwise in very fine strips

1. Stir the vinegar and salt together in a glass salad bowl. When the salt is dissolved, mix in the mustard until the mixture is smooth. Drop by drop, whip in the oil until the mixture is thick and pearly in appearance. This is a classic vinaigrette. Add the "killed" onion and stir everything together briefly.
2. Using your hands, dress the lentils with the onion vinaigrette, gently lifting the lentils and letting them drop from your fingers until all of them are coated with the dressing.
3. Add the lemon juice, thyme, finely chopped parsley, mint, and celery, working them through the lentils in the same fashion, with your fingers. Scatter the scallion ribbons over the top, cover the bowl, let it sit for a while in a cool—not frigid—place for at least 15 minutes, and serve.

N O T E : The gentle art of cooking is full of violent terms such as whipping, beating, bruising, cracking, crushing, and so on. "Killing" the onion is perhaps the most violent, but it simply means ridding the onion of its strong, persistent taste. Cucumber, eggplant, and some strong meats are regularly "killed" to make them more palatable. Here we kill the onion by sprinkling it liberally with coarse salt and a little vinegar and allowing it to sit and leach in a colander for 10 minutes. The onion is then rinsed under cold, running water, drained, and patted dry. Kill the onion before starting to prepare the lentil salad.

Chick-Peas

LES POIS CHICHES

Chick-peas, or *pois chiches,* as they have been called in France since Roman times, are very popular these days because they have been reintroduced by the great numbers of North Africans and Spanish now living in France. No one would think of serving a couscous without chick-peas, and today one often finds them sprinkled in the salad or served up as an hors d'oeuvre. Of course, in the Nice area they have always been a favorite. They are the main ingredient in a famous soup with a strong taste of sage, a large pancake called *socca,* and a tasty, deep-fried creation called *panisso*—all dishes found in and around Nice but practically unknown in the rest of France.

Chick-peas are so hard and require such long cooking from scratch that almost no one I know ever buys them in their dry stage. There are special merchants in France who prepare them and sell them already cooked. They can also be bought in tins, usually in their hulls to keep them from falling apart. They ought to be hulled before serving them. It is an easy task and it makes them easier to digest. Just empty a tin into a colander and hull them under gently running cold water. If you are adding them to a hot dish, do it at the end and don't cook them for more than a few minutes or they will begin to disintegrate and lose their unique appearance. There are many recipes for using chick-peas, but I have chosen only one. It is for a cold chick-pea salad—a very good choice for lunch on a hot day.

Cold Chick-Pea Salad
LES POIS CHICHES EN SALADE
SERVES 4 OR 5

3 tablespoons freshly squeezed
   lemon juice
1 teaspoon coarse salt
1 plump clove garlic, peeled and
   sliced paper-thin
½ teaspoon dried thyme leaves
½ teaspoon finely crumbled dried
   sage leaves
½ teaspoon freshly cracked black
   pepper
½ teaspoon cayenne flakes
1 tablespoon finely chopped
   flat-leaf parsley

1 firm, unripe tomato, unpeeled,
   cored, seeded, and coarsely
   chopped
3 tablespoons light olive oil
Two 10-ounce tins cooked
   chick-peas, rinsed, hulled, and
   well drained
1 bell pepper, flame-roasted (see
   page 45), cored, deribbed,
   seeded, and finely chopped
1 baked medium-sized onion,
   peeled and cut into thin
   crescents, top to root (see
   page 58)

1. Mix the lemon juice and salt until the salt is dissolved. Mix in the garlic, thyme, sage, black pepper, cayenne flakes, parsley, and tomato and set aside for 5 minutes.
2. Add the oil and stir gently.
3. Place the chick-peas, chopped pepper, and onion in a glass bowl and pour the dressing over them. Toss them gently with wooden implements.
4. Cover the salad and set it aside to meld for 15 to 20 minutes in a cool—not frigid—place and serve.

N O T E : Serve the cold chick-pea salad as a first course or as one of several hors d'oeuvre.

CHAPTER SEVEN

Eggs and Dishes Made with Eggs and Cheese

Les Oeufs

Eggs are essential, indeed irreplaceable in French cooking. To a French cook a fresh-laid, farmyard egg is a treasure, and most French cooks do wonders with them. The repertoire is very large and extremely varied, and it includes dishes that are both simple and elaborate. French householders will go to great lengths to obtain fresh eggs directly from farms where the hens are grain-fed and allowed to run free and forage for themselves. Before living in France I was never impressed by differences in taste and texture among eggs, but in fact eggs that come from hens that are well fed and allowed to range differ amazingly from those produced in establishments where the hens are formula-fed and never touch the ground. If you can find a farmer who will provide you with fresh eggs from barnyard hens, you are lucky. Most of us at present must depend upon our local supermarket and trust to its dating system.

The French have a way of satisfying themselves about the freshness of eggs. Two eggs are held near the ear and gently tapped, one against the other. If the eggs are fresh and uncracked, they will give off a clear, crisp sound. If they do not, they are considered defective. While I do not counsel "toquing" the eggs in a supermarket, I definitely advise you to open the cartons and look at the eggs carefully to see that they are not cracked or broken. While nutritionists assure us that there is no difference between white and brown eggs, I have always preferred brown eggs because they seem to have slightly thicker shells, making them easier to deal with when separating the white from the yolks. A truly fresh egg should have a yolk that stands up in a glossy bulge and a white that is not watery. It is a good idea to break eggs into a small plate or saucer before using them. That way you may inspect them carefully for specks and flecks of blood. Such things are harmless, but it is better to remove them. I keep a pair of tweezers in the kitchen for that purpose. Tweezers are also the best tools for removing the bits of broken shell that occasionally get caught in the whites. It is also good to keep a large darning needle handy for piercing the larger end of an egg before boiling it. There is a tiny air bubble at that end between the shell and the egg itself. Piercing it will often prevent the egg from cracking when it expands in the boiling water. However, it is a delicate operation. You should barely pierce the shell, otherwise you may crack the egg yourself. Sometimes, if the hole you have made is too big, the white will extrude in a little tail. It won't affect the egg. Simply remove it when the egg is ready. It is interesting to know that the air bubble at the end of the egg gets larger as the egg gets older. That is the reason for candling eggs to determine their age: the larger the air bubble at the end of the egg, the less fresh the egg. For that reason, beware of eggs that seem to move about when you shake them; they are sure to be old.

You should remove the eggs you plan to use from the refrigerator half an hour before using them so that they can warm to room temperature. A cold egg will crack if you put it into boiling water, and it will not emulsify properly if you are making a sauce such as mayonnaise. There is no question that keeping eggs in the refrigerator adds to their life, but if you use a large number of eggs, it is better to keep them in a cool rather than cold place.

Until the cholesterol scare, eggs were generally accepted for the excellent, almost perfect source of nutrition that they are. An egg contains as much protein as four ounces of meat. Eggs are also an important source of iron, phosphorus, and vitamin A. Two eggs contain only about 250 calories. The French believe, however, that eggs are hard on the liver, and since liver attacks are the national malady, they cannot understand our fondness for fried eggs. To most French people, the thought of fried eggs and bacon for breakfast is outlandish and not at all attractive to their somewhat squeamish livers.

There is a belief amongst some health food addicts that raw eggs are easier to assimilate than cooked ones. The French are quick to assure us that raw egg yolk is more difficult to digest than cooked egg yolk. Consequently, a cooked egg nourishes more than a raw one since the nutrients in it are more readily assimilated by the body.

THE PRINCIPAL WAYS THE FRENCH HOUSEHOLDER COOKS EGGS

BOILED EGGS (les Oeufs à la coque): Choose uncracked eggs at room temperature. Start them in slightly salted water that is tepid, not boiling.

Maintain the water at a simmer. If it boils too violently, the eggs will crack against each other while cooking. Counting from the minute that the bubbles begin to rise, use this time scale:

- 3 minutes for solid white and liquid yolk
- 4 minutes for solid white and half-solid yolk
- 6 minutes for solid white and solid but humid yolk
- 10 minutes for solid white and solid, dry yolk
  (Eggs boiled more than 10 minutes begin to develop an olive green color between the white and the yolk.)

As soon as the eggs have reached the desired doneness, remove them from the hot water with a slotted spoon. If they are not to be served hot in their shell, put them in a colander and run cold water over them at once. When they are cool enough to handle, crack them all over with the handle of a knife and peel them under running water. If you wish to serve the eggs in egg cups, crack them gently and carefully all around the top with the blade of a knife. Detach the little cap. It is customary to serve them without the cap, depositing a small knob of sweet butter or a drop of fine olive oil in its place, but that is up to you and the individual tastes of your family. By all means serve the eggs while they are still good and warm.

POACHED EGGS (les Oeufs pochés): To the French, poaching an egg means cooking it gently in simmering lightly vinegared water, plain milk, or, in some instances, wine and herbs so that the white forms a soft pocket or, as they like to call it, a *chemise* or shirt, with the soft, still liquid yolk nestling inside. The perfectly poached egg should be neat, compact, moist, but neither soaking wet nor dry, and the yolk should be only slightly thickened by the gentle heat. Most French cooks recommend that you follow 6 little rules to obtain the perfectly poached egg:

1. The egg must be fresh.
2. It must be broken onto a plate and gently slid into the water down the side of the pan.
3. The poaching liquid should be about 2 inches deep. If you are using water, add a few drops of vinegar. It helps to firm up the white and keep it white. The liquid simmers but never boils.
4. The egg should poach 3 minutes if the poaching liquid is water or milk, 4 minutes if wine. (Wine takes longer.)
5. Remove the egg promptly with a slotted spoon or skimmer. Let all the liquid drain away, then place the egg on a paper towel to make sure it is only moist. A wet poached egg makes a mess of whatever it is placed on for serving.

6. Trim the egg of whatever "tails" it has acquired in poaching with a sharp paring knife or shears.

This may seem at first much ado about nothing, but perfectly poached eggs are a considerable accomplishment. They are not only the sure credential of a fine cook, but they are also the main star in a number of French dishes that are common fare at home. There are countless ways of serving them, hot or cold, in sauces, often as a first course. The sauces can be as light as a little melted butter, lemon juice, and finely chopped herbs, or as heavy as a Burgundian *meurette* made of chopped bacon, shallots, and reduced Beaujolais. I love poached eggs cold in gelatin.

If you are planning to serve poached eggs to as many as 4 persons, you can prepare them beforehand. After trimming them, put them in a little cool water. This stops the cooking and keeps them moist. When you are ready to serve them, slip them for a few seconds into hot water, drain and blot them well, and serve them in whatever way you have planned.

FRIED EGGS (les Oeufs au plat): Though the thought of fried eggs for breakfast appalls the French and causes their sensitive livers to quiver, they often fry eggs for a snack or a light, impromptu supper. And they are fastidious about how this should be done. For the French, the perfect fried egg should be concentric. The white should be lightly firm right up to the yolk, and there should be no "brown lace" around the edges. The yolk should stand up and have the consistency of thick cream. The perfectly fried egg is easy to do, but it is so seldom encountered that many cooking schools require it as part of their examinations. The trick is not to be in a hurry. Here's how to do it:

1. Choose a light frying pan or an omelet pan that is either properly cured or has a nonstick surface. If the pan is too heavy, you will not be able to control the cooking of the egg except by removing it from the pan. (For curing pans, see page 9.)
2. Heat the pan slightly and rub the cooking surface with a little vegetable oil and coarse salt on a piece of cheesecloth or a paper towel until you are certain that there are no rough bits still sticking to the surface from previous cooking. If you are using a pan with a nonstick surface, omit this step.
3. Add a teaspoon of sweet butter to the pan and reduce the heat to very low. Be careful not to burn the butter solids. You may find it useful, if you are planning to fry a number of eggs, to prepare a quantity of clarified butter beforehand. Clarifying butter effectively removes the milk solids so that you don't have to worry about overheating the

butter and producing the unsightly black specks of carbonized milk solids in your otherwise perfectly prepared dishes. The easy process for clarifying butter is explained on page 113.

4. Break the egg carefully into a small bowl or saucer and slip it into the sizzling butter in the frying pan. Make sure the fire is low or the egg will cook too rapidly, turning the edges of the white into "brown lace" before the rest of the egg has a chance to cook properly.

5. Drop ½ teaspoon water into the frying pan and cover it tightly. Cook the egg for 3 or 4 minutes. The water will evaporate completely, causing the surface of the yolk and the white to cook perfectly. Serve the egg at once while it is hot.

If you have produced some "brown lace," all is not lost. You can always trim it off before serving the egg. If you fry several eggs at once and they fry together, you can easily snip them apart. Many cooks salt and pepper the eggs while they are cooking. I don't because it discolors the egg. Put a saltcellar and a peppermill on the table, and the guests can season their eggs for themselves.

SCRAMBLED EGGS (les Oeufs brouillés): As with almost everything in the world of cooking, the French household cook has a set of well-defined attitudes toward scrambled eggs and how they are to be prepared and served.

The French like scrambled eggs soft and creamy and supremely receptive to the countless sauces, sautéed vegetables, meat, fish, finely chopped fresh herbs, and other good things the French are fond of combining with them. The dry, overcooked curds that generally pass for scrambled eggs across the United States would receive a resounding vote of disapproval from the French. They insist that scrambling perfectly fresh eggs too hard deprives the eggs of their natural flavor and makes them incapable of absorbing the sauces and other delicious additions that they have thought up over centuries to enhance their already glorious soft scrambled eggs.

To scramble the eggs as the French do, you must have very fresh eggs and heavy cream, both at room temperature. Allow 1 teaspoon of cream for each egg. Beat the eggs and cream together lightly. (Overbeating, oddly enough, is apt to make them separate more easily in cooking.) Choose a light, well-cured frying pan or a frying pan with a nonstick surface. Add a little knob of sweet butter and rub it over the cooking surface.

The egg mixture must be cooked in a *bain-marie*. That means that the undersurface of the pan containing the egg mixture must be insulated from the source of heat by at least 1 inch of water. This is done not in a double boiler but by placing the frying pan in a larger receptacle containing water. The water is heated but must never be allowed to boil. (This wonderful invention dates back to the fourteenth century in France, though the Marie or Mary to whom it is attributed is Mary, the sister of Moses, who medieval churchmen thought was an alchemist! So much for that bit of cook's trivia. Now back to our soft scrambled eggs.)

Start cooking the mixture when the water is not yet hot so that it will heat very gradually. Never stop stirring the mixture with a wooden spatula, and continuously scrape the spatula across the bottom of the frying pan to assure that the bottom does not cook more rapidly than the rest of the mixture. When the mixture begins to thicken, watch it closely. Eggs are very sensitive to heat. When the creamy mixture is a little thinner than you wish it, take the frying pan out of the water. The heat of the pan will continue to cook the eggs. Some cooks insist on setting the frying pan in cool water to ensure that the cooking stops. Add a knob of sweet butter. Stir it in and your soft scrambled eggs are ready to dress and serve in whatever manner you choose.

This little master recipe is subject to at least a score of variations. Try it with finely chopped parsley or chives or tiny, unchopped sweet basil leaves. Try it with a hefty tablespoonful of anchovy paste mixed well into the eggs. For a very special occasion, rinse 2 tablespoons of red caviar with fresh lemon juice and toss the grains in the scrambled eggs. Very recently the French have discovered fresh dill, an herb rarely used in French cooking. A little finely chopped fresh dill scattered over the caviar and eggs is a fine addition. You might try the soft scrambled eggs with well-drained, grilled, ripe tomatoes and a generous sprinkling of thyme leaves, or with chopped fried bacon or ham, or grated Gruyère or Parmesan cheese. These eggs wed perfectly with croûtons that have been lightly rubbed with garlic and fried in butter or oil. There you have a few suggestions. It is now up to you to discover what delicious additions please you and your family most.

Soft scrambled eggs can be ruined by three things: too much heat, water from added ingredients, and acidity. Avoid the first by cooking the eggs very slowly. When adding vegetables that contain a lot of water such as mushrooms or zucchini (and there are many others) sauté the liquid out of the vegetables or squeeze them in a piece of cheesecloth or old linen. Acidity in tomatoes and other such vegetables can be neutralized effectively by adding ¼ teaspoon baking soda to them and mixing it in well before adding them to the eggs. Enjoy yourself exploring the endless possibilities of soft scrambled eggs à la française.

O M E L E T S (les Omelettes): The omelet is considered the greatest achievement of French egg cookery. The French did not invent the omelet, though it is attributed to them, and the term *French omelet* is universal. Of all the ways the French prepare eggs, surely the omelet is the easiest. At its simplest, an omelet is a way of serving soft scrambled eggs in a little package made of the eggs themselves. There are two main types of omelets: folded, generally called doubled, and flat. Both types may be very simple or very elaborate. They may be stuffed, puffed, solid, thick, or paper thin. An omelet should be cooked very quickly. It should be slightly crisp on the outside and soft and runny—*baveuse*—on the inside.

Here are the basic rules for making French omelets:
- If you haven't an omelet pan, use a frying pan with a reinforced bottom. The pan should be well cured or have a nonstick coating. (For how to cure frying pans, see the instructions on page 10.) It should be light enough to handle easily, in spite of the reinforced bottom. The handle should be long and heat-resistant. You must be able to swirl and tip the pan easily.
- The pan should be heated before adding the butter or oil.
- Use fresh eggs at room temperature. A classic omelet requires 2 eggs and a teaspoon of tepid water for each egg. Break the eggs one by one into a soup plate. Carefully remove any specks or bits of shell. Beat the eggs and water together lightly with a fork. Add ½ teaspoon coarse salt and give the eggs and water a couple more strokes with the fork.
- Add 1 or 2 tablespoons sweet or clarified butter to the hot pan and see that the surface is coated.
- Empty the egg and water mixture into the sizzling butter and swirl the pan about quickly so that the mixture catches and covers the entire bottom of the pan.
- With a fork—or a wooden spatula if you are using a coated pan—lift one edge of the omelet and double it over the other half.
- Lift the underside of the omelet a little and drop a knob of sweet butter under it so that the omelet will glaze.
- With a quick roll of the pan slip the omelet out of the pan and onto a warm plate, underside up. Serve at once.

If you tear or break the omelet in shifting it from the tipped pan to the plate, return it quickly to the pan, and if you haven't overcooked the omelet, the heat and the almost liquid interior will repair the damage.

Other than these simple rules, there are no tricks to making plain omelets. The whole cooking process should take no more than 60 seconds. If you are stuffing the omelet, have everything ready and near at hand to add quickly just before folding the omelet. You can make a 4- to 6-egg omelet if you have a pan that will accommodate it. The procedure is the same. Should you find the interior of the large omelet still too wet to double, simply lift the edge of the omelet, tip the pan, and let the liquid egg run under the omelet. It will immediately incorporate itself with the underside and you can then fold the omelet. After glazing it with butter, turn the large omelet out onto a warm platter and serve it with a knife or pie server so that it can be cut into portions.

As you can see, making omelets is simple. It takes a little practice so above all, don't get flustered. If you find the right pan, guard it carefully. Once it is well cured, don't wash it with detergent or scrubbing powder. Clean it with a little oil and coarse salt on a cloth or paper towel. Wipe out the salt and put the pan away, cooking surface down.

Soft Scrambled Eggs Provençal Style
LA BROUILLADE

SERVES 4 OR 5

3 tablespoons extra virgin olive oil

3 tablespoons coarsely chopped flat-leaf parsley

½ teaspoon dried leaf thyme

½ teaspoon crumbled oregano

3 medium-sized ripe tomatoes, skinned, seeded, and coarsely chopped

4 plump cloves garlic, peeled and crushed to a paste in 1 teaspoon coarse salt

3 tablespoons light vegetable oil

3 slices white bread, crusts removed, cut in ½-inch dice

9 large eggs, at room temperature

2 tablespoons water

½ teaspoon freshly ground black pepper

6 to 8 fresh basil leaves, stemmed and coarsely torn

Prepare the soffritto:

Heat the olive oil gently in a heavy-bottomed frying pan. When the oil is warm but not smoking, sauté the parsley, thyme, oregano, tomatoes, and half the garlic paste until the juice from the tomatoes is completely reduced and you have a paste. A true *soffritto* takes 12 minutes to make, so don't hurry it.

Prepare the croûtons:

1. In another frying pan gently heat the vegetable oil. Add the other half of the garlic paste and allow to sizzle for 15 seconds and no more!
2. Add the bread cubes and stir them about so that they absorb all the oil. Sauté the cubes gently until they are golden.
3. Remove the cubes from the frying pan, scatter them over the surface of a large baking pan, and finish crisping them in the oven at 325°.

Prepare the eggs:

1. Whisk the eggs and water together briefly.
2. Set the frying pan containing the *soffritto* in another pan containing 1 inch of water. Heat the water very slowly and make sure it does not boil.
3. Mix the eggs with the *soffritto* in the frying pan. Use a wooden spatula for this and keep scraping up the bottom as the water heats and the eggs begin to thicken.
4. Add the pepper and basil leaves and keep stirring.
5. When the eggs are thick and creamy, remove them immediately to an unheated platter, scatter the croûtons over the *brouillade*, and serve it while it is still warm.

N O T E : *La brouillade* is an old Provençal favorite. You will notice that the recipe contains no cream or butter. Most old Provençal recipes do not. Cow's milk was often hard to come by, and olive oil was abundant. At present, milk, butter, and cream are all available and are widely used in the Midi, but old villagers still think of them as outlandish luxuries.

• • •

Soft Scrambled Eggs Basque Style
LA PIPERADE

SERVES 5 OR 6

La pipérade *is perhaps the most popular way of serving soft scrambled eggs in France. It is even more familiar to most French householders than its Provençal cousin,* la brouillade. *Yet it is seldom prepared as it should be. All too often what passes for a true* pipérade *is a mass of stewed bell peppers, tomatoes, onions, garlic, and herbs and grainy, coagulated egg that may receive good marks for taste but fails badly in texture. A true* pipérade *takes time to prepare and is never watery. Nor is it grainy. The peppers must be flame-roasted to remove their outer skin and give them the correct roasted flavor. The eggs must be creamy and consistent. If you ever taste a perfect* pipérade, *you will never accept a less than perfect one as the real thing!*

2 large red bell peppers,
    fire-roasted (see page 44),
    cored, seeded, well rinsed,
    and finely chopped
¼ cup light olive oil
½ cup raw, dry-cured ham in
    ¼-inch cubes
1 medium-sized yellow onion,
    peeled and grated
1 plump clove garlic, peeled and
    finely chopped

1 tablespoon finely chopped
    flat-leaf parsley
1 teaspoon freshly cracked black
    pepper
1 teaspoon cayenne pepper flakes
¼ teaspoon ground cumin
9 to 12 fresh eggs, at room
    temperature
3 tablespoons water
1 teaspoon coarse salt

Prepare the soffritto:

1. Fire-roast the bell peppers and chop them very fine so that they sauté quickly when you prepare the *soffritto.*
2. In a heavy-bottomed frying pan heat the olive oil gently and sauté the ham. (Bayonne ham is used in Basque country. If you can't get it, ask a Spanish or Italian provisioner. Both *serrano* and Parma hams are reasonable substitutes. I have also used Virginia ham with good results.) The ham should just begin to whiten around the edges.
3. Add the onion, garlic, parsley, black and cayenne pepper, and cumin and sauté until the onion and garlic are softened and begin to turn gold.
4. Add the peppers and increase the heat so that the liquid quickly sautés out as you stir and press the mass with a wooden spatula.

5. This step is optional. Press the *soffritto* through a coarse sieve. This makes a wonderfully smooth *pipérade*, but I find it a bit refined. Actually I love to find the bits of ham and vegetables in the eggs. Every Basque I know would bristle at the idea of discarding even the smallest cube of mountain ham!
6. Though I have not included it in the recipe because the traditional recipe does not call for it, I suggest you add a pinch of baking soda—about ¼ teaspoon—to the *soffritto* at this point. You won't be able to taste it, but it will neutralize most of the acidity and help stabilize the eggs. Mix the soda in well and set the *soffritto* aside for a moment.

Prepare the eggs:
1. Whisk the eggs, water, and salt together until they are perfectly combined and lemon-colored.
2. Set the frying pan with the *soffritto* in another pan containing 1 inch of tepid water and put it over very low heat. Add the egg mixture and begin to stir it into the *soffritto*. As the mixture warms, scrape the bottom constantly with a wooden spatula, making sure that the whole *pipérade* thickens consistently until it is like a thick gravy. Remove it from the fire at once and serve it.

La *pipérade* is very often made with tomatoes—lots of them—in the *soffritto*, but I prefer not to include them. I prefer serving the tomatoes with the *pipérade* rather than in it. Many Basques have told me that they include lots of garlic in the *soffritto*, as well. I prefer rubbing the garlic liberally on long, narrow strips of French bread, sprinkling them with olive oil and coarse salt, toasting them in a 375° oven, and serving them with the *pipérade*.

I propose this delicious lunch: before you begin the *pipérade,* choose some fine, red, sun-ripened tomatoes—half as many as the number of people who will be eating your *pipérade*. Wash the tomatoes well and core them. Slice a small piece off each end so they will sit up, and cut them in half. With a spoon, remove a little of the pulp and seeds from the wider side of the halves. Sprinkle the halves with coarse salt, turn them upside down, and place them on a baking sheet covered with aluminum foil. Bake them for 10 minutes in a preheated 400° oven. When your *pipérade* is ready, turn the tomatoes over, sprinkle them with leaf thyme, and serve each guest a grilled tomato and 2 or 3 of the toasted breadsticks. Add a salad of young mixed greens, the season's fruit, and a good cheese, and you have a little gem of a Mediterranean lunch to offer your guests.

Fried Eggs Turkish Style
LES OEUFS A LA TURQUE
SERVES 5

I don't think this recipe came from Turkey, in spite of its name. I suspect that it must have originated not far from Marseille, where I first ate it in a friend's home. However, when I lived in the Middle East, I discovered that the people there made a similar dish. In my native Texas, we swear by an egg and tomato dish called ranch-style eggs. Whether French, Turkish, or Mexican, fried eggs are wonderful with tomato sauce. Here's the recipe as I learned it in Marseille.

1 fresh eggplant about 3 inches
   in diameter and 6 inches long
1 tablespoon coarse salt
½ cup flour
½ cup vegetable oil
5 large eggs
1 large yellow onion, peeled,
   halved, and sliced ½ inch
   thick
2 fat cloves garlic, peeled and
   quartered top to bottom

3 medium-sized ripe tomatoes,
   skinned, cored, seeded, and
   coarsely chopped
1 tablespoon tomato paste
   diluted in
      1 cup broth or water
1 bay leaf
¼ teaspoon thyme leaves
¼ teaspoon oregano
¼ teaspoon ground cinnamon
½ teaspoon freshly ground black
   pepper
1 teaspoon granulated sugar

1. Cut the stem end and the bottom from the eggplant and trim ½ inch from opposite sides. Hold the eggplant so that one of the un-cut sides is down, one up, and cut 5 slices lengthwise (top to bottom). Sprinkle these slices on both sides with salt, fit them back together, and set them on one of the flat sides. Place the whole eggplant between two plates, put a heavy weight such as an iron or a stack of plates on top, and allow the eggplant to leach for 20 minutes. This extracts the bitterness and makes it more resistant to the hot oil when frying. If you don't do this, the eggplant will drink up the oil like a sponge.

2. After 20 minutes, rinse the slices under cold, running water, squeeze them, and pat them dry with paper towels. Dredge the slices in flour, dusting off the excess.

3. Heat the oil in a large, heavy-bottomed frying pan and fry the 5 eggs

just until the whites are solid. The yolks should only be half cooked. Drain them on paper towels and set them aside.

4. In the same oil, fry the floured eggplant slices on both sides until they are golden. Remove them from the oil and drain them on paper towels. Set them aside.

5. Make a *soffritto* by sautéing the onion, garlic, and tomato in the oil until the onion is wilted and the tomato is almost dry. Add the diluted tomato paste, the bay leaf, the herbs, spices, and sugar and allow to simmer for 12 minutes.

6. Place the fried eggplant slices in the sauce like lily pads and braise them for 5 minutes.

7. Trim the egg whites neatly if they need it, and place a fried egg on each slice of eggplant. Cover the frying pan and continue simmering for 1 minute.

8. On a large, heated platter carefully place the slices of eggplant, each with its fried egg on top. Spoon over them any remaining sauce and serve.

N O T E : These eggs are excellent for a Sunday brunch. I suggest surrounding them with pilaf (see page 125). Eggs and rice go very well together.

Eggs in a Nest

LES OEUFS AU NID

SERVES 4

This is a dish that French children love. If you have a child who refuses to eat eggs, I suggest you try this recipe. Adults like eggs in a nest too. They are very easy to make.

1 tablespoon sweet butter	6 tablespoons heavy cream
1 tablespoon finely grated Parmesan cheese	2 tablespoons finely grated Gruyère or Emmenthal cheese
8 large fresh eggs, separated	
½ teaspoon coarse salt	½ teaspoon freshly ground white pepper
½ teaspoon cream of tartar	

1. Preheat the oven to 400°. Choose 4 individual baking dishes (ramekins). Butter them generously and powder them with Parmesan cheese. Tap out the excess.
2. Beat the egg whites with the salt and cream of tartar, slowly at first, then more rapidly, until the whites mount in soft peaks and keep their shape.
3. Divide the beaten whites among the four ramekins and make a depression in the center of each.
4. Place 2 yolks in each depression and spoon cream over them.
5. Pull the whites into peaks and scatter grated Gruyère or Emmenthal and pepper over them.
6. Set the ramekins on a cookie sheet and bake them in the oven for 10 minutes, or until the meringues are golden brown. Serve while they are hot and the toasted cheese is fragrant.

Hard-Boiled Eggs in Cider and Mustard Sauce
LES OEUFS AU CIDRE
SERVES 6

If you are tired of hard-boiled eggs in the eternal white sauce, here is an old Norman variation that your family might fancy. These eggs have a taste that can be described as zippy. They are a good first course because they can wake up sluggish appetites.

3 tablespoons sweet butter
4 medium-sized onions, peeled and finely chopped
3 tablespoons flour
½ teaspoon baking soda
2 cups cider or apple juice
½ cup heavy cream
3 tablespoons Dijon mustard
½ teaspoon coarse salt

½ teaspoon freshly ground white pepper
8 eggs, boiled 10 minutes according to the instructions on page 168, carefully peeled, and halved
1 tablespoon finely chopped chives

1. Melt the butter at medium heat in a heavy-bottomed saucepan and gently sauté the onions until they begin to turn pale gold.
2. Using a sifter, sprinkle the flour over the sautéing onions a little at a time, stirring it into the mixture with a wooden spatula.

3. Mix the baking soda with the cider and pour the cider into the onion mixture a little at a time, stirring it in well. Simmer the mixture at very low heat for 10 minutes, continuing to stir it.
4. Combine the cream, mustard, salt, and pepper and mix into the onion sauce. Remove the saucepan from the fire.
5. Pour ⅔ of the sauce into a warm serving platter. Place 12 of the egg halves, yolk side up, in the sauce, and cover them with the rest of the sauce.
6. Grate the remaining 4 egg halves coarsely and sprinkle them over the sauce. Sprinkle the chopped chives over the grated eggs and serve.

N O T E : This rather simple dish can be dressed up and served as a glamorous main course for a luncheon or brunch. Prepare individual canapés of freshly toasted, crustless sandwich bread lightly spread with pâté. Match a thin slice of ham to each so that it neatly covers the pâté. Cover the ham with the onion and mustard sauce, place two egg halves, yolks down, in the sauce, and cover them with more sauce. Finish the dish with the grated egg and chives.

Soft-Boiled Eggs Nice Style
LES OEUFS MOLLETS A LA NIÇOISE
SERVES 4

This is an easy first course that is simple but distinctive. Make it in summer when local tomatoes are at their best. I like the recipe because the eggs are sauced with a light lemon dressing and not the ever-present mayonnaise. I also like it because all the ingredients can be prepared hours ahead and assembled at the last minute.

4 large fresh eggs
1 bunch very fresh watercress
1 teaspoon coarse salt
3 tablespoons freshly squeezed
   lemon juice
2 medium-sized firm but red-ripe
   tomatoes
1 tablespoon Dijon mustard
5 fresh or ½ teaspoon dried
   tarragon leaves

1 small scallion, white part only,
   very finely chopped
¼ cup light olive oil
8 paper-thin slices Parma ham
   (you may opt for boiled
   Parisian-type ham, but the
   dry-cured ham has more
   flavor)

1. Boil the eggs for 5 minutes, following the instructions on page 168. Put them in cold water, then crack and peel them under cold running water. Set them aside in cold water.
2. Rinse the watercress well and dry it with paper towels or a salad dryer. Discard the coarsest stems and break up the rest into shorter pieces. Sprinkle the damp watercress with a little of the salt and a few drops of the lemon juice. Use the tips of your fingers to see that all the watercress gets a little of the salt and lemon juice. Set aside.
3. Wash and dry the tomatoes and cut a small slice off each end so they will sit up. Pare out the hard parts where the stems were attached, cut the tomatoes in half horizontally, and remove the core and the seeds from each half with a spoon. Use a little more of the salt to salt the insides of the tomato cups. Place them upside down to drain.
4. Prepare the lemon dressing by combining in a bowl the rest of the salt and lemon juice, the mustard, tarragon, and scallion. (I prefer doing this with a wooden pestle so that I can bruise and meld the ingredients more thoroughly.) Add the oil, a few drops at a time, and continue grinding until the sauce is pearly and lightly emulsified.
5. Choose some colorful plates (the yellow or green dishes from Provence are perfect for the color contrasts in this dish). Place a nest of watercress on each plate and put a tomato cup in the center of each. With a very sharp knife, score a cross on the narrow end of each egg (don't cut completely through the white or the yolk may begin to emerge). If the eggs don't fit neatly into the tomato cups, slice off a tiny piece of the white on the wide end of each egg and they will sit up properly. Roll the Parma ham into neat "cigarettes" and place two on each plate, opposite each other. Sauce the eggs with the lemon dressing by pouring a spoonful over each and letting it run down over the tomato and into the watercress. Serve very cold.

NOTE: You may prefer to cook the eggs for 10 minutes, making them hard. Like the French, I find the combination of soft yolk, lemon dressing, tomato, watercress, and Parma ham absolutely delicious. But suit yourself. One way or the other, I find this little egg dish well worth knowing.

• • •

Eggs Poached in Red Wine
LES OEUFS EN MEURETTE

SERVES 6

If you ever have the good fortune to stay with a family in Burgundy for a while, you will probably be served eggs en meurette. The dish is a great favorite in Burgundy, but Burgundians consider it very ordinary. To the rest of the world, this hearty dish of eggs poached in Beaujolais or Morgon wine is a delicious culinary curiosity.

1 cup smoked bacon, sliced in ¼-inch matchstick-like lardoons
2 tablespoons vegetable oil
2 carrots, scraped, trimmed, and cut in ½-inch dice
2 medium-sized onions, peeled and finely chopped
2 tablespoons flour
1½ cups good red wine (Beaujolais or Morgon are normally used)

½ cup broth or water
1 piece of bacon rind, at least 1 × 3 inches
3 plump cloves garlic, peeled and finely minced
6 large fresh eggs
½ teaspoon coarse salt
½ teaspoon finely ground black pepper

1. Blanch the bacon in boiling water for 3 minutes. Rinse it well and pat it very dry with paper towels.
2. In a heavy flameproof earthenware pot, heat the oil and sauté the bacon lardoons until golden. Add the carrots and onions and stir them about for 5 minutes.
3. Sift the flour over the mixture, stirring well so that no lumps form. Allow the flour to sauté until it begins to turn golden.
4. Add the wine and the broth, stir well, and bring sauce to a simmer.
5. Slip the rind to the bottom of the pot under the simmering sauce and allow the sauce to continue to simmer for 45 minutes at the very lowest heat.
6. Add the garlic and stir it in.
7. Break the eggs one at a time into a little bowl and slip them one at a time into the sauce. Allow the eggs to poach for 12 minutes. Sprinkle them with salt and pepper.
8. Remove the pot from the fire immediately. Cover it and allow the eggs to set in the sauce.

9. When the eggs have just set, bring the pot to the table and serve the eggs *en meurette* very hot.

French Omelet with Finely Chopped Fresh Herbs
L'OMELETTE AUX FINES HERBES
SERVES 1

In France this is by far the commonest of all omelets. Yet it is the test of the master omelettier. For it to be perfect, the eggs must be fresh laid, the herbs must have been gathered before sunrise on the day they are used, the butter must be fresh, sweet, and unsalted, and the omelet must be in and out of the pan in 45 seconds! Although it is the most common of omelets, it is perhaps the most delicious of all omelets. Have everything ready and at hand. If it comes out perfect, and I'm sure it will, it is a wonderful gift for someone you really care about, provided that person can appreciate its finesse. It ought to be served and the first bite taken in less than 2 minutes. I only make this omelet for myself, for one late riser who missed breakfast, or for a guest who arrives famished between mealtimes. I find it best to serve it right at the kitchen table.

2 large fresh eggs, at room temperature
¼ teaspoon finely milled salt
1 micropinch granulated sugar (for its browning power, not for sweetness)
½ teaspoon water
1 teaspoon very finely chopped flat-leaf parsley

2 fresh tarragon leaves, finely chopped
½ teaspoon finely chopped chives
⅛ teaspoon freshly ground white pepper
1 tablespoon plus 1 hazelnut-sized lump sweet butter

1. Break the eggs, one at a time, in a saucer to verify their freshness (see page 167).
2. Put the eggs in a mixing bowl or soup plate with the salt, sugar, and water and whisk them lightly. Add the chopped herbs and pepper and whisk lightly again.
3. Heat the pan. When it is quite hot, add 1 tablespoon butter. When the butter is sizzling, twirl the pan to coat the cooking surface.

4. Whisk the eggs briefly once more and pour them into the pan. With a wooden spatula, gently nudge them toward the center while tipping the pan in a circular motion so that the eggs "catch" on the already solidifying undersurface.

5. While the center is still liquid—*baveuse*, or drooly, as the French say—lift the right edge of the omelet if you are right-handed, otherwise the left edge, with the spatula and double one side over the other.

6. Drop the lump of butter into the pan just under the closed side of the omelet, lift the omelet a little and let the butter run underneath, glazing the underside.

7. With a quick tip of the pan and a sharp tap, turn the omelet out onto a warm plate, underside up, and serve it immediately.

N O T E : If the omelet drools a little in the plate once it's turned out, don't fret. That is a sign it isn't overdone. The heat inside the omelet will further solidify it. Fresh French bread is preferable to toast with this omelet. If you like watercress, you might also like a much-favored variation—watercress omelet: Just substitute 1 tablespoon very finely chopped watercress leaves for the parsley, tarragon, and chives.

French Country Omelet
L'OMELETTE A LA CAMPAGNARDE
S E R V E S 2 O R 3

Let's take a moment to discuss country omelets before we make one. Country omelets are traditionally flat and solid. They can contain almost anything, and can be eaten hot or cold. Their peasant lineage goes back centuries before the light, fluffy, wallet-shaped omelets we associate with French cooking were invented. Every region I have lived in or visited in France has its own country omelets, all with regional names. I suspect country omelets are as ubiquitous as noodles. No matter where I have found them—which is everywhere—they usually resemble each other. The rousolo *of beaten egg, leftover bread, and slices of sausage known to all the mountain folk in the Foix and Couserans area of France is just like the* Eierauflauf *that our beloved Austrian friend Gustl used to make for us when we were children. My friends in Spain make dozens of kinds of country omelets. They love to stack them up and slice them like layer cakes, and they call them all by the generic name* tortilla. *More than forty years ago Sicilian and Neapolitan friends in San Antonio used to make their own version of country omelets for us. They contained whatever was in season from tiny fresh artichoke hearts sprinkled with fennel seeds to zucchini flowers and sweet basil leaves. They called them* frittate. *To my delight, they have become the latest rage in some expensive New York restaurants.*

The French country omelet here is just made for hungry kids. You will like it too. The wedding of egg, parsley, spinach, bacon, and potato is a ménage à cinq *that was, I think, made in heaven.*

3 tablespoons vegetable oil
1 medium-sized potato, peeled and cut into ½-inch-thick roundels
1 rasher smoked bacon, blanched in boiling water, rinsed and dried, cut in ¼-inch matchstick-like lardoons
4 large fresh eggs
1 teaspoon water
½ teaspoon finely milled salt

½ teaspoon freshly cracked black pepper
2 tablespoons coarsely chopped flat-leaf parsley
1 scallion, root and part of green leaves trimmed off, coarsely chopped
½ cup fresh spinach, stemmed, well washed, and coarsely chopped
1 teaspoon freshly grated Parmesan cheese

1. Heat a 10-inch-wide nonstick frying pan. Add the oil and fry the potato roundels at medium heat until they are golden on both sides. Remove them from the oil, drain them on paper towels, and set them aside.
2. Fry the bacon lardoons until they begin to take on color, but don't let them get crisp or they will be bitter in the omelet. Remove them from the oil and drain them on paper towels.
3. Discard or save for another use all but 1 tablespoon of the oil.
4. Whisk the eggs, water, salt, pepper, and parsley together briefly. Add the potatoes, scallions, lardoons, and spinach and see that they all get properly coated with the egg mixture.
5. Heat the frying pan containing the 1 tablespoon oil and pour the mixture into it. Using a wooden spatula, push the potatoes toward the bottom and reduce the heat.
6. Introduce the spatula into the center of the omelet. Lift it a bit and allow the uncooked egg to run under the omelet. That will hasten the cooking.
7. Choose a kitchen plate that is larger than 10 inches across and invert

it over the frying pan. Holding it tightly against the frying pan, flip the pan over and leave the omelet, done side up, in the plate. Quickly slip the omelet, uncooked side down, back into the frying pan. Tidy up the edges, if they need it, by pressing them down toward the bottom with the edge of the spatula. Let the omelet brown on the undone side for 2 or 3 minutes.

8. Invert the plate over the frying pan and flip it to see if the second side is properly browned. If it isn't, return it to brown again. If it is, place it on a serving plate, sprinkle it with Parmesan, and serve it at once.

N O T E : Country omelets, unlike their more sophisticated Parisian cousins, the *omelette aux fines herbes* and the *omelette au fromage,* can take a lot of punishment in cooking and be none the worse for it. Good cooks know that dainty omelets should never be browned or wrinkled from too much cooking. But country omelets should be beautifully browned on both sides. In fact, some cooks in France refuse to call them omelets and refer to them, because of their solidity, as *galettes* or *pains,* literally cakes or loaves. Because of their solidity, they travel well and can be eaten warm or cold. They are a fine choice for picnics.

Cheese Omelet
L ' O M E L E T T E   A U   F R O M A G E
S E R V E S 2

This cheese omelet is a far cry from the deflated, leathery combination of eggs and vulcanized processed cheese that usually passes for cheese omelet in the United States.

4 large fresh eggs, at room
  temperature
1 teaspoon water
¼ teaspoon finely milled salt
¼ teaspoon finely ground white
  pepper
¼ teaspoon freshly grated
  nutmeg
¼ teaspoon fresh ground paprika

3 fresh tarragon leaves, finely
  chopped, or 1 large mint leaf,
  finely chopped
1 tablespoon finely grated
  Gruyère cheese
One 4-ounce piece plain, soft
  chèvre goat cheese without
  pepper, ash, or herbs
1 tablespoon plus 1
  hazelnut-sized lump sweet
  butter

1. Break the eggs, one at a time, into a saucer to judge their freshness. They must be very fresh.
2. Whisk the eggs, water, salt, pepper, nutmeg, paprika, and chopped tarragon or mint together until they froth.
3. Add the Gruyère and half the *chèvre* and whisk again.
4. Heat the frying pan. When it is hot, toss in 1 tablespoon of the butter and when the butter sizzles, pour in the egg and cheese mixture. Swirl the mixture around the pan and lift the center briefly with a wooden spatula, allowing the liquid egg to run under to the cooking surface.
5. Crumble the rest of the goat cheese and place it in the center of the omelet.
6. Lift the edge of the omelet with the spatula and double the omelet over. Then lift the closed side of the omelet with the spatula and drop the lump of butter under it so that the underside will glaze.
7. Quickly tip the pan and roll the omelet out onto a warm platter, underside up. Serve immediately.

Jam Omelet

L'OMELETTE AUX CONFITURES A L'ABRICOT

SERVES 1

Here is a real "kid-pleaser." Almost every schoolday afternoon Mme. Cabanès, my neighbor for a year in Aix, used to make this omelet for her little boy when he returned from school. He never grew tired of it. Maybe you will agree that it's better than a jelly sandwich. To do it just right you must be very quick indeed.

2 tablespoons apricot jam	1 teaspoon granulated sugar
1 large fresh egg, at room temperature	1 tablespoon plus 1 hazelnut-sized lump sweet butter
½ teaspoon water	
¼ teaspoon finely milled salt	1 tablespoon confectioner's sugar

1. Warm the jam in a pan over boiling water.
2. Whisk the egg, water, salt, and granulated sugar together until they froth.

3. Heat the frying pan. When it is quite hot, toss in 1 tablespoon butter and swirl the pan about to coat the cooking surface as it melts. When the butter is sizzling, pour in the egg mixture and swirl about quickly so the egg coats the bottom of the pan.
4. Add the jam to the center and quickly double the omelet over itself. Use a wooden spatula, and work very quickly.
5. Toss in the lump of butter. Lift the omelet to let the butter run under and glaze the underside.
6. Quickly flip out the omelet into a plate, underside up.
7. Sift confectioner's sugar over the omelet and serve it at once.

N O T E : This omelet cooks very fast, since it contains only 1 egg. You can slow the cooking by adding another egg, keeping all the other ingredients the same. If you want to dress up this little gem of an omelet, heat a skewer red hot and lay it on the sugared surface in opposing diagonals. It will caramelize the sugar and leave a wonderful dark design on the top. You don't have to do this for the kids, but when you make a larger dessert omelet for grown-ups, it is a handy technique to know.

Egg, Cheese, and Bacon Pie
LA QUICHE LORRAINE
SERVES 6

Years before the quiche lorraine was discovered, denatured, and betrayed by United States cooks, it was a treasured all-time favorite in French households. In those days it was made with nothing but eggs, fine Gruyère cheese, heavy cream, and smoked bacon. In my view, none of the "nouvelles quiches," even the fabulous ones made with puff paste and lobster, has ever met the mark of the hearty, homely, fragrant quiches lorraines that I was often served in French homes before the "quiche generation."

This recipe is an old-fashioned, completely authentic one. It was given to me back in the forties by a friend born and brought up in the Lorraine. Thanks to the hundreds of unworthy concoctions labeled quiche, the great old egg, cheese, and bacon pie has acquired a very bad reputation in the last twenty years. If you've never had a genuine quiche lorraine, you owe it to yourself to try the real article. It could be a revelation. However, you will have to find very fresh eggs, good farmhouse cream, aged Gruyère cheese, and excellent smoked slab bacon if you want to experience it at its primitive best.

FOR THE CRUST:

2 cups flour
2 fresh eggs
2 egg yolks
¼ teaspoon coarse salt

¼ teaspoon granulated sugar
2 tablespoons cold water
¼ pound (1 stick) cold, sweet
    butter cut in ¼-inch cubes

FOR THE FILLING:

Two ¼-inch-thick rashers
    dry-cured, smoked slab bacon,
    rind removed, cut in ¼-inch
    matchstick-like lardoons
6 paper-thin slices imported
    aged Gruyère cheese, each
    about 2 × 4 inches (a cheese
    sampler that produces thin
    lamelles [slices] is just the
    ticket)

3 fresh eggs
3 egg yolks
½ cup heavy cream
2 tablespoons milk
¼ teaspoon coarse salt
¼ teaspoon freshly ground white
    pepper
⅛ teaspoon freshly grated
    nutmeg

Make the crust:

1. On a clean, dry surface—preferably marble—heap the flour. Make a crater in the flour, and put the whole eggs, yolks, salt, sugar, and water in the crater.
2. With your fingertips, gradually work together all of the ingredients.
3. Put aside about 1 teaspoon of the butter for buttering the quiche mold and work the remaining butter cubes into the dough. The proper way to do this is by pressing the cubes into the dough by streaking it across the working surface with the heel of the hand. This really forces the butter into the texture of the dough. It is the same process used in making brioche dough. The dough should be smooth and shiny. If it is too sticky, add more flour. Cover the dough and let it rest for 20 minutes.
4. Grease the quiche mold. If you haven't one, use a 10-inch pie tin. Preheat the oven to 350°.
5. Roll out the dough ¼ inch thick. It shouldn't be thin. Originally, quiches were made with a crust of thick slices of stale bread, and the traditional quiche must have a thick crust. Line the mold or tin with

the dough, making sure that there is a high ridge of pastry around the edge of the mold. Flute the edge if you wish.

6. Cover the pastry carefully with buttered baking parchment or aluminum foil and press it down close to the pastry. Fill the mold with rice, beans, or pastry weights and bake it for about 20 minutes (it should be only ¾ done). Make sure you cover the edges of the pastry before subjecting the shell to heat or the edges may burn during the second baking.

7. Remove the mold from the oven and allow it to cool on a rack. When it is cool enough to handle comfortably, not before, empty out the weights. If you have used beans or rice, store them in a tightly closed jar for future baking. They can be used over and over again for baking, but baking makes them inedible.

8. Peel away the parchment or foil from the crust. Set aside the crust-filled mold and prepare the filling. (You can make the crust hours ahead of time if you wish.)

Make the filling:

1. Fry the bacon in a nonstick frying pan just until it becomes translucent. Drain the lardoons well and distribute them evenly over the bottom of the pastry shell. Distribute the thin pieces of cheese over the bacon.

2. Whip the eggs, yolks, cream, milk, salt, pepper, and nutmeg together until lemon-colored and ladle the mixture into the pastry shell over the bacon and cheese. Don't fill the shell too full: leave at least ¼ inch between the filling and the top of the crust or the filling will run over in baking.

3. Bake the quiche in the middle of a preheated 350° oven for 30 to 35 minutes or until a knife or skewer inserted in the middle comes out clean. Slow cooking is recommended. Traditionally the quiche should neither puff nor boil while baking.

4. Remove the quiche from the oven and serve it as soon as possible, using a sharp knife and a pie trowel to serve substantial wedges to your guests.

N O T E : Quiche lorraine is at its best straight from the oven while it is still sending forth its inimitable, country-kitchen aroma. But it is excellent warm or cold. A generous wedge, accompanied by a green salad, makes a fine lunch. Small wedges are a fine first course. Cold quiche is great picnic food. Quiche lorraine reheats well, but remember this: Quiche should cook slowly from beginning to end. I suggest covering the quiche with aluminum foil and reheating it for 5 to 10 minutes in a 350° oven. Pierce the aluminum foil in several places so that vapor doesn't condense between the foil and the surface of the pie.

Cheese Dishes

An entire book could and should be written about regional cheese cookery in France. With the exception of Brittany, all the regions and provinces of France have long histories of cheese production and consumption. Each possesses, as well, a repertoire of dishes in which cheese is the principal ingredient. This is not the time or place to treat it with the thoroughness it deserves, but I must at least tip my hat to that great area of French culinary ingenuity and shrewdness. So I shall speak here only of the fondue and the soufflé *au fromage.* The cheese soufflé is not regional; it is known to all French family cooks and deserves attention here as one of the most common and best cheese dishes in French household cooking. The fondue fad is pretty much over in the United States, but like the quiche, which also had its day, the fondue has suffered a great deal at the hands of cooks everywhere and, as a result, has gone out of fashion in the United States.

There are many kinds of fondue or melted cheese dishes in France. The objective with cheese fondue is to melt a significant amount of cheese in wine or beer so that the two substances mix perfectly. The pot is set in the middle of the table over a small spirit lamp, which keeps the fondue hot and creamy. Each guest is given a long fork to spear cubes of bread, and sometimes vegetables or meat, and dunk them in the warm, bubbling mixture. Except for Brittany, where aged cheese was disdained a century ago as "rotten butter," most of the regions in France have produced fondues of one sort or another.

The classic fondue is native to the eastern regions of France that lie along the Swiss border, and it is claimed by both the French and the Swiss. It is a marvelous convivial rite, not just a dish. The intention is twofold: to nourish the famished guests and to provide an attractive means for breaking with formalities. The host provides a good quantity of the same wine used in preparing the fondue to wash it down and to stimulate high spirits. The wine should be light, rather dry and fruity in flavor, and low in alcoholic content. The guests' glasses should be constantly refilled. The fondue is given an extra fillip by adding a small amount of kirsch, a dry spirit flavored with cracked cherry pits, and it is the custom for everyone to drink a small glass of kirsch when the fondue is half consumed. Like the Norman custom of having a glass of applejack during the meal, the little shot of kirsch, downed in the middle of the meal, makes room, it is believed, for still more fondue. This custom is called *le coup du milieu* or the shot in the middle!

There is another part of the rite that helps the festivities along when serving fondue: if you lose a bread cube when dunking it, you must pay a forfeit. You are obliged to kiss the persons seated beside you at table or provide an additional bottle of wine for your fellow diners. When the fondue has been exhausted, there is a crust at the bottom of the pot known as the *croûton.* Many fondue fanciers consider it the best part. They wait eagerly to claim a piece of it.

Christine's Fondue
LA FONDUE A CHRISTINE
SERVES 4 OR 5

Fondue can be made at any time, and it is always appreciated. It is, however, substantial fare and really at its best when cold, snowy weather, healthy appetites, and lively friends are all present. Here is a fine old family recipe for a genuine cheese fondue. It was given to me by my good friend Christine Eade, whose Swiss mother taught it to her.

2 plump cloves of garlic, peeled and cut in half

1 pound 5 ounces good, aged Gruyère (the legendary Gruyère of Fribourg is indicated, but any good Gruyère will do)

7 ounces Vacherin cheese

1 tablespoon flour

1 teaspoon baking soda

8 glasses dry white wine

1 jigger dry kirschwasser

¼ teaspoon freshly grated nutmeg

¼ teaspoon freshly ground white pepper

Seventy to eighty 1-inch cubes of bread, preferably a substantial sourdough made with unbleached flour

1. If you haven't a fondue pot, choose a heavy, nonstick, enameled braising pot with a short, stout handle. Rub the entire interior surface with garlic and leave the four pieces of garlic in the pot.
2. With a large-toothed grater, grate the cheeses. There is a long-standing argument amongst fondue makers over whether the cheese should be grated, cubed, or cut in thin *lamelles* (slices). The point is not to use a fine-toothed grater or the cheese will stick together and you will end up with hot, boiling wine and a lump of vulcanized cheese at the bottom of the pot.
3. Toss the flour, baking soda, and cheese together so that the cheese gets dusted and the flour and soda seem to disappear.
4. Put the cheese in the pot with half the wine and start heating the pot over a very low flame or the lowest reading on an electric burner. Stir the mixture in a figure 8 with a wooden spatula. (The ideal instrument is a wooden one with a flat, bladelike end with a large hole in it. Food specialty shops and kitchen suppliers usually stock this utensil.)
5. As the mixture begins to combine, add more wine, a little at a time, and increase the heat slightly, continuing to stir the mixture in a figure 8 until all the wine has combined with the cheese.
6. Just as the fondue begins to seethe, add the kirsch, nutmeg, and pepper and stir them in. Always stir the fondue in a figure 8.
7. Your fondue is now ready. Put it on the spirit lamp stand, open the aperture 2 points (or at a very low heat), light it, and place the whole apparatus in the center of the table.
8. Provide 2 platters for the bread cubes, so that the bread will be in easy reach of everyone. Each guest should have a plate, a fondue fork, a wine glass, and a tiny liqueur glass. Keep the wine glasses filled. Halfway through the meal, fill the liqueur glasses with kirsch and propose a toast.

N O T E : The wine should be light and slightly *pétillant* or alive. Neuchatel is an excellent choice, but Rhine wine, Alsatian hock, or Apremont, which Savoyard fondue makers swear by, are all good options. The fondue is the meal. Propose a toast with the first glass of wine as a starter, then begin! Follow the fondue with the simplest of green salads dressed with a light lemon dressing or vinaigrette. You'd be wise to offer only fresh fruit and a tiny cup of very good coffee to finish off this festive but heavy meal. It is an unlikely eventuality, but should there be any fondue left over, reheat it gently the next day and scramble an egg or two in it. *Voilà!* The makings of a light lunch or snack.

Cheese Soufflé

LE SOUFFLE AU FROMAGE

SERVES 4

The cheese soufflé is one of the great accomplishments of French cooking. As a lover of good food I still marvel at a perfectly browned, perfectly inflated, perfectly tender cheese soufflé. As a cook, I am even more impressed by the simple ingredients and the simple way in which they are used to produce this wonder. If you have never made a cheese soufflé, you will be surprised at how easy it is.

2 cups whole milk
4 tablespoons (½ stick) sweet
    butter
¼ cup flour
½ teaspoon coarse salt
¼ teaspoon freshly ground white
    pepper
¼ teaspoon freshly grated
    nutmeg

4 large fresh eggs, at room
    temperature
1 teaspoon water
⅔ cup finely grated Gruyère
    cheese
3 drops fresh lemon juice
⅛ teaspoon finely milled table
    salt

1. Preheat the oven to 375°.
2. Heat the milk to the boiling point and remove it from the heat.
3. With a knob of the butter, grease a straight-sided soufflé dish at least 4 inches deep and 7 inches wide.
4. Melt the butter at medium heat in a heavy-bottomed sauce pan. When it is completely melted, add the flour and stir the mixture to a thick paste. Allow this roux to cook for 2 minutes.
5. Add the hot milk gradually to the roux, stirring constantly with a wooden spatula or whisk as it thickens to a *Béchamel*. Stir in the coarse salt, pepper, and nutmeg and set the *Béchamel* aside to cool a bit.
6. Separate the eggs carefully.
7. Beat the yolks and the water together until frothy and combine them with the warm *Béchamel*. Stir in the grated cheese.
8. Add the lemon juice and finely milled salt to the egg whites and beat them until they stand in peaks. Add a little of the beaten whites to the *Béchamel* to soften it a bit, then fold in the rest of the whites carefully, so as to keep the mixture as light as possible. By all means don't stir it.
9. Pour the mixture into the buttered soufflé dish and bake it on the

middle rack of the oven for 20 minutes or until it is beautifully golden and well puffed.

10. Take the soufflé directly from the oven to the table and serve it immediately, before it begins to cool and deflate.

N O T E : A perfect soufflé works exactly like a hot air balloon. The outside must be sealed so that when the air in the egg whites begins to expand and ascend, it is trapped and causes the entire soufflé to inflate. The soufflé will deflate if you rupture it or allow the air to cool and lose its buoyancy. That is the scientific explanation, but it does not in the least dispel the culinary magic of this splendid invention.

This basic soufflé recipe can be used to make many kinds of savory soufflés. Try adding 3 or 4 thinly sliced, lightly sautéed mushrooms or ½ cup purée of fresh spinach to the *Béchamel* before adding the beaten egg whites. Some cooks like to powder the top of the soufflé with a little grated cheese. Fine! But don't gild the lily. The recipe as it is will produce a fine, pristine cheese soufflé.

French Pancakes

LES GALETTES ET LES CREPES

Pancakes, in one form or another, were once eaten instead of bread in many rural districts of France. That has changed in the last fifty years, but pancakes are still sold on the street corners of Paris, where they are as familiar to Parisians as the frank is to New Yorkers. However, it is Brittany and not Paris that is the true home of the French pancake. By pancake I do not mean the tiny, paper-thin crêpes we remember from the craze a few years back. I mean the thin but hefty 12- to 16-inch *galettes bretonnes* made with buckwheat flour and usually containing no eggs. It is these *matefaims*, or "hunger killers," that are now sold on the streets of Paris. You can buy them glazed with melted butter and rolled around a choice of stuffings.

Formerly, these great pancakes were made by the grandmother in the family during the meal. She baked them on a *bilig*, or griddle, heated with embers. Each person at table tore a piece off the *galette*, slathered it with salted butter, and ate it with whatever was being served. My Bretonne friend Joséphine Le Bec informs me that the fancy dessert crêpes we are served in the the United States were unknown to most Bretons when she was a child forty years ago at Plowan in Brittany. When the evening meal was near its end, if there was any batter left over, the grandmother would make a small *galette* for each child, drop on some thin slices of apple, turn them, cook them briefly, and serve them to the children with melted butter and a little sugar. "That," says my friend, "was as fancy a pancake as we ever knew, and it was considered a real treat."

Nowadays many kinds of pancakes are produced in Brittany for the tourists. Some are made only with buckwheat flour, some with white, some with both, some with egg, some without egg, some with water, some with milk, and some with both. Some are even made with cider.

Though I have made French pancakes most of my adult life, I do not consider myself a master *galettier*. That takes years of daily experience. But I am not in the least ashamed of my French pancakes, and I have several excellent French pancake recipes to pass on to you. You can easily become proficient, too, if you use these recipes enough. I strongly recommend that you master José's wonderful "Batter for Beginners," which follows. When you get the feel of it, invite some friends to a *galette* party. Pancake parties are good almost anytime, but they are usually held to celebrate the Feast of Lights, Candlemas, which falls on February 2, in the coldest, darkest part of the winter. True Bretons disdain *galettes* that are more than five minutes old. They swear that they are best just off the griddle. I agree, but I am not such a purist. I suggest that you do as I do and make a stack of 20 or 30 *galettes* beforehand for your party. But don't try to reheat them in an oven or a microwave. The heat will produce steam inside the stack and make your *galettes* soggy. The trick is to heat several pans and reheat the galettes a few at a time. That certainly beats making them one at a time for a crowd of hungry guests. When planning for a *galette* party, calculate that each guest will eat 5 or 6 pancakes. Be prudent and set aside some of the batter just in case you need a few more.

• • •

José's Pancake Batter for Beginners
LA PATE A GALETTES POUR DEBUTANTS

MAKES 20 TO 25 8-INCH *GALETTES*

Master pancake makers in Brittany refuse to give exact measurements for water or milk in a pancake batter recipe. They insist that different flours will absorb varying amounts of liquid and that it is far more important to the success of the recipe that the pancake maker recognize the right consistency for the batter. They simply say " . . . de l'eau jusqu'à ce que la pâte soit à point," which translates ". . .add enough water to make the batter just right." In this case, "just right" means that the batter should have the consistency of a rich cream that coats the hand lightly but runs off the stirring fingers in a continuous, thin stream. In any case, if you are unfamiliar with galettes, you can test the consistency of the batter by judging the first pancake. It should be very thin and paperlike. If it isn't, add more water to the batter and stir it in well.

1 cup freshly ground buckwheat flour (get this from a health food store or grind your own from buckwheat groats)
6 tablespoons white flour
1 whole egg

1 egg yolk
1 teaspoon coarse salt
Cold water
3 tablespoons salted butter, melted, for greasing the pan

1. Mix the flours together in a large mixing bowl and make a crater in the center.
2. Place the whole egg, the yolk, and the salt in the crater and start combining the ingredients with the fingers of one hand. Keep one hand free to hold the edge of the mixing bowl. Continuously but slowly work through the ingredients with your fingers until the liquid has been completely absorbed by the flours.
3. Add the water, a little at a time, but don't get in a hurry and "drown the batter." This patient *pétrissage* will take about 10 minutes, but it is necessary if the *galettes* are to turn out light and thin. At the end of 10 minutes the batter should coat the hand lightly but fall away from the fingers in a thin, continuous stream when they are clutched and lifted a few inches from the rest of the batter. If you are concerned about working the batter with your hand, you can perform Steps 1

through 3 with a food processor in about 3 minutes. The processor will do an excellent job, but you will be deprived of learning the feel of the batter, an important accomplishment in *galette* making.

4. If you have a large, round griddle that resembles a *bilig*, the enormous griddle used in Brittany, use it. If not, heat an 8- to 10-inch nonstick frying pan over moderate heat. Coat the cooking surface lightly with melted butter using a piece of old linen or a folded paper towel.

5. Stir the batter before making each *galette*, and pour just enough batter onto the griddle or frying pan to coat the bottom when you tip the pan and swirl it about. If you are using a heavy griddle, you will have to provide yourself with a wooden *rouable* or *rozell*, a kind of hoe-shaped spreader (or an improvised substitute) to spread the batter paper-thin over the griddle, or you will end up with plain griddle cakes. Should the batter sputter and make lacy holes, the cooking surface is too hot. Reduce the heat. The first pancake is always a guinea pig.

6. When the edges of the *galette* begin to dry and curl, shake the pan to loosen the pancake and flip it over. You can do this in one of three ways. If you are not using a griddle, you can toss the pan, flipping the pancake in the air and catching it in the pan, done side up, or you can seize the edges of the *galette* with your fingertips and flip it over, or, if you are using a griddle, slip a wooden instrument under the *galette* and flip it over.

7. Cook the undone side for about 1 minute. Turn the *galette* out onto a warm, buttered plate. Judge it. If it is too thick, the batter should be thinned with water. If it is full of holes, the cooking surface is too hot. Reduce the heat. Rub the pan with butter. If any part of your *galette* stuck, rub the spot in the pan with coarse salt and butter on a bit of cloth until it is perfectly free of the stuck batter and takes on a high polish. Wipe away the salt and continue making the *galettes*, stacking the finished ones. You may want to have 2 or 3 pans going at the same time. I often do. The stack of *galettes* grows more rapidly that way.

N O T E : If you give a *galette* party, and I hope you will, show your guests how to fill and fold their own *galettes*. Lay the *galette* flat and coat it with melted butter. Spread the center with one of the fillings you have provided. Fold the lower half toward the top. Fold the sides in toward the center. Fold the sides again toward each other. You now have a compact roll. Wrap a paper napkin around it, and eat it like a hotdog. You should provide a brush or large goose feather for the melted butter, and bowls of sautéed onions and mushrooms, chopped, fried ham and bacon, grated Gruyère cheese, applesauce, and jam. Have fun!

CHAPTER EIGHT

Meats

LES VIANDES   *203*

Some Things Every Cook Should Know About Meat   *204*

BEEF AND VEAL (le Boeuf et le Veau)   *205*

The Provençal Daube   *216*

Les Viandes

The ideal of most French householders is to offer meat in one form or another as the principal course at about three-quarters of the week's major meals and yet stay within their food allowance. Meat accounts for about one-third of the food budget in most French homes, so a great deal of thoughtful planning is required. Expensive prime cuts of meat rarely appear on French family menus. Large cuts are bought for such favorites as boiled beef *(le pot-au-feu)*, but householders feel obliged to justify such a purchase by making those cuts provide for two or three meals. To that end, the French cook resorts to a vast traditional repertoire of ingenious ways of preparing the leftovers, and in general there is no disdain in a French home for dishes made from leftover meats. In fact, I know several families in France with whom *boeuf miroton* and *hachis parmentier,* both dishes traditionally made from leftover boiled beef, are great favorites.

I do not wish to give the impression that they manage so well that there is never a slipup. As Elizabeth David pointed out long ago, French household cooks have no special exemption from tough meat or an occasional culinary failure. However, good food is part of the French national culture, and the French manage to provide delicious meals that are nutritious, appetizing, and economical. Cooks in France make a practice of being on good terms with their butchers. If their butcher sells them a tough or faulty piece of meat, there is sure to be a personal confrontation the next shopping day. Everyone in a French family grows up thinking he or she is a fine judge of good food; consequently, every member of the family will have passed judgment on the offending piece of meat.

In the meal plan, the meat is the primary consideration. The choice of meat and its preparation will determine the vegetable or staple that will accompany it, what is to precede it, and what is to follow. That means that a good household cook must know a great deal about meats and their preparation. French meat lore, as I have suggested, is exhaustive, but that should excite rather than discourage the lover of good food. Mastering this vast tradition of French meat cookery may take a lifetime, but can you think of a more enjoyable task? Naturally, in this book I cannot tell you all you should know about the French ways of cooking meat. However, I can give you, to start with, a few general principles and encourage you to begin.

SOME THINGS EVERY COOK SHOULD KNOW ABOUT MEAT

Like us, the contemporary French householder is becoming aware of the correlation between controlled cholesterol levels and good health. This is a very great problem in French cooking, but not insurmountable. The French, as a whole, are not fond of excess fat and always advise skimming off whatever fat rises to the surface, even resorting to leaving certain dishes overnight in the refrigerator so that the surface fat will solidify and be much easier to remove. Yet they usually employ a great deal of butter and pork fat in their cooking, and many regional dishes contain notable amounts of goose and duck fat. The great chefs of the past who framed the canons of French meat cookery were unaware of cholesterol. They knew, however, that fat content was an essential consideration in controlling both the tenderness and moisture in meat dishes. There is the problem: We must learn to prepare meats so that they maintain their tenderness and juiciness, but that requires, in most cases, a good deal of animal fat. Therefore, we must find out how to eliminate as much of that fat as possible from the finished product. Here are some suggestions:

- Follow the recipe indications where bacon lardoons, a layer of pork fat, butter, or other cholesterol-laden ingredients are required. These ensure tenderness, juiciness, and taste. Carefully remove every vestige of fat from the finished dish before serving it.
- Where possible, rack roasts and *grillades* (grilled chops and the like) so that the fat drips down and off the meat. It can then be separated from the juices and discarded before serving the natural sauce or gravy.
- Be very prudent in planning meals. A normal menu should contain at most only one-quarter fat, in whatever form, to the other three-quarters of nonfat ingredients. Remember that egg yolks, organ meats such as liver, kidneys, and so on, sausage and cold cuts, pâté, butter, cream, hard and cream cheese, vegetable shortening, and

beef and poultry fat must all be counted when calculating the one-quarter of fat in the menu.

- The nutritional value is the same in a piece of red meat and a piece of white meat, in a piece of meat cooked slowly and the same piece of meat grilled or roasted, or a piece of meat that is rare and the same piece of meat well done.
- It is wise to see that the interior of a piece of meat attains 140°, the heat at which most bacteria and parasites are killed. Use a meat thermometer if you feel you need to.
- Ordinarily meat should not be salted before cooking. Salt will inevitably draw out the juices in the meat. If you insist on salting meat at the beginning, sear it so that the juices are sealed in. Once meat is salted, the salt does not disappear in cooking. It concentrates as the juices evaporate. It is always prudent, then, to adjust the seasoning after cooking the meat unless there is a very good reason to do otherwise.
- All chopped meat spoils more quickly than meat in any other form because it has more surfaces for the bacteria to attack. When possible, have meat chopped at the time you buy it, and if it is not used at once, wrap it well and refrigerate it.

Beef and Veal

LE BOEUF ET LE VEAU

Given their preference, the French would probably choose thick cuts of good red beef over all other meats. It is a luxury. Good French beef is very costly. Mature beef must be fed a long time before it goes to market, and most French farmers prefer to sell off their herds while they are young. Accordingly, good veal is plentiful and reasonably priced. For that reason, the French ordinarily eat more veal at home than beef. The beef offered for sale in French butcher shops is almost never fattened for market to the point it is in the States, where prime beef is heavily marbled with fat. Because the beef and veal are usually rather lean, French cooks used to lard the thicker cuts before cooking them. Today very few French cooks bother to lard roasts. The neighborhood butcher inevitably presents beef and veal roasts for sale already wrapped in thin sheets of white pork fat and neatly trussed with string to prevent the meat from drying out when cooking.

Here are some of the favorite ways my friends in France taught me to prepare beef and veal.

Grilled Steak French Style
LE STEAK-FRITES
SERVES 4

If a poll were taken in France to determine the favorite lunch of office workers and a host of others, steak-frites-salade verte-fromage, *which means a small grilled beefsteak, french fries, green salad, and cheese, would win by an overwhelming majority. By* bifteck *the French do not mean the large, thick, expensive steaks we adore in the United States. They mean a small, thin slice of round steak or rump steak or from between the ribs, oiled or buttered, grilled, and eaten before the steak cools and the tendons toughen. This little steak is inevitably served with shoestring potatoes. When I was a child I remember my mother preparing just such steaks; imagine my surprise to find that the French beat them with the edge of an old dinner plate exactly as she used to do!*

4 thin steaks cut from the round or rump	¼ cup vegetable oil or clarified butter
1 teaspoon freshly ground black pepper	1 teaspoon dried thyme leaves (optional)

1. Heat the grill or broiler. A cast-iron serrated grill is best for this steak, as it is for grilling most pieces of meat, but serrated grills are not so common in the States. There is nothing wrong with grilling the steaks on a griddle or in your oven.
2. Pepper both sides of each steak and lay the steaks out flat on a clean, hard surface. With a serrated meat pounder or the edge of an old dinner plate pound the steaks all over on both sides.
3. With a brush or a stiff feather oil the steaks on both sides and grill them. If you want them rare, grill the first side 3 minutes, the second side 2. If you want them medium rare, add 1 minute for each side.

Should you prefer them well done, grill the steaks 5 minutes on the first side, 4 minutes on the second.

4. Sprinkle the steaks with thyme, if you choose to, and serve them at once with a generous portion of shoestring potatoes. I suggest you try my recipe for Crispy Fried Potatoes on page 103.

N O T E : There is a knack with these little steaks that will keep them from curling while they are grilling. Simply take a pair of kitchen shears and snip the tiny ribbon of fell or ligament that encircles the steaks at 1-inch intervals and the steaks will relax.

Be sure you have coarse salt and a pot of Dijon mustard on the table for these steaks. If you want to be a little fancy, serve the steaks with a knob of parsley butter or Anchovy Butter (pages 28–29) on them. Follow the steaks with a simple salad of Bibb lettuce dressed with a good *Sauce vinaigrette* made with a light, excellent olive oil (page 38), and finish the meal with a ripe Brie or Camembert cheese (I like to serve the cheese along with the salad). A tiny cup of good, black coffee should be the full stop to this little lunch, and you and your guests can go back to work immediately without feeling heavy. I am told by a nutritionist friend that such a lunch is almost perfect. But that is no secret; the French have known it for ages.

Pepper Steak Normandy Style
LE STEAK AU POIVRE A LA NORMANDE
SERVES 4

This is the simple, old-fashioned village version of pepper steak, a far cry from the flamboyant steak au poivre *served in many fancy restaurants. For the right taste you will need a very good Calvados, Norman applejack. However, Cognac or whiskey are perfectly acceptable substitutes. This is a beautifully uncomplicated way to serve first-rate beef. I specify filets mignons because they are generally available in the United States. In France this recipe is often made at home with a cut similar to our London broil, but your best bet is to make it with very good 2-inch-thick slices of fillet of beef.*

I normally do not counsel salting steaks before grilling them, but this recipe was given me by a venerable cook in Valencienne more than thirty years ago. Having made the recipe many times, I find no argument with it.

1 teaspoon coarse salt
4 filets mignons
¼ cup freshly cracked black
     pepper
2 tablespoons sweet butter
2 tablespoons vegetable oil

2 plump shallots, peeled, root
     end removed, sliced
     paper-thin
⅔ cup whipping cream
¼ teaspoon leaf thyme
1 jigger very good Calvados

1. Salt the steaks lightly with half the salt. Coat them on all sides with the coarsely cracked pepper, pressing the pepper into the surface of the meat with your fingers. The coating on the 2 flat surfaces should be thick and even. Cover the steaks and put them in a cool place while you prepare the sauce.
2. Heat a heavy frying pan and slowly melt the butter and oil. Sauté the shallots gently until they are transparent and almost melted. It is essential that this be done very gently.
3. With a slotted spoon remove the shallots from the pan and set them aside. Strain the butter and oil through a fine sieve. Clean the frying pan with a paper towel and put the strained fat back into it.
4. Increase the heat, but do not let the oil smoke or the fat will be spoiled and you will have to discard it and begin again. Fry the steaks in the fat for 4 minutes on each side. (You may be concerned about the rareness of the steaks, but do not fry them much longer or the pepper will become too strong for the sauce.)
5. Remove the steaks to a warm platter. Put the platter in a warm oven, but keep the oven door open.
6. Reduce the heat under the frying pan and add the cream, thyme leaves, and Calvados in that order, stirring with a wooden spatula. Increase the heat and reduce the cream to half its volume. Add the rest of the salt. Add the melted shallots and stir briefly. Spoon the sauce carefully over the steaks and serve them immediately.

NOTE : The perfect accompaniment to this version of *steak au poivre* is plain boiled potatoes with a little sweet butter and chopped parsley scattered over them. Of course, since it is a Norman dish, thickly sliced, sautéed apples are always a welcome addition.

If you make this dish with a good cut of London broil, proceed

exactly as for the filets, but cook each side for 8 minutes. Slice the
entire London broil against the grain before you serve it, and spoon
the sauce down the center.

Madame R.'s Boiled Beef and Vegetables

LE POT-AU-FEU

SERVES 6 TO 8

*For anyone who has spent even a short time in a French household, the importance
of pot-au-feu is impossible to ignore. The great French chef Escoffier said it was
the symbol of French family life, and indeed it is. At Madame R.'s, where I was
a frequent visitor during my student days in Aix, pot-au-feu was made about twice
a month. A whole day was consecrated to its preparation. The great pot would
begin to simmer at midmorning, and it would continue to fill the kitchen and the
adjoining rooms with the aroma of leeks, boiling beef, and herbs for the entire
afternoon.*

*The ceremony of serving it at the evening meal would begin with the emergence
of the familiar white covered tureen. As soon as it was uncovered, a cloud of steam
would ascend, filling the dining room with the most delicious perfume. The clear,
amber broth was ladled into our soup plates. When you tasted the first spoonful
of that broth, you understood why so much attention had been lavished on the
pot-au-feu and were immediately convinced that it was worth it. Later came the
boiled beef and vegetables and the plate of potatoes boiled in their jackets. Potatoes,
we were told, should never be cooked with the rest of the vegetables because they
would cloud the broth. But they were always there alongside, and very welcome.
The beef and vegetables were always accompanied by generous dollops of eyewater-
ing Dijon mustard, coarse salt, freshly milled pepper, and tiny, supersour cornichons—the only cucumber pickle used in French homes. There indeed was the
symbol of French family life as well as a step-by-step demonstration of the tradition
of French household cooking at its best.*

*If you undertake this elaborate dish, devote yourself to it and observe each step
in its preparation religiously. Only then will you understand all the brouhaha
about a plate of broth, boiled beef, and vegetables.*

3 or 4 pounds rump steak, 2 inches thick

3 or 4 pounds beef short ribs

1 large beef or veal marrow bone, cracked

1 calf's foot, sawed in 2 or 3 pieces

1 tablespoon coarse salt

5 quarts cold water

1 large bouquet garni containing 1 large stalk celery; 1 large carrot; 1 bay leaf; 2 leeks, white part only, slit and well washed; 1 branch thyme; 3 sprigs fresh parsley; 1 medium-sized onion spiked with 3 cloves; one 3- to 4-inch piece dried orange skin; 2 plump cloves garlic unpeeled; and 8 peppercorns

4 medium-sized turnips, peeled and trimmed

4 medium-sized carrots, scraped, trimmed, and cut in 2-inch pieces

1 head escarole, poached 10 minutes, squeezed out, and tied up with string

½ small head cabbage, poached 10 minutes, squeezed out, and tied up with string

2 stalks celery, threads removed, cut in 2-inch lengths

4 or 5 medium-sized waxy boiling potatoes, scrubbed and slit around their circumference to prevent their skins from bursting while cooking

Prepare the meat:

1. Wash the meat and bones well under cold running water and dry them with paper towels. Salt the meat. (In principle, meat should usually not be salted before cooking it. Here it is done to facilitate the escape of the juices from the meat into the broth.)

2. Trim off any excess fat. Truss the meat stoutly with cotton string. This keeps the meat from losing its compact shape during the long simmering, making it easier to carve when cooked.

3. Put the meat and bones in a large, deep, 4- to 5-quart heavy pot and cover with cold water. Heat the water slowly to a boil. When it boils, skim off the froth and fat that rise to the surface. Add 2 cups of cold water and allow the pot to boil again. Keep skimming off the froth and scum that rise.

Prepare the bouquet garni:

Break the large stalk of celery in two and make a packet of the celery, the large carrot, bay leaf, leeks, thyme, parsley, spiked onion, orange skin, garlic, and peppercorns. Wrap them neatly in cheesecloth and tie them securely with cotton string.

Cook the pot-au-feu:

1. After the meat and bones have been brought to a boil and skimmed the second time, add the bouquet garni, reduce the heat, and simmer the meat, bones, and bouquet garni at the very lowest possible heat for 1 hour with the lid on but tipped to leave about a quarter of the pot uncovered. Skim the surface from time to time.
2. Add all the other vegetables and let the pot simmer without boiling for 3 to 3½ hours.
3. Start the potatoes in cold, salted water and boil them for 40 minutes.
4. When the meat is tender, lift it out of the broth. When it has cooled for 5 minutes, remove the string, carve into serving pieces, and place them on a warm platter. If the bones have any marrow left, add them to the platter. Otherwise discard them.
5. Discard the bouquet garni. Carefully remove the vegetables and untie and drain the cabbage and escarole. Arrange all the vegetables on the meat platter. Cover with foil and keep in a warm oven.
6. Strain the broth through 3 thicknesses of cheesecloth wrung out in cold water. Make certain that all the fat has disappeared from the broth. If necessary, strain it again. (The hallmark of a perfect pot-au-feu broth is that it hasn't one *lunette* of fat floating on its surface.) Reheat the broth and serve it first, with or without toasted bread in the plates.
7. Serve the meat and vegetables and the boiled potatoes. Provide plenty of good, hot, Dijon mustard, coarse salt, a peppermill with fresh black peppercorns in it, and a crock of tiny French gherkins.

N O T E : Making a proper pot-au-feu is a major undertaking. It is also more expensive than the ordinary main course, but it is a meal-in-one. Most French householders manage to get at least one extra meal out of the leftovers. The expense is justifiable from several standpoints.

There are arguments about preparing a pot-au-feu, as there are about any classic item in French household cookery. Some cooks believe that the meat should be put in only after the water is boiling because it seals in the juices and keeps the meat from getting stringy. They have a point. But Madame R. simmered her pot-au-feu so gently that the meat never became dry or stringy. I have always had good luck with her recipe. I hope you will, too.

• • •

Gratin of Boiled Beef with Onion Sauce
LE BOEUF EN MIROTON

SERVES 4

Boeuf en miroton, sometimes called boeuf miroton, *is one of the classic ways the French household cook deals with boiled beef left over from a pot-au-feu. It goes back at least to the 1690s, but it is a great favorite all over France today.*

2 tablespoons vegetable oil
3 medium-sized onions, peeled, trimmed, and finely grated
1 tablespoon flour
1½ cups broth from the pot-au-feu, or water
1 tablespoon wine vinegar
½ teaspoon coarse salt
¼ teaspoon freshly ground white pepper
1 bay leaf
1 plump clove garlic, peeled
12 to 16 preserved capers
2 tablespoons coarsely chopped sour pickle
16 to 20 thin slices cold boiled beef
1 cup fine dry breadcrumbs
2 tablespoons sweet butter

1. Heat a heavy frying pan and add the oil. When it is sizzling, add the grated onions and reduce the heat to its lowest mark. Sauté the onions slowly, stirring them with a wooden spatula from time to time so that they cook evenly and do not burn.
2. When the onions begin to turn a bit golden, sift the flour over them and stir it in carefully. Crush and smooth out any lumps. Let this roux cook for 3 minutes, stirring it constantly.
3. Add the broth and stir vigorously. Add the vinegar, salt, pepper, bay leaf, and garlic and allow to simmer for 8 minutes.
4. Preheat the oven to 400°.
5. Lightly oil a shallow baking dish. Discard the bay leaf and garlic and put a little of the sauce in the bottom of the dish. Spread it lightly over the bottom and sprinkle it evenly with capers and chopped pickle. Arrange the slices of boiled beef in overlapping layers on top of the capers and chopped pickle. Cover the beef with all the sauce, spreading the rather thick sauce evenly so that it covers all the beef and touches all the sides of the dish.
6. Sprinkle the sauce with an even cover of breadcrumbs and dot the surface with little knobs of butter.
7. Bake until golden. Serve hot.

N O T E : This dish is best if the thick sauce does not dry out in baking. Since all the ingredients are already cooked, it is only a question of heating the beef through and browning the top. If the browning in the top of the oven takes more than 5 minutes, I suggest that you put the dish under the broiler to brown it. Then move it to the top of the oven and turn off the heat. That way it will be completely browned and completely heated through without the sauce drying out.

Boiled Beef Hash with Mashed Potato Topping
HACHIS PARMENTIER
SERVES 4

This fragrant, delicious hash with its mashed potato topping gets its name from A. A. Parmentier, the man who is credited with introducing the potato to the French. Hachis parmentier *may be the most popular way in France to present the leftover boiled beef from a pot-au-feu. The dish is so much loved that it is often made from freshly ground beef when there is no leftover boiled beef handy.*

4 medium-sized potatoes, peeled and quartered
4 tablespoons (½ stick) sweet butter
2 medium-sized onions, peeled, trimmed, and coarsely grated
2 ripe tomatoes, skinned, seeded, and coarsely chopped
1 tablespoon finely chopped flat-leaf parsley
1 small clove garlic, peeled and chopped very fine
2 cups broth from the pot-au-feu, or water

2 tablespoons flour mixed with ¼ cup water
2 cups cubed leftover boiled beef
¼ teaspoon freshly ground black pepper
¼ teaspoon freshly grated nutmeg
½ teaspoon coarse salt
¼ teaspoon freshly ground white pepper
½ cup light cream
1 tablespoon freshly grated Parmesan cheese
½ cup fine dry breadcrumbs

1. Put the potatoes on to boil in cold, lightly salted water.
2. Heat a heavy frying pan. Melt 2 tablespoons of the butter gently in

it. When the butter is sizzling, add the onions. Stir them with a wooden spatula as they sauté. Continue to cook the onions very slowly until they are wilted and almost transparent.

3. Add the tomatoes, parsley, and garlic. Increase the heat and reduce the liquid to half its original volume. Keep stirring the mixture and pressing it against the bottom of the frying pan until it is a paste.

4. Add the broth and the flour-and-water mixture. When the sauce begins to thicken, add the cubed beef and continue stirring and cooking the mixture for 5 minutes.

5. Add the black pepper, the nutmeg, and ¼ teaspoon salt and remove the frying pan from the fire.

6. Preheat the oven to 400°.

7. When the potatoes are very tender, drain them. Add the remaining 2 tablespoons butter, ¼ teaspoon salt, the white pepper, cream, and cheese. Mash and whip the potatoes. If the purée seems too thick, add a little more cream.

8. Butter a shallow baking dish lightly. Add the hash and cover it with the mashed potato topping. Decorate the top with a fork, if you like. Sprinkle the top with breadcrumbs.

9. Bake the *hachis* until it is nicely browned. Serve the dish straight from the oven. It is best eaten hot.

N O T E : I have on occasion made a version of this dish with 2 cups crumbled, well-browned hamburger. The taste is slightly different, but it is quite acceptable.

Occasionally American cooks have asked me whether Parmesan cheese is used throughout France in household cooking. The answer is yes, it is available in every region of France, usually in packets. While Gruyère is the time-honored favorite for gratins, Parmesan is often used, and sometimes both cheeses appear in the same dish.

• • •

Boiled Beef Salad Lyon Style
LA SALADE TIEDE A LA LYONNAISE

SERVES 3 AS MAIN COURSE,
4 TO 6 AS FIRST COURSE

Salade tiède *or warm salad is another instance of a fine dish made from the boiled beef left over from the pot-au-feu. Despite the raw green onion and garlic, both of which appear rarely in lyonnais family cooking, warm salad is a great favorite in the Lyon area.*

One of the cardinal rules of dishes made from leftovers is that they should have an attractive appearance. Take pains to see that the various elements in this salad remain recognizable and don't become an unattractive mass.

1 pound leftover boiled beef
2 large boiled potatoes
1 small clove garlic, peeled, crushed, and teased to a paste with
   1 tablespoon coarse salt
3 tablespoons red wine vinegar
¼ teaspoon granulated sugar

2 tablespoons finely chopped scallions
1 tablespoon Dijon mustard
½ cup light olive oil
1 teaspoon freshly cracked black pepper
¼ teaspoon freshly grated nutmeg

1. Slice the cold beef in very thin slices.
2. Slice the potatoes slightly thicker. If you slice them too thin, they will fall apart when you heat and toss the salad.
3. Mix the garlic paste with the vinegar and sugar until both the salt and sugar are dissolved and lose their grittiness. Add the scallions and let them marinate for 3 or 4 minutes. Add the mustard and stir until it is evenly absorbed. Add the olive oil little by little, stirring it into a smooth emulsion. This will be easier if all the ingredients are at room temperature.
4. Slowly warm the meat and potato slices in a frying pan, shaking them from time to time so that they warm through. Do not stir them or you will break them up into a hash.
5. Add the pepper, nutmeg and the dressing and toss the meat and potato slices with a wooden spatula so that they are coated thoroughly with the dressing and the pepper and nutmeg are scattered throughout.
6. Serve the warm salad in a nest of lettuce leaves and encourage your

guests to help themselves to the lettuce. The salad is delicious but somewhat heavy.

N O T E : Many lyonnais householders slice up the other vegetables left over from the pot-au-feu and add them with the potatoes. Purists may object, but I sometimes add thinly sliced raw celery and carrots. They not only lighten the salad, they add a welcome contrast in texture.

THE PROVENÇAL DAUBE

Long before I went to live in Provence, Virginia Woolf's vivid allusions to the *boeuf en daube* in the dinner scene in *To the Lighthouse* had me interested in the famous Provençal recipe. The entire dinner scene is scattered with impressions of the great dish that the cook had spent three days preparing. Listen to this passage:

> . . . an exquisite scent of olives and oil and juice rose from the great brown dish. . . . There it was, all round them. It partook [Mrs. Ramsay] felt, carefully helping Mr. Bankes to a specially tender piece, of eternity . . .

Now, forty years later, the word *daube* conjures up for me suppers in remote villages in Provence and dear, hospitable friends long since disappeared.

No one is quite sure of the origin of the dish or its name. We know that something called *addobbo* was known in both Italian and Spanish cookery as early as the sixteenth century, and Latin-American, Philippine, and present-day Spanish recipes still use the word *adobo* for a highly seasoned preparation of meats, fowl, and even fish. However, today the word *daube* in Provence—indeed, wherever the dish is known throughout the world—refers uniquely to a regional specialty in which beef and salt bacon are layered into a big-bellied earthenware pot called a *daubière* with garlic, onion, thyme, rosemary, juniper berries, and orange peel, a bottle of good, dry red wine, a little vinegar, water, a pinch of sugar, and a jigger of country brandy. The pot is sealed and cooked at low heat for 4 or 5 hours. The seal is broken, and the wonderful braise is eaten with boiled noodles, rice, or potatoes.

Daube is usually made with beef, but there is a famous Avignon *daube* made with mutton. I myself have made a fine *daube* of big turkey legs; I find it an excellent solution for dealing effectively with the almost intractable toughness of those huge drumsticks. Recently a fellow cook told me about a delicious *daube* he had eaten in a restaurant; it used thick chunks of fresh tuna.

Nicole Roman, a good friend and a fine household cooking teacher from my earliest years in Aix, taught me how to make *daube.* Her arlésienne grandmother taught the dish to her. My version of the great recipe follows.

Braised Beef in the Style of Arles
LE BOEUF EN DAUBE A L'ARLESIENNE
S E R V E S 6 T O 8

4 pounds lean bottom round, chuck, or boneless shank of beef in 2 × 4-inch pieces
1 teaspoon freshly milled black pepper
2 plump cloves garlic, peeled and crushed with 4 flat anchovy fillets
1 pound streaky salt bacon with its rind
1 bouquet garni made of 2 branches dried thyme; 1 branch dried rosemary; 6 dried juniper berries, crushed; 2 bay leaves; 1 large carrot; 1 medium-sized onion spiked with 3 cloves; 1 branch celery; and one 4-inch piece dried orange peel
10 to 12 black oil-cured olives, pitted
1 bottle (1 liter) good, dry red wine
2 cups water
½ teaspoon sugar dissolved in 2 tablespoons wine vinegar
1 jigger brandy
Parsley, for garnish

The night before you plan to serve the daube:
1. Carefully trim away and discard any fat you find on the beef. Rinse the beef well in cold running water and dry it thoroughly with paper towels. With your fingers rub the pepper well into all the surfaces of the beef. Repeat the process with the garlic and anchovy paste. (Rub your fingers with a lemon wedge and odor will disappear.)
2. Remove the rind from the salt bacon. Cut the bacon into ¼-inch-wide lardoons (cut across the rasher). Poach both the rind and the lardoons

in boiling water for 5 minutes. Drain, rinse, and dry the rind and lardoons well.

3. Put the bouquet garni together. Make a neat packet of the thyme, rosemary, juniper berries, bay leaves, carrot, spiked onion, celery, and orange peel by wrapping them in a piece of cheesecloth and tying it securely with cotton string. The packet should not measure more than 2 × 4 inches. (If you have no branches of thyme or rosemary, substitute 2 teaspoons of dried thyme leaves and 1 teaspoon dried rosemary leaves.) Fresh orange peel may be used instead of the dried, but be sure not to use the white part.

4. Find the right pot. If you haven't a *daubière*, try to find a big-bellied earthenware 3- to 4-quart pot with a tight-fitting lid. I have sometimes used a heavy enameled pot. A big baked-bean pot works rather well. Place the rind at the bottom of the pot, layer the beef and lardoons around the sides, and put the bouquet garni and the olives in the center.

5. Pour the wine, water, the sugar dissolved in the vinegar, and the brandy over the contents of the pot. Cover the pot and place it in a cool place overnight.

The next morning:

1. Seal the lid on the pot with a little flour, water, and a strip of dampened cloth. If this daunts you, simply cover the top of the pot with heavy aluminum foil and force the lid down over it into its groove.

2. Set the oven at 350°. Place the pot in the center of the oven and let the *daube* cook there undisturbed for 3½ hours.

3. Break the seal. Remove and discard the bouquet garni and continue to cook the *daube*, uncovered, for 30 minutes.

4. Remove the *daube* from the pot to a serving bowl. If you like, cut up the rind so that it can be eaten by those who like it. (It is considered a treat by *daube* lovers.) Skim off all the fat you can before serving. A little finely chopped parsley may be sprinkled over the top for color. Serve with plain boiled noodles, rice, or potatoes. The sauce will not be thick, but because of the lardoons it will be rich.

N O T E : *Daube* is often eaten cold. Like most highly aromatic braises it will be even more luscious if it is allowed to chill overnight in the refrigerator. That will make it possible for you to remove every vestige of fat from the surface. *Daube* is a rough, country braise. Its sauce becomes a delicious jelly overnight. It will be dull and never sparkle like a refined, clarified aspic. It was never meant to. But try it cold. Brighten the presentation with a little finely chopped parsley and some lemon and tomato wedges. Both lemon and tomato enhance the rich taste of the jelly. A tossed salad of mixed greens goes well with chilled *daube*.

Veal Stew in White Sauce Mâcon Style
LA BLANQUETTE DE VEAU
A LA MACONNAISE

SERVES 4 OR 5

Blanquette is one of the tastiest veal dishes ever invented, and a standard favorite all over France. This recipe was provided by my old friend Marguerite Béchet in whose home I have eaten it often.

1½ to 2 pounds breast of veal or stewing veal cut in bite-sized pieces

½ teaspoon freshly milled white pepper

1 bouquet garni made of 1 bay leaf, 1 branch celery, and 1 branch thyme

1 medium onion, peeled, trimmed, and coarsely chopped

1 medium-sized carrot, scraped, trimmed, and cut in thin, coinlike roundels

½ cup dry white wine

6 cups cold water

16 small white mushrooms, wiped clean and trimmed

3 tablespoons sweet butter

3 tablespoons flour

1 teaspoon coarse salt

2 egg yolks

1 teaspoon freshly squeezed lemon juice

1 teaspoon finely chopped flat-leaf parsley

1. Wash the meat in cold water, drain it, and dry it with paper towels. Sprinkle it well with the pepper.
2. Bind the bay leaf, celery, and thyme together with cotton string.
3. Put the meat, onion, carrot, wine, and the bouquet garni in a heavy-bottomed stewpan and cover them with the water. Bring the water to a full boil and let it continue to boil for 3 minutes. Skim the froth and scum from the surface and reduce the heat to the lowest mark.

4. Simmer for 1 hour. Keep skimming off the froth that rises.
5. Add the mushrooms and simmer for another 15 minutes.
6. With a skimmer, remove the meat and vegetables and set them aside. Discard the bouquet garni. Strain the broth into a bowl and set it aside.
7. Wash the pot and dry it well. Heat it and gently melt the butter. Stir in the flour with a wooden spatula and keep mixing as the roux sizzles for 1 minute. (Do not let it burn.) Add the broth and stir well.
8. Add the veal and vegetables. Cover the pan and simmer the *blanquette* for 20 minutes. Add the salt.
9. In a small bowl beat the egg yolks and lemon juice together until smooth and lemon-colored. Stir a little of the hot sauce from the *blanquette* into the yolks.
10. Remove the pan from the fire and stir the yolk mixture into the *blanquette* very quickly. Continue stirring for 15 seconds. Put the *blanquette* in a serving dish, sprinkle the surface with the chopped parsley, and serve.

N O T E :   For a very rich *blanquette*, add 3 tablespoons of heavy cream or *crème fraîche*. (You will find the recipe for a good substitute for *crème fraîche* on page 304.)

Blanquette is rich. The traditional accompaniment is plain boiled rice or potatoes. Provide plenty of crusty bread to dip in the sauce. You won't want to waste a drop.

Veal Chops La Savoyarde Style
LES COTES DE VEAU A LA SAVOYARDE
SERVES 4

I coaxed this recipe out of a pink-cheeked old lady more than thirty years ago. She ran a small pension in Annecy called La Savoyarde *and did all the cooking herself. I was impressed with the way she did veal chops. She was amused and incredulous when I pressed her for the recipe. Both she and her pension disappeared years ago, but here's how she told me to do her famous veal chops.*

First-rate veal is expensive and often difficult to come by in the United States, but you must insist upon top quality veal for this recipe. Be sure the chops are perfectly shaped and equal in appearance and weight. If you pay a lot for good veal, make sure the butcher gives you what you pay for.

¼ teaspoon freshly milled white pepper

Four 1-inch-thick veal chops

3 tablespoons sweet butter

1 tablespoon vegetable oil

2 or 3 plump shallots, peeled and sliced paper-thin

8 large, white mushrooms, wiped clean, trimmed, and sliced in ¼-inch slices

3 tablespoons freshly squeezed lemon juice

½ teaspoon dried tarragon leaves, coarsely crumbled

1 tablespoon finely chopped flat-leaf parsley

½ glass dry white wine

1 cup water mixed with 1 teaspoon arrowroot powder

½ teaspoon coarse salt

1 tablespoon Cognac

¼ teaspoon granulated sugar

1. Pepper the chops on both sides.
2. Choose a large, heavy skillet with a tight-fitting lid that will accommodate the 4 chops without crowding them. Heat the skillet and melt the butter with the oil. When they are sizzling, brown the chops for 3 minutes on each side. The idea is to sear the juices in, not to cook the chops through.
3. Remove the chops to a heated platter, cover them with aluminum foil, and set them in a warm oven with the door open.
4. Sauté the shallots very slowly until they are transparent. Take the time to do this properly and don't allow them to brown. When they finish sautéing they should be almost melted.
5. Coat the mushrooms with the lemon juice. Add them, the tarragon, and parsley to the shallots in the pan, tossing them together well with a wooden spatula. Cover the pan and cook the mixture at very low heat for 5 minutes.
6. Add the wine and, as it begins to heat, scrape up all the browned juices that have adhered to the bottom of the pan. Take time to do this deglazing thoroughly.
7. Add the water mixed with the arrowroot powder and stir well. The mixture should begin to thicken immediately. Add the salt and keep stirring the sauce so that it is smooth and without lumps. Add the Cognac and sugar. (There is an ancient belief that a tiny pinch of sugar

added with the Cognac will cinch taste. It cannot be detected at all as sweet, and it seems to work.) Give the sauce a good stirring and remove the pan from the fire.

8. Arrange the chops in the pan so that they nestle in the sauce and mushrooms. Cover the pan and return it to the fire. Reduce the heat to the lowest mark and smother the chops for 10 minutes. Then test the chops by running the point of a sharp knife between the bone and the flesh. If the meat looks very pink and clings to the bone, cook them another few minutes.

9. Arrange the chops on a hot platter and spoon the sauce and mushrooms over them. Serve at once.

N O T E : If you plan to offer these magnificent chops for lunch, I suggest you let them go it alone. They are well garnished with the mushrooms. Should you want to serve them for dinner, I can think of no more wonderful accompaniment than Braised Belgian Endives (page 101). If you want to be perfectly consistent and regional, serve them with a *gratin dauphinois* (page 106), and follow the chops with a simple green salad of Bibb or Boston lettuce with a light *sauce vinaigrette* (page 38).

Lamb and Mutton

L'AGNEAU ET LE MOUTON

I grew up in Texas where lamb and mutton were despised by most of the locals. Given a choice, good Texans eat only beef. Fortunately my mother, a non-Texan, had no such prejudice. She was a thrifty householder who managed her food allowance to the penny. Since lamb and mutton were very cheap in Texas in those days, we ate a great deal of both. My mother prepared them in such an appetizing fashion that she actually won over many of our friends.

It is easy to explain why sheep were hated by ranchers in Texas. Sheep overgraze the grasslands and foul the waterholes and streams, making it next to impossible to raise cattle where sheep have grazed. However, the prejudice against lamb and mutton is much more widespread in the

United States than one would believe, and it isn't for the same reason at all. It stems from the fact that lamb and mutton have a gamier taste and odor than beef. This, I believe, accounts for the prejudice in most of the people I know who would not choose lamb or mutton to prepare at home.

Lamb and mutton are greatly esteemed in France. Lamb from seaside fields is perhaps the all-time favorite meat in French households, no matter what the region. Of course, it is also the most expensive. French homemakers rarely buy it, preferring to purchase cheaper varieties and cuts. The French household cook is usually quite successful at controlling the gamey taste and odor and in preparing these meats in such a way that even the most squeamish eater would find them delicious. There are two knacks to remember in dealing effectively with the former. Take a very sharp boning knife and remove every vestige of fell, the pearly membrane that covers the meat. It is the origin of most of the gaminess. The other knack is to rub the meat all over with half a fresh lemon. The lemon will also effectively remove the smell from your hands after you have finished cutting away the fell.

When shopping for these meats remember that lamb is younger than mutton. Fresh, young lamb has a pale rose color. A darker plum color is natural for mutton. Lamb is more expensive than mutton, so do not accept a dark lamb. You will be paying for lamb and receiving mutton. The only exception I can think of is the excellent New Zealand lamb that we now find in our markets. It is dark, I am told, because it is frozen. (I tell you these things because mutton as a designation has disappeared from supermarket labels. Both lamb and mutton are designated as lamb, so be an alert shopper.)

Every good cook needs to know that in addition to garlic, there are three herbs that seem to have been created for lamb and mutton. They are mint, thyme, and rosemary. I have listed them in ascending order of strength. It is almost impossible to overpower lamb or mutton with mint, so you may use as much as you like, especially if the mint is fresh. Thyme is stronger. It works its magic very well if you use it with discretion. Rosemary is the strongest of the three. Many people love its strong, pine-resin taste and perfume, but use it with the greatest care. Like garlic, it seems to concentrate with frying and grilling. A wise old cook once told me that one rosemary leaf for each side of a lamb chop was plenty. He suggested breaking up each leaf into several bits and scattering them over the surface of the meat.

A last note: the fat from lamb and mutton congeals at a higher temperature than the fat of most meats, so be very solicitous about removing it from sauces made from the roasting juices of these meats before serving them. Otherwise a perfectly delicious sauce will congeal on the warm plate. Skimming the sauce, then straining it through several thicknesses of dampened cheesecloth will help you to deal with this problem effectively.

Leg of Lamb in the Style of Aix
LE GIGOT D'AGNEAU A L'AIXOISE
SERVES 6 TO 8

Years ago I was invited for lunch at l'Ermitage, a beautiful estate just outside Aix, near the Route de Nice, where there was a spectacular vista of Cézanne country and Mont Ste.-Victoire itself. Our elegant hostess served us the best leg of lamb I have ever eaten. In keeping with the surroundings, the lamb was unmistakably à la provençale, yet there wasn't a clove of garlic in sight. When I asked her about it, she told me that leg of lamb prepared in the traditional Provençal manner was her husband's favorite dish but that the customary 15 to 20 piquets of garlic in the roast always gave him terrible indigestion. Her mother, a provençale of many generations, recalled that in the time of her grandmother the garlic had been boiled and then added to the sauce and that it had been done especially for those who loved the dish, yet could not digest the broiled garlic. This is my version of my friend's superb leg of lamb. Once you have eaten it, you may never want to prepare leg of lamb any other way.

One 6-pound leg of lamb
2 fresh lemons, cut in half
1 teaspoon dried leaf thyme
8 to 10 rosemary leaves
1 tablespoon freshly cracked
   black pepper
1 tablespoon ground coriander

2 large crowns garlic, 16 to 20
   cloves
1 cup mild olive oil
1 large bunch fresh mint, 6 to 8
   well-leafed stems
2 tablespoons flour
1 teaspoon coarse salt

1. Have your butcher remove the bones from the leg of lamb. (Ask for them. Freeze them if you cannot use them at once. They may be used for soup.) With a very sharp boning knife remove and discard all but

1 layer of the lamb suet. Carefully remove the fell—a thin layer of loose, fatty tissue which belongs to the hide but often adheres to the flesh and suet after the animal is skinned. It is mainly the fell that imports a strong muttonlike taste to the lamb. Leave the upper part of the leg, which is covered with suet, intact. Remove and discard the fell from the lower half of the leg.

2. Rub the meat all over, inside and out, with the lemon halves, squeezing the lemon as you go to get plenty of the juice into the meat. Squeeze what is left of the juice into a bowl and discard the lemon rinds. Set the juice aside.

3. Mix the thyme, rosemary, pepper, and coriander together and rub the mixture all over the surface of the meat, inside and out.

4. Smash open the crowns of garlic by striking them with the outer side of your fist. Remove and discard the central stems, roots, and loose, paperlike partitions. Peel 3 of the garlic cloves and place them on the meat where the bone was removed. Put the unpeeled cloves aside.

5. Put the leg of lamb back together as it was before the bones were removed. With stout cotton string draw one end together with a slip knot and, working very slowly and carefully, make running bowlines up and down the surface until the entire piece of meat is trussed in a snoodlike mesh of string. Reinforce the mesh anyplace where the meat bulges out. The more perfectly you do this, the better the meat will roast and carve.

6. Mix the olive oil with the reserved lemon juice and paint the trussed meat all over.

7. Preheat the oven to 375°.

8. Wash the mint well, drain it, and place it in a shallow baking dish. Place the meat on top of it. Put the unpeeled garlic cloves in the dish at one end. Pour 1 cup of water into the dish.

9. Place the roast on the middle rack of the oven and roast it for 1½ hours, basting it with the oil and lemon juice every 15 minutes. Add more water when necessary to maintain ½ inch of liquid in the bottom of the baking dish at all times.

10. After 1½ hours, pierce the roast with a sharp knife. The juice should be pink. This indicates that the meat is medium rare. If you want it less rare, cook it more, but don't cook it more than 15 minutes longer or it will start to dry out. Remove the roast from the oven and place it on a carving board to rest for 10 minutes while you make the sauce.

11. Strain the pan drippings, pressing the mint and garlic cloves with a wooden spoon to extract all the juice and pulp. Discard what does not pass through the sieve.

12. Skim 2 tablespoons of the fat from the pan juices and mix it with the flour. Heat the juices in a wide pan. Add the flour and fat mixture and 1½ cups water and stir well. Let the sauce boil and reduce to about half its original volume. Salt to taste. Skim all the fat you can off the top and discard it. Put the sauce in a sauceboat.

13. Remove the string from the roast and discard it. Carve the roast into generous slices and arrange them on a serving platter. Serve the roast at once. Pass the sauce.

NOTE: The traditional accompaniment for this fine dish is Provençal-style Grilled Tomatoes (page 100). *La Ratatouille aixoise* (page 56) is an excellent substitute. You should serve some potatoes that have been peeled, quartered, half-boiled, then baked in the oven until brown. They go very well with this dish.

Lamb Steaks Grilled with Garlic and Potatoes

LES TRANCHES DE GIGOT DE MOUTON GRILLEES AUX GOUSSES D'AIL ET AUX POMMES DE TERRE

SERVES 4

Offer this grillade *for lunch when you are feeling festive and want to enjoy the meal with two or three friends yet don't want to wear yourself out with the preparations. Every time I prepare this dish I think of the first time it was offered to me: the meal was served outside under a trellis of grapevines at Mougins, high above the Mediterranean. It was noon on a glorious sunny day. One whiff of these grilled lamb steaks and it all comes back. The dish is magic, but it is simplicity itself to prepare. It is always a success with the guests and, of course, with the cook. If you want to impress a guest who loves to eat, this is the recipe.*

Don't be dismayed by the quantity of garlic in this recipe. Boiling it causes it to lose its strength, but popped out of its husk it becomes a perfect, buttery sauce for the lamb.

Four ½-inch-thick lamb steaks
½ fresh lemon
1 teaspoon freshly cracked
    pepper
4 rosemary leaves, broken into
    tiny bits
4 medium-sized baking potatoes

13 plump cloves of garlic,
    unpeeled
4 bay leaves
2 tablespoons mild olive oil
1 teaspoon coarse salt
1 teaspoon leaf thyme

1. Rinse the steaks well in cold running water and dry them thoroughly with paper towels. Spread out the steaks and rub them all over both surfaces with the lemon half. Squeeze out a little of the juice as you rub. Sprinkle both sides of the steaks with the pepper and rosemary leaves. Set aside.

2. Peel the potatoes and quarter them. Put them in a pan of cold water with the unpeeled garlic, and cook them 12 minutes. Drain and put them aside.

3. Choose a shallow broiling pan that will accommodate all the steaks and the potatoes. Cover it with aluminum foil. Place the steaks on it with a bay leaf and 3 cloves of boiled garlic under each steak, and the potatoes arranged alongside. Paint the surface of the steaks with olive oil and sprinkle them with the salt and thyme.

4. Place the broiling rack 6 to 8 inches from the heat source. Preheat the broiler.

5. Grill the steaks and potatoes 7 minutes on one side, then turn them over. Paint the ungrilled surface of the steaks with olive oil and grill for 7 more minutes. Take care that the potatoes do not burn. They will cook faster than the steaks. Turn off the broiler, but leave the steaks and the potatoes in the oven for 5 more minutes with the oven door closed.

6. Discard the bay leaves. Serve each person a steak, 3 cloves of garlic, and 4 quarters of potato. Spoon some of the meat juices over each steak.

I suggest you serve the steaks with wedges of lemon and *la Ratatouille aixoise* (page 56). Grilled tomatoes or fire-skinned bell peppers are also good possible choices. Be sure to provide plenty of crusty bread and a good, cold Tavel or a very light red Bordeaux. Anything with an alcoholic content higher than 9 percent would be a mistake.

Let's compose a perfect menu around this wonderful *grillade:* Serve the steaks and grilled tomatoes at once. Follow them with a simple green salad of Bibb or Boston lettuce or rocket sauced with a light vinaigrette dressing. Offer next a hard cheese and a soft one, and a selection of fresh fruit. For those who have decided to make an afternoon of it, a tiny cup of good coffee and maybe a drop of liqueur, and plenty of time to talk!

Lamb Stew French Style
LE NAVARIN

SERVES 4

The French discovered a long time ago that turnips and lamb have a great affinity. This famous lamb stew will hold its own with the best Irish stew or any other. Navarin appears often on French household menus in winter because it is both hearty and economical. It is also a great favorite with French children.

1½ pounds breast or neck of
  lamb cut into bite-size pieces
½ teaspoon freshly milled white
  pepper
½ cup flour
3 tablespoons sweet butter
2 tablespoons vegetable oil
3 medium-sized carrots,
  scraped, trimmed, and cut
  into ¼-inch roundels
3 medium-sized onions, peeled,
  trimmed, and coarsely
  chopped

1 cup dry white wine
2 cups water
1 bouquet garni made up of 1
  bay leaf, 1 branch celery, 1
  branch rosemary, and 1
  branch fresh parsley, tied
  together with cotton string
6 medium-sized turnips, peeled,
  trimmed, and quartered
1 teaspoon coarse salt

1. Wash and dry the meat. Sprinkle it well with pepper and dredge it with flour.
2. Heat the butter and oil in a Dutch oven. When the fat is bubbling, add the meat and brown it. Stir it about with a wooden spatula from time to time to see that it does not stick.

3. Add the carrots and onions. Stir them into the browning meat and coat them well with the hot fat.

4. When the onions have become almost transparent, add the wine. Deglaze the bottom of the Dutch oven completely, then add the water and the bouquet garni. Cover the pot and simmer at very low heat for 1 hour.

5. Add the turnips and salt and stir them in well. Continue to simmer at the lowest heat for 1 hour uncovered.

6. Carefully skim off and discard all the fat that has risen to the top Discard the bouquet garni. Taste the stew and correct for salt. Serve very hot.

N O T E : Like most stews, *navarin* improves overnight. The turnips will darken a little if you leave the surface exposed, so if you are planning to serve the *navarin* the next day, cover it tightly before you put it in the refrigerator. The next day, carefully remove any bits of coagulated fat that have formed on the surface. Heat the stew very gently. A squeeze of fresh lemon juice will freshen the taste wonderfully, and 2 tablespoons of finely chopped parsley will brighten the presentation. Though butter is rarely eaten in a French household at any meal except breakfast, I like to serve this stew on a cold night with sourdough bread and lots of sweet butter to spread on it.

Lamb Shanks Braised with Green Beans
LES JARRETS DE MOUTON BRAISES AUX HARICOTS VERTS
SERVES 4

Lamb shanks are not as cheap as they once were, but they are still a good bargain for lamb-loving households. This recipe comes from a French householder who spent many years in North Africa when Algeria was a French colony. It is the French version of a North African tagine, *or stew.* Tagines *are prepared in special ceramic pots. If you have a fireproof earthenware casserole, I suggest you make this dish in it rather than in a metal pot.*

4 lamb shanks
1 fresh lemon, cut in half
3 plump cloves garlic, peeled, crushed, and teased to a paste in
   1 teaspoon coarse salt
1 teaspoon ground ginger
1 small package saffron powder or 12 saffron threads, toasted and crumbled
1 teaspoon ground cumin

1 teaspoon freshly milled black pepper
½ cup mild olive oil
1 medium-sized onion, peeled, trimmed, and coarsely grated
1 pound green beans, washed, stemmed, tailed, and broken into 2-inch pieces
1 tablespoon flour
3 tablespoons water
Lemon wedges, for garnish
Mint sprigs, for garnish

1. With a very sharp boning knife, remove the excess fat and as much of the fell as you can from the shanks. (The fell is the nacreous tissue that covers the muscles.)

2. Rub the shanks all over with the lemon halves, squeezing the lemon as you rub so that a lot of the lemon juice comes in contact with the meat. Lemon juice not only improves the taste and odor of lamb, it also acts as a tenderizer.

3. Mix the garlic paste, ginger, saffron powder, cumin, and pepper. Rub this mixture well into the shanks. Rub your hands with a few drops of lemon juice before washing them and the lemon juice will effectively remove both the garlic and lamb odor from them. Don't discard the lemon halves yet.

4. Heat a large, deep, earthenware casserole that has a lid. If you have no such casserole, use a Dutch oven. Add the oil. When it is hot but not smoking, brown the shanks on all sides. This will take about 12 minutes. (Tongs are by far the best utensil for turning the shanks. The browning helps the shanks to retain what natural juice they have. Piercing them with a fork will only cause them to lose some of their juice.)

5. When the shanks are nicely browned, add the onions and stir them well so that they are coated with the oil. Reduce the heat and sauté the onions until they are transparent and soft.

6. Add the green beans, stirring them until they are also coated with the oil and onions. Reduce the heat to its lowest mark. Cover the pot tightly and braise the shanks and beans for 1½ hours. Check from time to time to see that they are not drying out. Add a little water if necessary.

7. After 1½ hours remove the pot from the heat. Squeeze whatever juice

is left in the lemon halves into a cup and mix it with the flour and 3 tablespoons water into a smooth paste. Stir the paste into the contents of the pot. Return the pot to the burner and cook gently for 5 more minutes until the juice from the beans has thickened. Taste the beans and add salt if necessary.

8. Serve the dish hot or warm with lemon wedges and sprigs of fresh mint.

N O T E : This dish has a rather thick consistency that is absolutely right for it. It can be made with artichoke hearts or greens instead of green beans, and it is particularly delicious with chopped broad-leaf escarole, which becomes very sweet when braised. If you use escarole, add a sprinkling of fennel seeds at the very beginning of the braising process.

Pork

LE PORC

Since time immemorial the French have been famous for the excellence of their pork and pork products. The traditions surrounding French pork go back to prehistory. Ancient Gaul was covered with thick forests where the ancestors of the present-day French kept enormous herds of swine, fattening them on the acorns and mushrooms that grew there in abundance. It was the Gauls who discovered and developed the fine art of smoke-curing hams. Those hams were the delight of the Roman world. In fact, it is often said in jest that the Romans conquered Gaul to assure themselves a constant supply of Gallic hams.

Every region in France has its pork specialties. The catalog of regional culinary wonders in the form of hams, bacons, sausages, *boudins*, *rillons* and *rillettes*, and pâtés is endless. When I think that I have tasted them all, others appear that I never heard of. Those wonders of regional *charcutiers* and cooks continue to be the delight of the locals and the occasional travelers who are fortunate enough to discover them.

It is difficult to conceive of French cooking without French pork and French pork products, so difficult, in fact, that you may wonder which came first, French pork or French cooking. Pork, in one form or another, finds its way into the majority of French household recipes. What would French regional sauces be without a little blanched and sautéed French salt pork? Would the famous French stuffings and pâtés be as famous without the fresh French pork and ham that they always seem to call for? Would the celebrated *rosbif* (roast beef) and roasted veal be as juicy and tasty without that neatly tied jacket of French pork fat? I could conjure up for you gargantuan coils and chains of sausages; flitches of smoked or salted bacon; hillocks of rosy chops; sooty Auvergnat hams, scrubbed and pared on one side, showing a pale, fragrant interior ready to be sliced; and so many other things from my years of knocking about and hobnobbing with food lovers in rural France, but enough! Here are a few pork recipes for you to try.

Pork Chops Baked with Potatoes Country Style
LES COTES DE PORC A LA CAMPAGNARDE

SERVES 4

One ¼-inch-thick slice streaky salt pork
½ teaspoon freshly cracked black pepper
Four ½-inch-thick pork loin chops
3 tablespoons flour
4 juniper berries, crushed

2 medium-sized onions, peeled, trimmed, and quartered
½ teaspoon rubbed sage
1 bay leaf
½ teaspoon coarse salt
2 cups whole milk
3 large potatoes, peeled and quartered

1. Remove and discard the rind from the salt pork. Cut the pork into ¼-inch lardoons (matchstick-like slices). Blanch the lardoons in boiling water for 5 minutes, drain, and rinse them in running water. Pat them completely dry with paper towels.
2. Heat a heavy skillet and sauté the lardoons very gently until they are just golden. Remove them from their fat and set them aside.
3. Pat the pepper into the chops and dredge them all over with flour.

Brush off and save the excess flour. Brown the chops well on both sides in the lardoon drippings, remove them from the frying pan, sprinkle them with the crushed juniper berries, and set them aside.

4. Add the onions, sage, and bay leaf to the drippings and sauté them briefly, stirring all the while with a wooden spatula so that the onions come apart and are coated well with the hot fat.

5. When the onions begin to turn translucent, sprinkle the reserved flour and the salt over them and stir until the flour is absorbed. Add the milk and stir until the sauce begins to thicken. Set aside.

6. Preheat the oven to 325°.

7. Transfer the lardoons and the chops to a heavy braising pan with a lid. Pour the sauce over them. Cover the pan and put it on the center rack of the oven to bake for 1 hour.

8. Boil the potatoes in lightly salted water for 15 minutes. Drain and put them in the braising pot with the chops. Bake the chops and potatoes uncovered for 20 minutes or until the potatoes are nicely browned.

9. Serve the chops in a heated serving dish with the onion sauce poured over them and the roasted potatoes arranged around the sides of the dish.

N O T E : These chops are real Alsatian country fare. I have never served them without someone asking me for the recipe. If you want to sharpen their taste slightly, add 1 tablespoon cider vinegar, ½ teaspoon granulated sugar, and ½ jigger gin to the sauce before pouring it over the chops at serving time. You will want to let the alcohol evaporate completely, so let the sauce simmer 3 minutes after these additions. Your sauce will be marvelously aromatized by the juniper in the gin, slightly acidified by the vinegar, and softened and cinched by the tiny quantity of sugar you have added.

• • •

Grilled Pork Chops Norman Style
LES COTES DE PORC A LA NORMANDE
SERVES 4

Everyone, it seems, has discovered that pork and apples make a great pair. This festive recipe vaunts that discovery. It not only makes use of fresh apples to enhance the pork chops but of cider and Calvados, the splendid Norman applejack, as well.

Four ¼-inch-thick pork loin
　chops
2 cups sweet cider
3 tablespoons sweet butter
Four ½-inch slices unpeeled apple
　cut from the center (remove
　the core, leaving a small, neat
　circular hole)
1 tablespoon flour
6 plump shallots, peeled,
　trimmed, and cut paper-thin
1 medium-sized carrot, scraped,
　quartered, and finely chopped

4 small mushrooms, wiped clean,
　trimmed, and finely chopped
¼ teaspoon marjoram leaves,
　finely crumbled
½ teaspoon freshly milled white
　pepper
1 tablespoon Dijon mustard
½ teaspoon coarse salt
1 tablespoon vegetable oil
¼ cup heavy cream
1 jigger warmed Calvados

1. Wipe the chops well with paper towels. Place them in a large glass or other noncorrosive dish and pour the cider over them. Let them marinate for 1 hour at room temperature.
2. Heat a heavy frying pan. Add the butter and melt it at medium heat.
3. Dust the apple slices lightly on each side with flour. Brush off the excess and save it.
4. Cook the apples in the butter for 3 minutes on each side, remove them, and set them aside.
5. Sauté the shallots, carrot, and mushrooms in the butter remaining in the skillet. Take sufficient time to do this very gently. When the shallots are almost melted and the juice from the mushrooms is evaporated, sprinkle in the marjoram and the reserved flour and stir them in very well.
6. Remove the chops from the cider and dry them very well with paper towels. Sprinkle them with pepper and work it in with your fingers.
7. Empty the cider into the sautéing vegetables and stir it all together as it thickens. Increase the heat and allow the sauce to reduce to about 1 cup. Stir in the mustard and salt.

8. Preheat the broiler and fix the tray 5 or 6 inches from the source of heat.

9. Coat the chops on both sides with oil and broil them 6 or 7 minutes on each side. Make sure that they are properly cooked, but be careful not to let them burn. If your broiler is good and hot, 14 minutes should be sufficient.

10. Spread the sauce over the bottom of a baking dish large enough to accommodate all 4 chops. Arrange the chops in the dish and place an apple slice on each one. Put 1 tablespoon heavy cream in the center hole of each apple slice. Put the dish under the broiler for 3 minutes. Put a little warm Calvados on each apple slice. Light it, and serve the dish immediately.

N O T E : If you make this dish properly, it won't need an accompanying vegetable. I suggest you follow it with a salad of mixed greens with a very light *Sauce vinaigrette* (page 38).

Braised Loin of Pork with Prunes

LES NOISETTES DE FILET DE PORC AUX PRUNEAUX

SERVES 4

This delicious dish from the region of Tours is the only meat dish I am aware of in French household cooking that has a sweet sauce. Most French home cooks are a little dogmatic about never mixing sweet and savory or sweet and salty in their cooking. (You do find them mixed at present in expensive restaurants in France, since nouvelle cuisine has flown in the face of this proscription.) I am sure that there are many households in France where this dish would be looked upon as outlandish. However, it is so wonderful that I feel you ought to know about it. Since the French, by and large, find American cooking far too sucrée, or sweetened, they would find it only natural that I should suggest it to United States household cooks.

I have often wondered why this great dish, which is justly famous, should have originated in the very center of France. I suspect the answer is no more mysterious than that Tours produces magnificent prunes. In any case, since the fabulous prunes of California are easily available in the States, here is a great dish to show them off. I think you will agree that braised loin of pork with prunes deserves to be better known here.

1 pound large, unpitted prunes
2 cloves tied together with a
   long thread
1½ cups dry white wine
¼ teaspoon freshly milled white
   pepper
½ teaspoon coarse salt
Eight ¼-inch slices fresh, boneless
   loin of pork

2 tablespoons flour
3 tablespoons sweet butter
2 tablespoons vegetable oil
2 tablespoons red currant jelly
   (Concord grape jelly is an
   acceptable substitute)
1 cup heavy cream
Finely chopped parsley, for
   garnish

1. Put the prunes and cloves to soak overnight in 1 cup of the wine. (Why the long thread on the cloves? So you can locate and discard them later.)
2. If the prunes soak up all the wine overnight, add ½ cup water the next morning. Cover the prunes tightly and cook them in a 250° oven for 1 hour. The juice must not evaporate.
3. Work the pepper and salt into the pork with your fingers. Dredge the pieces well in flour, patting them so that the flour adheres.
4. Heat a large, heavy frying pan that is large enough to accommodate the 8 slices of loin at once without crowding them. Melt the butter and oil. When they are bubbling, put in the meat and brown it very slowly on both sides. Take your time and don't let the butter scorch.
5. Add the remaining ½ cup wine. Cover the pan tightly, reduce the heat to its lowest point, and braise the meat for 40 to 50 minutes. The pieces should be quite tender.
6. Carefully remove the pieces of pork to a large, ovenproof serving dish at least 2 inches deep. Cover the dish with aluminum foil and keep it warm in the oven.
7. Pour the juice from the prunes into the frying pan with the braising juices from the pork. Return the frying pan to the burner and increase the heat. Add the jelly and stir it in completely. Little by little add the cream. It should thicken at once. Don't let it thicken past the pouring stage. If it does you must add more cream.
8. Remove the meat from the oven, uncover the plate, and pour the sauce over the meat. Discard the cloves. Place the prunes around the serving dish. A little finely chopped parsley sprinkled over the surface of the sauce will give the dish a nice contrasting color.

N O T E : Serve the dish hot and wait for the surprised but delighted reaction to the pork, the prunes, and the tasty sauce. Plain boiled rice tossed with a generous amount of sweet butter and 3 or 4 tablespoons of finely chopped parsley makes an excellent accompaniment to this beautiful dish.

Fresh Ham Baked in Port Wine
LE JAMBON FRAIS ROTI AU PORTO
SERVES 8 TO 10

A whole ham is rarely prepared in a French household because it is large and therefore costly, it takes at least 2½ days to prepare a whole ham decently, and the pork butcher prepares ham several times a week and sells it by the gram. The occasion would have to be exceptional, but for Christmas, New Year, or the Feast of Kings, a French householder might indeed undertake the long preparation of a fresh ham, knowing that the leftover ham would serve very well for at least 2 meals after the festivities are over. This is truly an extraordinary recipe for fresh ham. It is time-consuming, but I consider it time well spent. Even the cold cuts from this recipe make it worth the effort.

F O R   T H E   H A M   A N D   M A R I N A D E :

One 6- or 7-pound ham, boned, skinned, and the fat trimmed to ½ inch
8 peppercorns, bruised
8 juniper berries, crushed
1 bottle port wine
1 tablespoon coarse salt
1 large carrot, scraped, quartered, and finely sliced
1 medium-sized onion, peeled and spiked with 3 cloves

¾ cup vegetable oil
1 bouquet garni consisting of 2 bay leaves, 1 branch thyme, 1 branch sage, 1 branch rosemary, and 3 branches fresh parsley, securely tied with cotton string
½ cup white raisins
1 dried orange skin (fresh orange peel without the white pith may be used)
2 cups Perrier water or seltzer

F O R   T H E   P A S T E :

3 tablespoons Dijon mustard
3 tablespoons honey

3 tablespoons ham dripping
6 tablespoons flour

To prepare and marinate the ham:

1. Ask your butcher to remove the bone, skin, and a bit of the fat from the ham, but have him leave a ½-inch layer of fat. It will ensure the juiciness and tenderness of the ham. Be sure to ask for the bones, skin, and fat if you will have occasion to use them. They can be frozen.
2. Truss the ham all over with a web of cotton string. Do this carefully so that the meat will keep its shape.
3. Wrap the peppercorns and juniper berries in a piece of cheesecloth and tie them securely.
4. Put all the listed ingredients except the Perrier, ham, and paste ingredients in a kettle and bring them to a boil. Let this marinade cool.
5. Put the trussed ham in a large crock or noncorrosive bowl and pour all the contents of the marinade, including solids, over it. Add the Perrier. The ham should be at least half covered with marinade. Cover the crock or bowl with aluminum foil and put it in a cool place for the next 2 days. Every 12 hours turn the ham so that all of it gets exposed to the marinade.

To bake the ham:

1. Preheat the oven to 300°.
2. Dry the ham with paper towels and place it in a braising pan, fat side up. Pour the marinade around the bottom. Discard the orange peel, *sachet,* the bouquet garni, and the spiked onion, but spoon the raisins and carrot slices around the bottom of the ham. Bake the ham for 3½ hours, basting it from time to time with the marinade.
3. Remove the ham from the oven and allow it to cool for 20 to 30 minutes. Remove the trussing string.
4. Mix all the paste ingredients and spread the paste all over the exposed surface of the ham. Return it to the oven, increase the heat to 400°, and bake the ham until the paste is a golden crust.
5. Remove the ham from the oven to a carving board.
6. Skim away and discard the fat from the marinade and juices that have accumulated in the braising pan. Put the pan on a burner and reduce the juices at high heat, scraping up all the browned bits. If the marinade has evaporated considerably, then add water to constitute a sauce. Strain the sauce into a sauceboat and serve it along with the carved ham.

• • •

A WORD ABOUT HOMEMADE PÂTÉS

Like French pancakes, now referred to everywhere in the United States
as crêpes, whether sweet or savory or both, and quiche, which now
designates anything mixed with egg and baked in pie crust, pâté, another
distinguished classic of French regional and household cooking, has suffered at the hands of the ubiquitous "me-too" guys who want to claim
the prestige of the French food tradition without earning the right to it.
Thanks to the compulsive "creative" meddling that characterizes so much
of what is called "gourmet cooking" in the United States, almost anything
processed to a pulp and baked in a terrine or a loaf pan now masquerades
as "pâté-whatever." I was recently served a nasty, pretentious, all-
vegetable pâté that really caused my hackles to rise. I do not feel up to
the job of setting the pâté world right. The most I can do about it is to
encourage you to make a simple *pâté de campagne* or *pâté maison* for
yourself from the best ingredients you can find. Short of a stay at a French
country inn where you could taste a real French country pâté, about the
only way you are going to experience the real article is to make one
yourself.

Pâtés lend themselves to all kinds of variations, but do not fall into the
trap of thinking that a great many expensive ingredients processed to a
mousse will produce the best pâtés. Leave the really elaborate ones to the
trained *charcutiers.* Concentrate on learning to make the country varieties
from simple, first-class ingredients. Country pâtés should be robust, both
lumpy and buttery, redolent of shallots, garlic, aromatic herbs, and
brandy. They cry out for stout appetites.

Making pâté is not a simple enterprise. It takes time and patience and
a considerable number of good ingredients. French householders do not
make pâté often. Some never undertake it at all. The expert pork butchers
in France do such a wonderful job of making all kinds of pâtés that it is
easier just to buy a good-sized slice rather than go to the trouble to make
it. But many householders all over France make special pâtés for Christmas and New Year. Personally, I love making pâté for the holidays, and
I take at least two whole days to do it. I like to make two large terrines
of pâté to have on hand for the festivities and enough for little pots to
give to my special friends as gifts. It is always rewarding to see how much
they appreciate those little pots of homemade pâté.

• • •

French Country Pâté

LE PATE DE CAMPAGNE

MAKES 1 8 × 6-INCH OVAL TERRINE, 3 INCHES DEEP OR 1 8 × 5-INCH LOAF PAN, 2½ INCHES DEEP

Here is a good, dependable recipe for country pâté, the kind you find only in out-of-the-way villages in the central highlands of France. It calls for neither truffles nor goose liver, but when eating it you won't miss either one.

1½ pounds salted pork belly
½ pound pork liver, cut in
    ½-inch-wide strips
1½ jiggers Cognac
1 teaspoon lard
2 plump shallots, peeled and
    sliced paper-thin
2 large mushrooms, wiped,
    trimmed, and finely chopped
¼ teaspoon thyme leaves
¼ teaspoon marjoram leaves,
    finely crumbled
6 juniper berries, crushed
¼ teaspoon ground allspice
1 teaspoon freshly cracked
    black pepper
1 plump clove garlic, peeled,
    crushed, and teased to a
    paste in
    1 tablespoon coarse salt

1 slice white bread, crust
    removed, soaked in
    ½ cup port wine
1 pound lean, coarsely minced
    pork
½ pound lean, coarsely minced
    veal
¼ teaspoon saltpeter (optional)
2 large egg yolks
3 thick rashers smoked
    breakfast bacon, rind
    removed, cut in ¼-inch
    strips the length of the
    rasher
8 rosemary leaves
1 bay leaf

1. Prepare the pork belly:
    - Cut the slab of salt pork in two.
    - Using a very sharp slicing knife, cut as many thin, even sheets across the two pieces as you can. You will use them to line the terrine. If you have access to a slicer, use it. (In France sheets of pork fat, called *platine de porc*, are sold at the butcher's. They are used to wrap roasts.)
    - Scald the sheets of salt pork with boiling water. Drain them, pat them dry, and refrigerate them. They are more manageable when very cold.

2. Put the liver in a noncorrosive dish and marinate it in ½ jigger of Cognac.
3. Heat the lard in a heavy skillet and gently sauté the shallots and mushrooms until the shallots have wilted and almost melted and the juice from the mushrooms has evaporated.
4. Add the thyme, marjoram, juniper berries, allspice, pepper, and garlic paste and stir them into the shallot and mushroom mixture. Add the bread and the port it was soaking in and stir them in.
5. In a large mixing bowl, using your hands, combine the pork, veal, saltpeter, egg yolks, and the sautéed mixture. Mix all of these ingredients very thoroughly. Cover the mixing bowl and set it aside.
6. Cover the bottom and sides of the terrine with the chilled sheets of pork fat. If you haven't a proper pâté terrine, you may use a loaf pan. I use a pair of kitchen shears to help me cut the sheets of fat to the right sizes. They should fit neatly into the bottom. The pieces you use for the sides should not be cut off at the top. Whatever is too long will be used to lap over the top. The point of covering the terrine with sheets of fat is to insulate the pâté from the heat. The entire pâté must be covered so that no part of it browns or it will harden and grow bitter during the slow cooking.
7. Drain the liver and dry it with paper towels. Pour the marinade into the bowl with the meat mixture and mix it in well.
8. Preheat the oven to 325°.

Assemble the pâté:
1. Pack about half of the meat mixture into the terrine.
2. Place the bacon and liver strips in straight, alternate lines the length of the terrine and press them gently into the mixture. Do this neatly so that when the pâté is sliced there will be a handsome layer of liver and bacon in the center.
3. Pack the other half of the meat mixture around and on top of the bacon and liver and fill the terrine. Sprinkle the rosemary leaves over the top and place the bay leaf in the center.
4. Lap the overhanging pork fat over the top. It should cover the top completely. If it doesn't, cut a few more bits from the rind and patch the places that are exposed. Discard the rind or save it for another use.

Baking and storing the pâté:
1. Place the terrine in a baking tin that is 2 inches deep and large enough to allow at least 2 inches all around between the terrine and the edge. Put 1 inch of water in the tin around the terrine (a *bain-marie*).

2. Place the entire setup on the center rack in the oven and bake the pâté for 2½ hours. Keep replenishing the water in the tin during the time the pâté is baking.
3. Remove the pâté from the oven and tip up a piece of the fat on the top. If the juice and hot fat are clear, the pâté is done. If pink juices are still bubbling forth, you will have to bake it a little more.
4. When the pâté is done, remove the entire setup from the oven and place it on a cake rack to cool in the *bain-marie.* When the terrine is cool enough to handle comfortably, remove it from the baking tin, dry it off, and place it on a solid surface. To weight the pâté, find a piece of plywood cut a little smaller than the top of the terrine, fit it over the pâté, and place a 2-pound weight on it. I use an old flatiron for this purpose. You can use canned goods, but make sure the weight is equally distributed. You weight the pâté to make it more compact and sliceable. Pressing it also gets rid of some of the juices that might cause it to spoil after a few days' refrigeration.
5. When the pâté is completely cool, remove the weight and the board and take it out of the terrine. Wash the terrine well and dry it. Rinse the interior with a little of the Cognac.
6. Remove the pork fat. Discard the bay leaf and pick off the rosemary leaves and discard them. Heat the pork fat gently in a frying pan until it has rendered a good deal of its fat.
7. Put the pâté back in the terrine and pour the rest of the Cognac over it.
8. Strain the solids out of the melted fat and pour it over the pâté. There should be enough to cover it. (This is very essential. If there is enough to cover all the meat, the pâté will keep very well, if refrigerated, for 2 weeks.) Cover the terrine and keep it refrigerated.

N O T E : The pâté should not be eaten for 24 hours. The flavors must be given a chance to mature. This is a very full-bodied pâté, just like the ones made in the Auvergne. If you find it too stout, cut a slice and process it with one-half its weight of sweet butter. Rinse a porcelain pot with Cognac and pack the pâté into it. Cover the top with a skin of buttered paper or foil cut to fit exactly. When serving time comes, simply peel back the covering and allow your guests to serve themselves. When they have finished, if there is any of the pâté left, all you have to do is press the paper or foil down again and the pâté will keep for another 24 hours in the refrigerator. Never leave pâté uncovered. It discolors.

Pork Spread

LES RILLETES DE TOURS

MAKES ABOUT 1 POUND

Rillettes *are a delight. They are indigenous to the Loire valley around Tours, and I have never found them in the United States except in my own kitchen. I make them at Christmas time, and they have become a great family favorite. I can recall the very first time I tasted* rillettes. *A fellow student and I had decided to see the châteaux on the Loire and Cher rivers. We bought an inflatable boat and criss-crossed between the two rivers, paddling and visiting the castles during the day, camping along the rivers at night. After a morning of paddling, we stopped near Tours to buy some provisions for lunch. We bought a strange, grayish spread from the local* charcutier. *He assured us that we would like it. We bought some newly baked bread and went back to the boat. We spread the* rillettes *on the split loaves and tried them. A few minutes later we were back at the shop buying more* rillettes. *The good* charcutier, *amused by our enthusiasm, explained how he made the spread. Here is the simple recipe.*

¾ pound fresh pork fatback	1 branch dried thyme
1 tablespoon coarse salt	1 bay leaf
1½ pounds fresh, lean, boneless	3 peppercorns
pork	1 cup water
2 plump cloves garlic, unpeeled	

1. Remove the rind from the fatback. Discard it or save it for another purpose.
2. Work the salt into all the surfaces of the meat. Place it in a noncorrosive bowl, cover it, and refrigerate it overnight.
3. Next day, dry the meat by patting it with paper towels. Don't be at pains to remove the salt. Cut both the fat and the lean meat into small thin pieces about 2 inches by ¼ inch.
4. Preheat the oven to 300°
5. Wrap the garlic, thyme, bay leaf, and peppercorns in a piece of cheesecloth and tie it up securely. Put this *sachet* at the bottom of an ovenproof earthenware pot. (I use a beanpot with a lid.) Put the chopped meat in the pot and add the water. Seal the pot with a piece of aluminum foil and press the lid down over the foil into the lid groove of the pot.

6. Put the pot on the center rack of the oven and bake it for 3½ hours. Turn off the oven, but leave the pot there for another ½ hour.
7. Place a large, stout sieve over a bowl. Break the seal on the pot and empty the contents into the sieve. Discard the *sachet.*
8. Break the bits of meat apart with your fingers. Then, working with 2 forks, pull all the fibers apart. This operation is very essential for genuine *rillettes*, which are not a paste. They are finely shredded pork and pork fat. (Don't make the mistake of putting the meat into the food processor and making a fine pâté of it.)

N O T E : You may eat the *rillettes* at once, if you like, but mix the shredded meat with a little of the dripping in a ratio of 2 parts shredded meat to 1 part dripping. You may also pack the *rillettes* into jars or pots and pour the dripping over them. Make certain that the dripping covers the *rillettes* at least ¼ inch deep. Cover the tops of the pots or jars with foil. They will keep for a month or so under refrigeration. Make sure your pots are sterilized. An easy way to do that is by washing them well and rinsing them out with a few drops of Cognac.

Be sure the spread is at room temperature when you serve it. If you try to eat it cold, you will be astonished at how tasteless and greasy it seems. When it is served at room temperature you get the full benefit of the long cooking and the faint, savory perfume and taste of the garlic and herbs. The spread is at its best on crusty, freshly baked French bread.

Alsatian-Style Sauerkraut and Pork Feast
LA CHOUCROUTE GARNIE
SERVES 4 TO 6

This fabulous Alsatian feast once belonged uniquely to the Alsace-Lorraine. For almost a century it has belonged, by universal adoption, to all of France. Chou-croûte garnie is a permanent item on the menus of brasseries from Lille to Marseille and from Bordeaux to Grenoble. It is really winter fare and at its best on a cold, blustery night, but I have often eaten it with Parisian friends in summer

and enjoyed it, despite the beads of perspiration it brought out on our brows. The
dish is sumptuous and has a spectacular appearance, piled high on the serving dish
as it always is. It is impressive, but it is very easy to make at home, and it often
is made at home in France. It is a favorite with household cooks who find themselves
faced with the problem of serving a good number of guests in a way that will
impress and please them without having to spend two days slaving away in the
kitchen. An Alsatian sauerkraut feast is a wonderful solution. It requires minimal
effort and yields maximal results.

¾ pound streaky salt pork in 1
    piece, with its rind
2 pounds bulk or tinned
    sauerkraut
2 tablespoons vegetable oil
3 medium-sized onions, peeled,
    trimmed, and sliced very thin
1 bay leaf
8 juniper berries
¼ teaspoon freshly cracked black
    pepper

1 teaspoon coarse salt
1 teaspoon granulated sugar
1 cup dry white wine
3 cups water
2 Granny Smith apples, peeled,
    cored, and sliced in ¼-inch
    roundels
4 to 6 small potatoes, peeled
4 to 6 smoked pork chops
4 to 6 frankfurter sausages
4 to 6 slices boiled ham

Prepare the salt pork:
1. With a very sharp slicing knife, cut into the pork as if you were going
   to make 4 to 6 rashers, but do not cut through the rind. Put the pork
   in a noncorrosive bowl or dish, scald it with boiling water, and let it
   steep in the hot water for 5 minutes.
2. Rinse the pork in cold running water, opening up the incisions and
   allowing the water to wash away the saltiness. Dry it well with paper
   towels.
3. With cotton string, truss the pork so that it does not fan open when
   cooking. Set it aside.

Prepare the sauerkraut:
1. Put the kraut in a large sieve or colander in the sink and wash it well
   under cold running water. Pull the shreds apart with your fingers and
   wash away all of the saltiness. Squeeze the kraut, fluff it, and leave it
   in the sieve.
2. Heat the oil in a large, heavy kettle and toss the onions in the hot oil
   until they are completely coated. Reduce the heat, cover the pot, and
   smother the onions until they are wilted. Stir them from time to time
   to see that they do not scorch.

3. Add the kraut, bay leaf, juniper berries, pepper, salt, and sugar to the onions and toss them all together until they are well mixed.
4. Place the trussed pork deep in the kraut and onions. Add the wine and water. Place the apple roundels on top of the kraut, cover the pot, and simmer very gently for 3 hours.

Prepare the meat and potatoes:
1. Stir the apples into the kraut, then bury the potatoes and the chops in the kraut mixture.
2. Prick the franks all over and place them on top of the kraut. Arrange the ham slices over the frankfurters, like a cover.
3. Cover the pot and simmer the kraut and meat and potatoes for 40 minutes.

Assemble the dish:
1. Choose a large, circular, rimmed serving dish about 2 inches deep.
2. Using a skimmer, lift the kraut out of the pot and pile it high in the middle of the dish. The skimmer will allow the kraut to drain. It won't pile high if it is too wet. Discard the bay leaf.
3. Arrange the slices of ham around the mound of kraut, and the frankfurters and chops around the sides.
4. Cut away and discard the trussing string and cut the pork rashers apart. (For heaven's sake, don't discard the rind. It is delicious to eat as is or cooked in a pot of beans for another meal.) Arrange the rashers nicely around the bottom of the dish.
5. Arrange the potatoes around the serving dish next to the rim.
6. Ladle some of the pot juices over the entire arrangement to moisten it. (If there is much extra juice, save it to make sauerkraut soup.) Serve the dish at once.

N O T E : Light, white Alsatian wine such as Gewürztraminer or Sylvaner is usually drunk with this meal, but many prefer a very light Alsatian beer. Be sure you provide hot mustard, coarse salt, a pepper-mill full of fresh black peppercorns, and a dish of sour gherkins. I also serve an assortment of good, hearty, country bread: a sourdough white and both dark and light rye. Though the French are not used to eating buttered bread with this meal, my family and friends in the United States expect it. I always put out a few little crocks of sweet butter with the bread. Both disappear as if by magic!

A WORD ABOUT CASSOULET
AND CASSOULETS

The cassoulet is often considered the great star of Languedoc regional cooking. It is a great earthenware crock of white beans baked with an assortment of aromatic herbs, garlic, onion, tomato, and various fresh and preserved meats. It is an undertaking that requires time and expense, for the ingredients are many and they must be of excellent quality. For that reason, most household cooks make it only on a very special occasion, and some simply will not attempt it because it literally takes over the kitchen for at least half a day.

The cassoulet has a troubled history. Cook disagrees with cook, town with town, district with district, about what a true cassoulet must and must not contain. The disagreements are surprisingly vehement. One school disdains lamb; another avows dogmatically that there can be no authentic cassoulet without several large pieces of preserved goose and quite a lot of its fat. Yet another school maintains that the cassoulet must be almost solid in consistency and turns the crust under three times during the baking to see that it is. Still others maintain that there should be a crust but that the consistency of the cassoulet under it should be creamy and liquid.

Listening to these endless disagreements, I have often thought of the princess and the pea. It is not my business here to defend one of these schools against another. I have eaten excellent cassoulets with and without lamb, with and without preserved goose. I have eaten almost solid cassoulets and I have eaten very creamy, even soupy ones. My concern here is simple. I want to convince you that a well-made cassoulet is a wonderful dish, whatever the particular variety. Not to know this famous dish is to ignore one of the great regional specialties of France. The contra-lamb and pro-preserved goose schools may disagree with my recipe, but I think you will find it, *malgré tout*, very good indeed.

• • •

Baked Beans Languedoc Style
LE CASSOULET A LA LANGUEDOCIENNE

SERVES 6 TO 8

½ pound streaky salt pork, with its rind

¼ pound smoked slab bacon, with its rind

1 pound Great Northern navy beans

1 tablespoon coarse salt

¼ teaspoon dried thyme leaves

3 dried rosemary leaves, broken into small bits

1 teaspoon freshly milled black pepper

2 plump cloves garlic, peeled and crushed to a paste with 1 teaspoon coarse salt

1½ pounds neck of lamb, cut up for stewing

2 tablespoons light olive oil or pork lard

1 large, ripe tomato, skinned, seeded, and coarsely chopped

1½ garlic sausages (Polish or Czech kielbasa are excellent choices and are usually available in supermarkets)

1 medium-sized onion, peeled and spiked with 2 cloves

1 cup fresh breadcrumbs

2 tablespoons finely chopped flat-leaf parsley

½ teaspoon freshly cracked black pepper

2 small cloves garlic, peeled and very finely chopped

Prepare the salt pork and bacon:

1. Cut the rind from the pork and bacon. With a very sharp knife dipped in boiling water, or a pair of heavy-duty kitchen shears, cut the two rinds into ½-inch squares.
2. Slice the pork and bacon into ¼-inch rashers.
3. Put the pieces of rind and the rashers you have cut in a glass baking dish and scald them with boiling water, leaving them there for 5 minutes. Discard the leaching water. Put the rind and rashers in a colander and rinse them very well with cold running water.
4. Dry the pieces of rind and the rashers thoroughly. Separate the rind from the rashers and set both aside.

Prepare the beans:

1. Spread the beans on a clean, flat surface and remove and discard any stones, foreign matter, or imperfect beans.
2. Wash the beans in a colander under cold running water, then put them in a small, heavy kettle with 3 cups of water and bring them to a boil.

3. Take the kettle off the fire immediately and set it aside for 40 minutes to allow the beans to plump.
4. Return the beans to the colander and wash away all of the water in which they were soaking. Wash the kettle out well and dry it.
5. Spread the rind all over the bottom of the kettle. Put the beans on top and add 1 tablespoon coarse salt and 4 cups tepid water. Cover the kettle and simmer the beans at just a murmur (low flame) for 1½ hours.

Prepare the lamb:
1. Mix the thyme, rosemary, 1 teaspoon milled pepper, and garlic paste together and rub the mixture well into all the pieces of lamb. You will need to do this with your fingers, then rub your fingers with half a lemon. It will remove the lamb and garlic smell.
2. Heat the oil or lard in a large, heavy skillet and gently brown both the lamb and the bacon. Take time to do this well. The taste of the finished cassoulet will be the better for it. Just don't allow either the bacon or lamb to scorch.
3. Remove the lamb and bacon and set them aside, discard the drippings, and deglaze the skillet with the tomato and a tiny bit of water. Reserve this sauce for the assembling of the cassoulet.

Assemble the cassoulet:
1. Preheat the oven to 300°.
2. Choose a large, deep earthenware casserole or crock. In a pinch I have used a large cast-iron pot. This will rumple the sensitivities of the purists, but, frankly, a trusty iron pot makes a very good substitute for the traditional casserole.
3. Lay the rashers of pork across the bottom of the casserole or pot. Using a skimmer so that you leave the juice in the kettle, ladle a layer of beans over the pork.
4. Cut the sausage into 2-inch pieces, prick them in a few places, and put them on the beans. Place the browned bacon among the pieces of sausage.
5. Ladle in another thin layer of beans. Place the lamb on top of the beans. Pour the tomato sauce over the pieces and bury the spiked onion in the middle.
6. Ladle in the rest of the beans. Gently pour the juice from the beans down one side of the casserole so that it slowly invades all the layers of the cassoulet. There should be enough juice to come up to the top

layer of beans. If there isn't enough, pour a little warm water down the side until the liquid reaches the proper depth.

7. Mix the crumbs with the parsley, cracked pepper, and chopped garlic. Spread this topping evenly over the top of the cassoulet.

8. Place a baking plaque or cookie sheet on the middle rack of the oven. (This is to protect your oven in case the cassoulet boils over, so you may want to cover the plaque or sheet with foil.) Place the cassoulet on the plaque or sheet and bake it for 2 hours.

9. During the baking, keep watch over the topping. It should not burn. If it seems on the point of doing so, you may take a spoon and turn it under. That is the general practice. I prefer covering it with foil.

Serve the cassoulet:

1. Remove the cassoulet from the oven and let it rest for 15 to 20 minutes.

2. Serve the guests from the casserole or pot in which the cassoulet was cooked. (Place the *cassoulet* on a trivet on the dining table for all to see before you begin to delve into the depths of the dish.) Serve each guest a little of the topping and a bit of each ingredient in the dish. Cassoulet-lovers are particularly fond of the rind and the pork, so be at pains to give each guest a little of everything.

N O T E : Cassoulet is a complete meal so you won't need to provide any accompanying vegetables. To accompany or follow, I suggest a salad of bitter greens such as curly endive or chicory in a stout mustard vinaigrette. Serve a light red Bordeaux rather than a red burgundy. Any of the red wines from the Languedoc region would be acceptable, but they are more difficult to find in the United States. A jug of California mountain red is a good choice.

C H A P T E R N I N E

Domestic Fowl and Game

Domestic Fowl and Game on
the French Household Menu

I have chosen to speak here only of chicken, duck, turkey, quail, and rabbit. All of these are available in United States supermarkets. Turkey is certainly not eaten as often in French homes as it is here, but I have included it because it is very cheap and easily available, and I have proposed that it be substituted in a few instances for goose. Goose is a very important item in many regions in France, but because it is rather difficult to come by in the States, I give no recipes for preparing goose in this book. However, I have found a way of transforming the almost intractable turkey leg into a perfectly wonderful substitute for preserved goose.

French householders still consider chicken special as we did in the United States before chickens were mass-produced on an industrial scale and became so cheap and so tasteless. The French are already mass-producing them in some regions. Fortunately in France you can still get good farm chickens in most villages and in many city shops. The best-tasting chickens in France come from the rich, verdant Bresse area in Burgundy. They are good indeed—just like the chickens I remember from my great-grandmother's farm when I was a child. The chickens from Bresse are grain fed, and are allowed to vary their diet by foraging. That accounts for their wonderful taste. Their ability to move about keeps them from becoming too fat. If you can find a reliable source for supplying you with good, lean farm chickens, you are fortunate. Most of us must depend on our supermarkets, and those chickens are usually flat tasting and excessively fat. In spite of the fact that our grandmothers treasured chicken fat more than butter, chicken fat is not good for us. Since it is to be discarded, why pay for the added weight? Ask your supermarket to try to obtain grain-fed chickens for you. Kosher chickens are good, though they are usually frozen.

Most French household cooks are very fastidious and quite skillful about removing excess fat from meat and fowl. They skim the fat from sauces while they are still simmering and, when they can, allow fatty sauces and broths to sit overnight in the refrigerator so that all of the fat that rises to the top and solidifies can be removed.

There are, of course, sections of France such as the Cévennes, Gascony, the Béarnais, and the region around Foix where goose and duck fat are highly esteemed. In those regions goose and duck fat are used for preserving, stewing, flavoring, and frying. Many people from those regions swear that the best french fries in the world are fried in goose fat. They may be delicious, but they are disastrous for most digestions, and I don't dare think what they do for most persons' cholesterol levels. I shall go on insisting that, where possible, animal fats should be used with the greatest discretion.

Frozen Long Island duck and duckling are available in most large supermarkets in the United States. We should all be aware, too, that the French, who eat quite a lot of duck, have discovered better ways for preparing duck than the ubiquitous duck *à l'orange*, with its cloyingly sweet sauce. I shall give you one of them.

The French householder eats game birds more often than we do, but quail are the only small birds I find in good supply in my supermarket, so I have included a good recipe for them. Even though the supermarket quail are raised on farms and not brought in by hunters, their domestication is so recent that they pass muster as game birds. I think you should try them.

A last note about game birds and their preparation. Game birds get a lot of exercise in the wild. For that reason they develop little or no fat. Unlike the industrially produced chicken that never gets any exercise at all and develops excess fat that we must then get rid of, game birds have to be larded and basted or they cook up tough. Turkeys and some Cornish game hens need the same attention. They are not many generations away from their wild stage and their dryness attests to that fact, so they sometimes require fat and basting to make them tender and juicy. The ones I have bought recently in my supermarket are fatter than usual, so perhaps their raisers are giving this point their attention.

• • •

Chicken Braised in Red Wine Burgundian Style

LE COQ AU VIN A LA BOURGUIGNONNE

SERVES 6

Coq au vin, literally cockerel in wine, is a genuine Burgundian recipe that has been adopted by households in many other regions in France. It is perhaps the French home cook's favorite way of preparing a large hen or rooster. Because the sauce of reduced, concentrated red wine, herbs, and vegetables is very full-bodied, it is not a suitable recipe for young, tender pullets. Their best qualities might be overpowered by it. It is ideal for a good-sized hen, one that weighs 3 1/2 to 4 pounds. The sauce, much like the meurettes *or* matelotes *so loved by the Burgundians, is also made by reducing an entire bottle of Beaujolais or Mâcon red to about half its volume. The result is tremendous.*

One 3½- to 4-pound chicken
¼ cup flour
6 tablespoons (¾ stick) sweet butter
¼ pound streaky salt pork, rind removed, cut into ¼-inch lardoons (matchstick-like strips), blanched, rinsed, and carefully dried with paper towels
12 pearl onions, peeled
½ pound small mushrooms, wiped clean, trimmed, and cut in half top to bottom
1 jigger *marc de Bourgogne* (brandy or whiskey may be substituted)

1 bottle Beaujolais or other red burgundy (mountain red is a suitable substitute)
3 plump cloves garlic, unpeeled, skewered together with a toothpick
1 bouquet garni, consisting of 1 celery branch, cut in half; 1 medium-sized carrot, scraped and trimmed; 1 bay leaf; 1 sprig thyme; and 3 sprigs fresh parsley bound together with cotton string
Freshly milled black pepper
Coarse salt
3 tablespoons chicken blood
½ pound crôutons

1. Cut the chicken up into the traditional 8 pieces. Put the liver aside. Flour the pieces only lightly, brushing off all the excess flour.
2. Heat a heavy-bottomed kettle or braising pan and melt 2 tablespoons of the butter. In it sauté the lardoons until they begin to take on color. Remove them. Sauté the pearl onions and mushrooms briefly. Remove them after 3 minutes.

3. Gently brown the chicken in the same fat. When all the pieces are browned, toss in the *marc* and light it. Continue to shake the chicken pieces about in the *marc* until the alcohol has completely burned off and the flame goes out.

4. Return the lardoons, onions, and mushrooms to the kettle and add the wine, garlic, and the bouquet garni. Cover and simmer at the lowest mark for 45 to 50 minutes.

5. Remove the chicken, lardoons, onions, and mushrooms and keep warm. Discard the garlic and bouquet garni. Strain the sauce.

6. Wash out and dry the kettle and heat it again.

7. Chop the chicken liver and sauté it in the kettle with 2 more table-spoons of the butter for 3 minutes. If you have the chicken blood, add it at this point and remove the kettle from the heat while you stir the blood and liver together. Pour in the strained sauce, heat to the boiling point, and remove from the fire. Salt and pepper to taste.

8. Arrange the chicken, lardoons, onions, and mushrooms in a deep serving dish and pour the hot sauce over them.

9. Melt the remaining 2 tablespoons of butter and toss the crôutons in it. Sprinkle the crôutons over the coq au vin and serve hot.

NOTE: Buttered rice or noodles go well with this great-tasting dish. It usually makes a fair amount of sauce, so some good, thick-crusted bread will come in handy.

Purists will object to my flouring the chicken, insisting the flour be sprinkled in after the chicken is browned. Do as you like; the taste will be the same.

If you are wondering what to do with the neck, gizzard, and heart of the chicken, you may put them right in with the other pieces and sauté and braise them. On Burgundian farms even the well-cleaned and trimmed feet and part of the head are included.

• • •

Basque-Style Chicken
LE POULET A LA BASQUAISE

SERVES 4 TO 6

Recipes for Basque-style chicken can stimulate some pretty violent arguments. Some Basque cooks swear that you cannot make an authentic Basque-style chicken without including a considerable quantity of unblanched mountain ham from the Pyrenees. Others insist that the real thing must contain half a dozen roundels of strong, Basque garlic sausage. Still others hold that no other oil can be used except the fruity, green olive oil of the Basque country and that the dish must contain two dozen cloves of garlic. All agree on only one thing: Basque-style chicken is delicious. Your family and friends will agree. My recipe produces a chicken that is subtler, less salty, and much lighter and less oily than most versions you will find in the Pyrenees. All the ingredients the recipe requires can be found in a good supermarket.

1 large hen cut into the 8 traditional pieces
3 tablespoons sweet butter
3 tablespoons vegetable oil
6 to 8 cloves garlic, separated but unpeeled
One ¼-inch slice streaky salt pork, rind removed, cut into ¼-inch lardoons (matchstick-like strips), blanched, rinsed, and dried with paper towels
1 jigger dry red wine
1 jigger brandy
1 quart water
1 bouquet garni made up of 1 carrot, scraped and trimmed; 1 bay leaf; and 2 sprigs fresh parsley, bound up securely with cotton string
2 medium-sized onions, peeled, quartered, and coarsely sliced
2 large bell peppers, one green, one red, fire-roasted (see page 44), cored, seeded, and cut into ½-inch strips
1 small, dried hot pepper pod
2 medium-sized ripe tomatoes, skinned, seeded, and coarsely chopped
8 oil-cured black olives, pitted
Coarse salt

1. Remove the excess fat from all the chicken pieces. Remove the skin from all the pieces except the wings and drumsticks.
2. Gently heat the butter and oil in a large, heavy-bottomed kettle or braising pan. Brown the chicken with its gizzard, heart, liver and neck, the garlic, and lardoons very slowly. It should take about 20 minutes.

3. Remove the chicken, garlic, and lardoons and set them aside. Pour off and discard the fat.
4. Deglaze the pan with the wine and brandy, rubbing loose all the browned bits that have stuck to the bottom. Reduce the wine and brandy to about 1 tablespoon of liquid.
5. Add the water, bouquet garni, onions, sweet and hot peppers, and the tomatoes. Stir well, then reduce the heat to a simmer and cook uncovered for 40 minutes or until the liquid has reduced to ⅔ its volume.
6. Add the chicken, lardoons, garlic, and olives and simmer very gently for 20 minutes. Salt to taste.
7. Remove and discard the bouquet garni and the hot pepper pod.
8. Arrange the chicken and all the other components in a deep serving dish and pour the sauce over them. Serve warm but not hot.

N O T E : Basque-style chicken improves in taste if allowed to sit for a while. Before you reheat it, carefully skim off all the fat that has risen to the top. By all means insist on trying one of the garlic cloves. They are all buttery and mild inside. The Basques like to grab the point of the husk and pull the garlic cloves through their half-closed teeth, leaving the soft, delicious interior on their tongues. This chicken goes very well with plain rice and rough, country bread.

Chicken Thighs Dijon Style
LES CUISSES DE POULET
A LA DIJONNAISE

SERVES 4 TO 6

In Burgundy and in the Lyon area, Dijon mustard is often added to cooked sauces. It produces a distinctive fillip that is subtle and enhancing, not at all what we in the United States would associate with a mustard sauce. This recipe usually employs very young chickens, almost chicks. In the States we never eat chickens that young. However, we can buy entire packages of chicken thighs in our supermarkets. I have adapted the famous recipe for chicken thighs. Use the whole leg, thigh and drumstick left intact. If you and your family are tired of chicken, this preparation may restore it to your good graces.

6 to 8 large chicken thighs, trimmed of their excess fat and overlapping skin (they should be plump, have unblemished skin, and be of equal size)
1 tablespoon coarse salt
1 tablespoon cracked black pepper
½ teaspoon dried leaf thyme
½ teaspoon crumbled marjoram
3 tablespoons sweet butter

3 tablespoons vegetable oil
¼ cup Dijon mustard
6 to 8 large white mushrooms
4 small white onions, peeled and trimmed
3 plump garlic cloves, peeled
1 tablespoon flour
½ cup dry white wine
½ cup heavy cream

1. Preheat the oven to 350°.
2. Sprinkle the chicken thighs with salt, pepper, thyme, and marjoram and work everything well into the skin and flesh.
3. Heat the butter and oil gently in a large, heavy skillet. Brown the thighs slowly on both sides, turning them with tongs so as not to puncture them.
4. Place the browned thighs skin side up on a baking tray that has been lined with aluminum foil and brush them liberally with Dijon mustard. Bake them on the middle rack of the oven for 40 minutes.
5. Wipe, trim, and slice the mushrooms in thick lengthwise slices. Quarter the onions. Slice the garlic cloves lengthwise. Dredge these sliced vegetables in the flour.
6. Discard half the fat from the skillet. Add the mushrooms, onions, and garlic and toss them in the hot fat with a wooden spatula. Cover the skillet tightly and smother the vegetables at the lowest possible heat for 7 minutes.
7. Pour in the wine and stir it well into the vegetables, scraping up from the bottom any browned bits that may have adhered to it. Add the cream. Stir it in well and allow the liquid to reduce with the skillet uncovered.
8. When the sauce is like thick cream, remove the skillet from the fire and stir in whatever is left of the mustard.
9. Strain the sauce. Arrange the vegetables caught in the sieve over the bottom of a buttered baking dish that can be used as a serving dish. Arrange the chicken thighs on top of the vegetables and carefully ladle the sauce over them. If you like—I always do—allow the dish to brown under the broiler before serving it. Serve hot.

NOTE : I think you will marvel at the many tastes in this dish. Very few of your guests, if any, will guess that the secret ingredient is the celebrated Dijon mustard. Sautéed green beans or Sautéed Leaf Spinach (page 119) go well with this dish.

A WORD ABOUT TRUSSING FOWL

French household cooks normally truss fowl with string if they are planning to cook the birds whole. Binding the wings and drumsticks close to the fowl's body not only ensures that all parts of the bird will cook uniformly, it also helps the bird to keep a presentable shape that can then be carved up into neater, more attractive servings at table. Only cotton or linen string are recommended for trussing. Synthetic strings will sometimes melt and give way during cooking, though I admit that once in a pinch I trussed a number of chickens with dental floss and it held very well!

In large restaurant kitchens fowl are usually trussed with the help of an enormous trussing needle, but I never knew a household cook in France who owned a trussing needle. As far as I am concerned, there is no need for an ordinary home cook to own one, since fowl may be trussed quite easily without having to pierce their bodies and lose some of their delicious juice. Here is how I was taught to truss fowl:

1. Wash the fowl well, inside and out, with cold running water, and dry it inside and out with paper towels. Salt and pepper the cavity lightly.
2. Place the fowl breast up on a clean, flat working surface, with the drumsticks toward you. Pull each wingtip up toward the neck and wedge it behind the second joint of the wing. This will force the breast slightly forward and high, making it easier to carve once the bird is cooked.
3. Cut an 18- to 24-inch length of light-gauge cotton or linen string and find its exact center. Place the center point immediately under the tail of the fowl and tie a simple knot around the tail.
4. Cross the string ends, run each twice around the ankle of the drumstick nearest it and pull the ankles together until they meet. Tie them together securely.
5. Run each string up along the groove on each side where the drumstick lies against the body and force each string deeply into the groove.
6. Turn the bird over, breast down, and cross the strings over the back.
7. Run each string twice around the third joint of the wing nearest it.

8. Pull the strings toward each other and tie them together securely. Clip the string ends neatly.

The fowl is now ready for cooking. Once the bird is done, allow it to cool for a few minutes and "set." Snip the trussing strings loose and discard them before arranging the fowl on the platter or serving dish.

Butter-Roasted Chicken
LE POULET ROTI AU BEURRE

SERVES 4 OR 5

Many cooks have admired this beautiful French way of roasting a chicken. It has been written up many times, but I have not yet run across this version in print, though I have eaten it in the upper Rhône valley. I am very fond of this recipe because it seems to give a heightened taste to any hen, however lowly its pedigree, and you end up with all that luscious rice stuffing to boot!

½ cup (1 stick) sweet butter
¾ cup short-grain rice, cleaned
    and dried according to
    instructions on page 125
1 small onion, peeled, trimmed,
    and finely grated
The chicken liver
½ cup dry white wine
16 saffron threads, crumbled
½ teaspoon tarragon, crumbled
¼ teaspoon rubbed sage
¼ teaspoon freshly milled white
    pepper
1 slice white bread, crust
    removed and discarded,
    soaked in
    ½ cup milk

1 large egg
½ teaspoon marjoram, crumbled
2 tablespoons finely chopped
    flat-leaf parsley
½ teaspoon finely milled salt
One 3- to 4-pound roasting
    chicken
2 tablespoons freshly squeezed
    lemon juice
½ teaspoon coarse salt
½ teaspoon freshly grated
    nutmeg
1 cup water

Prepare the stuffing:

1. Heat a heavy skillet and gently melt 1 tablespoon of the butter. Sauté the clean, dry rice in the butter, stirring it about with a wooden spatula, until it whitens.

2. Add the onion. Chop the chicken liver and add it. Sauté for only 3 minutes.
3. Add the wine, saffron, tarragon, sage, and white pepper. Cook together for 3 minutes, stirring thoroughly. Remove from the fire.
4. In a large mixing bowl combine the half-cooked rice, liver, and herbs, the bread and milk, the egg, marjoram, parsley, and finely milled salt. Mix well. Set aside.

Prepare the chicken:
1. Rinse the chicken inside and out in cold running water. Dry inside and out with paper towels.
2. Paint the chicken inside and out with 1 tablespoon of the lemon juice, and salt the interior of the chicken with a little of the coarse salt.
3. Using a wooden spoon, stuff the chicken loosely, leaving some room for the rice to expand.
4. Close the opening by running 3 or 4 skewers or stout, round toothpicks through the skin on each side of the opening and lacing the opening closed with cotton string. Leave a little opening for the steam to escape.
5. Truss the chicken firmly as explained on page 260. Preheat the oven to 400°.

Prepare the coating:
1. Mix the rest of the butter, the rest of the coarse salt, and the nutmeg. Rub the trussed bird all over with this mixture.
2. Place the chicken on its side in a rack on a roasting pan. Using half the remaining mixture, coat the exposed side of the chicken. The layer must be rather thick. Reserve the other half for later.
3. Add the water to the bottom of the roasting pan.

Roast and serve the chicken:
1. Bake the chicken for 40 minutes, basting it from time to time with its own juices.
2. Turn the chicken carefully and coat the other side with the butter mixture. Reduce the heat to 350° and bake the chicken for another 30 minutes, basting it occasionally. If the chicken hasn't browned properly, broil it for 3 minutes before removing it from the oven.
3. Remove the chicken from the oven and allow it to cool 5 minutes.

4. Strain the juices, mix them with the remaining 1 tablespoon lemon juice, and pour into a sauceboat.
5. Remove the skewers and trussing strings from the chicken. You may carve the chicken before or after taking it to the table. Each person should receive a generous serving of the stuffing with the chicken. Pass the sauceboat.

NOTE: You won't need to serve another vegetable with the chicken and stuffing, but Grilled Zucchini (page 96) is a good addition to each serving. I have sometimes baked the chicken without stuffing it. It cooks 10 minutes more quickly. Without stuffing, you will need to serve a vegetable or risotto with the chicken.

Sautéed Chicken Livers
LES FOIES DE VOLAILLE SAUTES
SERVES 4

If you like chicken livers, this recipe is bound to become a trusty standby. It is light and delicious as a main course, and I have often made an impromptu meal with it. The investment of half an hour, which is all it requires, gives rich, luscious returns.

12 fresh chicken livers, cleaned and patted dry, bits of fat, ligaments, and gall marks removed
1 jigger brandy (whiskey may be substituted)
¼ teaspoon freshly cracked black pepper
3 thick rashers very streaky breakfast bacon, rind removed and discarded

4 plump shallots, peeled, hard bits cut out, sliced paper-thin
15 fresh rosemary leaves
¼ teaspoon freshly grated nutmeg
½ teaspoon coarse salt
½ cup dry white wine
2 teaspoons freshly squeezed lemon juice
1 tablespoon finely chopped flat-leaf parsley

1. Rinse the livers and pat them dry with paper towels. Put them to marinate in a noncorrosive bowl with the brandy and pepper.

2. Cut the bacon into ¼-inch lardoons (matchstick-like strips).
3. Heat a heavy skillet and gently sauté the lardoons until they begin to take on color along the edges. Remove them and set them aside.
4. Add the shallots to the hot fat and gently sauté them until they are completely wilted.
5. Drain the livers but save the marinade. Sauté the livers, stirring them about lightly with a wooden spatula, for exactly 5 minutes.
6. Add the rosemary, nutmeg, salt, and wine and increase the heat. Deglaze the bottom of the frying pan quickly. This should take only 3 minutes. Do not overcook the livers. Add the marinade and the lemon juice and stir for 1 minute at high heat.
7. Remove the livers and their sauce immediately to a warm serving dish and serve while still hot, sprinkled with chopped parsley.

N O T E : These sautéed chicken livers can be served on a bed of buttered rice or spaghettini. For simple elegance, serve the livers on individual canapés of toast spread with a thin layer of good, tinned Strasbourg goose liver spread. For wine I suggest a simple Merlot.

Country-Cured Turkey Wings and Legs
LE CONFIT DE DINDE
MAKES 2 OR 3 CROCKS

Confit *is one of those typical French concoctions that account for the unique taste and aroma that distinguish French country cooking from any other. French households generally do not make* confit *or preserved fowl. They buy it when they need it for cassoulet or some other regional dish. Goose and duck, as well as other meats, are country-cured in this fashion in great quantities and sold throughout France. Those products are very expensive in the United States. Goose is difficult to come by, and duck is so expensive that I do not try to make my own* confit *of either one here. But turkey wings and legs are cheap and in very good supply in the United States. I make* confit *of them once or twice a year, and that gives me a good supply of country-cured fowl for my cassoulets. Turkey wings and legs are usually pretty tough and intractable, but country-curing transforms them into something wonderful—pink, tender, and juicy. Making* confit *takes about a day and a half, but the reward is a year's supply!*

3 turkey wings, dismembered
3 turkey legs
3 tablespoons coarse salt
½ teaspoon saltpeter (ask your pharmacist for it under the name niter or potassium nitrate; it is essential to this recipe)

1 tablespoon fresh, finely milled black pepper
2 bay leaves, broken into small pieces
3 pounds pork lard
3 plump cloves garlic, peeled
2 branches dried thyme
1 branch rosemary
½ jigger brandy
Coarse salt

Cure the turkey parts:

1. In a deep kettle bring 4 quarts of water to a rolling boil. Plunge the turkey parts into the boiling water. When the water begins to boil again, remove them. Drain them and wipe them dry.
2. Mix the 3 tablespoons salt, saltpeter, and pepper together and rub the mixture well into all the turkey parts. Work quickly while the parts are still warm.
3. Place the parts in a large glass or ceramic dish. Sprinkle the rest of the salt mixture over the pieces and scatter the crumbled bay leaves over them.
4. Cover the dish and refrigerate the turkey parts for 6 to 12 hours, turning the parts about every 2 or 3 hours.

Cook the turkey parts:

1. Rinse the parts under cold running water and dry them well with paper towels.
2. Preheat the oven to 300°.
3. Melt 3 tablespoons of the lard in a large, heavy skillet and lightly brown the parts.
4. Melt the remaining lard in a large, ovenproof kettle. Submerge the turkey pieces, garlic cloves, thyme, and rosemary in the warm fat and place the kettle in the oven.
5. Bake the pieces and the aromatics for 2 hours. Remove the kettle but leave the oven on.

Preserve the turkey parts:

1. Sterilize 3 crocks by washing them well, drying them, and swabbing them with brandy.
2. Ladle a little of the melted lard into the bottoms of the crocks. Care-

fully place the turkey parts in the crocks, discarding the garlic and the herbs.

3. Cover the turkey pieces with lard. They must be completely covered or whatever is exposed will spoil.

4. Place the crocks in the oven and heat them for 20 minutes.

5. Let them cool. When the lard is cold and solid, sprinkle the surface with coarse salt and cover with aluminum foil. Place the crocks in the refrigerator or in a cool place.

N O T E : When you wish to use the *confit*, scrape away the surface salt, put the crock in the oven, and melt the lard. Remove the pieces you want. If any pieces are not used, reseal the crock and put it back in the refrigerator. Brown the turkey pieces well before using them. If any juices accumulate at the bottom of the crock, discard them. Country people in France often sterilize twigs and put them at the bottom of the crocks to keep the pieces of *confit* free of any juices that accumulate.

I doubt if there is anything except a good-sized truffle that will successfully create for you the distinctive taste and aroma of French country cooking as well as this *confit de dinde*. You could certainly be a successful French household cook without ever making or using *confit*, but if you have the time and interest, I suggest that you get on good terms with this uniquely French way of preserving fowl. Thick hunks of pork loin, rabbit, and pheasant can also be preserved in this fashion. The lard is greatly prized for sautéing, frying, and flavoring dishes. *Confit* should be allowed to sit for 2 weeks before using it, though it is delicious to eat when it comes out of the oven. When I am making it, I must watch over it carefully or my ever-hungry nephews make off with pieces just as they emerge from the hot fat; wrapping them in slabs of bread, they devour them at once.

Confit will keep for months. You should look at it every 60 days and carefully remove any mold that may form on the top. Swab the surface with a little brandy.

• • •

Young Rabbit Sautéed with Green Olives

LE LAPIN SAUTE AUX OLIVES VERTES

SERVES 4

One 2-pound rabbit with liver, dressed and cut up into 6 pieces
16 small pitted green olives
1 teaspoon coarse salt
1 teaspoon finely milled pepper
½ cup flour
3 tablespoons vegetable oil
2 plump shallots, peeled and sliced paper-thin
1 plump clove garlic, peeled and thinly sliced

6 medium-sized white mushrooms wiped clean, trimmed, and thinly sliced
¼ teaspoon dried thyme leaves
½ cup dry white wine
½ cup water
One 8-ounce tin light tomato sauce
2 tablespoons cornstarch dissolved in:
    1 cup cold water
1 jigger brandy
2 tablespoons sweet butter

1. Rinse and thoroughly dry the rabbit pieces. Reserve the liver.
2. Put the olives in a sieve and rinse them thoroughly under cold running water. Drain them and set them aside.
3. Mix the salt and pepper and rub the mixture well into the rabbit pieces, then dredge the pieces well with flour, brushing off the excess.
4. Heat the oil at medium heat in a large, heavy skillet and brown the rabbit pieces lightly on all sides. This should take about 20 minutes. Prick the pieces; if the juice is pink, allow them to cook a little longer. Set the rabbit pieces aside to drain.
5. Reduce the heat under the skillet and sauté the shallots and garlic until they have wilted. Chop the liver and stir it in. Add the mushrooms and thyme and stir the mixture until the mushrooms are thoroughly coated with the hot oil.
6. Add the wine, water, and tomato sauce and deglaze the pan. Add the cornstarch and water. Stir in well and simmer for 5 minutes.
7. Add the rabbit pieces, olives, brandy, and butter, stir well, and simmer for 2 minutes. Dish up and serve at once.

NOTE: A very good accompaniment for this rather elegant little rabbit dish is small boiled new potatoes, peeled and sautéed in a little olive oil with a little crushed garlic. Salt and pepper the potatoes and scatter a tablespoon of finely chopped parsley over them. Many people in the United States do not eat rabbit, mainly because they are not familiar with it. French householders grow up eating rabbit, just as I did.

Terrine of Duck Norman Style
LA TERRINE DE CANARD AU CALVADOS

MAKES ONE 2½- TO 3-POUND TERRINE

Terrines were once the rough country version of pâtés. They get their name from the crocks in which they were made and stored. At one time you could be sure that any kind of rural celebration would bring forth half a dozen kinds of these aromatic meat loaves. Today, unless you have the good fortune to know a country inn or a large farm that still makes old-fashioned terrines, you won't get one unless you make it yourself. Here is the recipe for a simple but extraordinary terrine made principally of duck. Prepare it for the holidays or for a special birthday or anniversary. It will be greatly appreciated.

One 4-pound duck or two
2-pound ducklings*
2 or 3 dried morels, pulverized
   or pounded into bits
½ cup Calvados applejack (gin
   may be used in a pinch)
½ pound ground veal
½ pound ground pork or
   unseasoned sausage meat
4 fresh sage leaves, finely
   chopped, or ¼ teaspoon dried
   rubbed sage

1 teaspoon finely chopped
   orange peel, pith carefully
   removed
1 teaspoon coarse salt
1 tablespoon finely milled black
   pepper
2 large egg yolks
1 Golden Delicious apple,
   peeled, cored, and finely
   chopped
2 scallions, white part only,
   finely chopped
1 bay leaf

*If you are using frozen duck it should be allowed to thaw for 24 hours in the refrigerator before you start the terrine.

Prepare the duck:
1. Set the liver aside.
2. In a deep kettle bring 4 or 5 quarts of water to a rolling boil. Plunge

the duck into the boiling water and leave it there until the water returns to a boil. Remove the kettle from the fire and allow the duck to cool in the water.

3. When the duck has cooled enough to handle, but is not cold, discard the water and dry the duck with paper towels. With a pair of heavy kitchen shears, cut through the back of the carcass from top to bottom and start detaching the skin from the flesh. If you can get it all off in one piece, fine, but if you tear it, never mind. Do the best you can. Get it all off. Pat the skin dry with paper towels, Wrap it in paper towels and set it aside.

4. Slice the breast meat in long, neat slices. Set them aside with the skin.

5. Remove all the meat from the carcass, cleaning and scraping the bones well. (Save the carcass and bones for soup. They can be put in freezer bags and frozen for later use.)

6. Place the slices of breast and all the meat you have removed in a glass or enamel dish. Scatter on the dried morels and then pour the Calvados over them. Cover and set aside.

Prepare the other meats:
1. Mix the veal, pork or sausage meat, sage, orange peel, salt, pepper, egg yolks, apple, and scallions thoroughly.
2. Cut the liver into several pieces and set aside.

Assemble the terrine:
1. With a darning needle prick the duck skin all over. Spread it, skin side down, fat side up, over the bottom and up the sides of a terrine or loaf pan. Let the extra skin hang over the sides.

2. Pack half the ground meat mixture into the terrine against the fat side of the skin.

3. Press half the duck meat into the layer of ground meat and arrange the slices of breast and pieces of liver on top. Arrange the other half of the duck meat over the slices of breast and liver.

4. Pack the rest of the ground meat on top and pat it down well into the skin-lined terrine.

5. Place the bay leaf on top, in the center of the meat. Pour the Calvados in which the duck was marinated over the terrine. Lap the duck skin over the ground meat to close it in.

6. Cover the terrine with aluminum foil and press the cover of the terrine down over the foil.

Bake the terrine:
1. Preheat the oven to 325°.
2. Place the terrine in a pan of water and bake it for 1½ to 2 hours.

Finish the terrine:
1. Remove the terrine from the oven and pour off and discard the accumulated hot fat. Discard the bay leaf.
2. Cut a piece of corrugated cardboard the shape of the interior of the terrine. Cover it with aluminum foil. Place the foil-covered cardboard against the surface of the meat in the terrine and put a 2-pound weight or its equivalent on top. Canned goods are fine for this.
3. When the terrine is cold, remove the weights and the cardboard. Put the terrine cover back in place and refrigerate the terrine 24 hours before serving it.

N O T E : This delicious dish can be served in its terrine. I prefer to do the slicing myself. This is a beautifully layered terrine that slices very well when quite cold. Use a thin, sharp knife dipped in hot water. The slices can be served country style, with the skin still attached, or they can be trimmed up elegantly for a neater presentation. The usual accompaniment is a crock of tiny French *cornichons* (gherkins): Although French householders are not fond of sweet relishes, my family and friends love sweet pickles, mustard pickles, pickled cauliflower, cranberry relish, and a sweet-salty relish called Ploughman's Lunch with this rich terrine.

Suzie's Braised Quail
LES CAILLES BRAISEES A LA SUZIE
SERVES 4

This extra-special recipe for quail was given to me thirty years ago by my late friend Suzie Larmignat. Quail is often tough and dry because it spends its life running and has almost no fat on its body. Wrapping the tiny birds in lettuce leaves keeps them from drying out in cooking. It also imparts a bittersweet taste to the birds that seems to offset the gaminess we often encounter in wild fowl.

16 white raisins
1 jigger Calvados applejack
4 large quail, dressed, heads and
   feet removed and discarded
2 tablespoons cider vinegar
½ teaspoon coarse salt
½ teaspoon finely milled black
   pepper
4 tablespoons (½ stick) sweet
   butter
4 large leaves Boston lettuce
1 small onion, peeled and finely
   grated
1 medium-sized carrot, finely
   grated

1 Granny Smith apple, peeled,
   cored, and finely grated
1 teaspoon lemon juice
16 dried juniper berries
4 rashers lean breakfast bacon
1 cup dry white wine
1 teaspoon granulated sugar
3 tablespoons red currant jelly
   (grape jelly is an acceptable
   substitute)
4 slices white bread, crusts
   removed, toasted
1 small tin liver pâté

1. Rinse the raisins in warm water and put them to marinate in the
   Calvados.
2. Brush the quail inside and out with vinegar. Lightly salt and pepper
   the quail inside and out. Set aside the salt and pepper left over.
3. Heat 2 tablespoons of the butter in a frying pan and gently brown
   the quail all over. Remove them and set them aside.
4. Plunge the lettuce leaves into boiling water for 3 minutes. Rinse
   them carefully under cold running water. Spread the leaves on paper
   towels and set them aside for the moment.
5. Sauté the onion, carrot, and apple in the frying pan. Sprinkle them
   with the remaining salt and pepper and the lemon juice. Remove this
   sauté from the frying pan to cool.
6. Stuff each quail with 4 juniper berries, 4 raisins, and as much of the
   sauté as the cavity will accommodate. Wrap each quail in a lettuce
   leaf, folding the edges in neatly, then encircle each of these little
   packets with a rasher of bacon and secure each with cotton thread or
   string.
7. Melt the remaining 2 tablespoons of butter in the frying pan over
   medium heat and sauté the trussed birds again so that the bacon is
   browned, and remove them from the pan.
8. Deglaze the pan with the white wine, the Calvados used to marinate
   the raisins, and the sugar. Return the birds to the pan, roll them in
   the sauce, cover the pan, and simmer the birds for 30 minutes at the
   lowest heat.
9. Uncover the pan and increase the heat. Stir in the jelly and allow the

sauce to reduce to half its volume, basting the birds as the sauce thickens.

10. Spread the toasts with a thick layer of pâté. Place each on a plate. Remove and discard the trussing strings and bacon from the birds. Place a bird on each canapé, spoon a little sauce over each, and serve.

N O T E : These little birds are good to serve as a first course on a very special occasion. Garnish each plate with a small bunch of white seedless grapes and a few crisp leaves of arugula. Serve a well-chilled Sylvaner with them or, better still, a very cold demi-sec champagne.

CHAPTER TEN

Variety Meats

Les Abats

The French householder uses many variety meats such as liver, kidney, brains, sweetbreads, heart, and tripe regularly in planning the weekly menus. Organ or variety meats are usually cheaper than many prime cuts. They are also rich in nutrients, especially minerals. That combination of virtues is very appealing to the thrifty French householder.

We have to marvel at the ingenious ways in which the French prepare these foods. They have created some delicious and delightful dishes from variety meats. In the United States, ordinary households are unlikely to undertake the preparation of such meats, apart from veal liver, for their families. Although we had sweetbreads from time to time at home when I was a child in Texas, my mother was much more successful with preparing liver and making us relish it. Brains appeared only once or twice a year on our table. They were invariably scrambled with eggs and were considered a great Texas treat. My mother simply did not know how to prepare them any other way. I have the impression that this is the case with many other American cooks. Almost without fail, when I am buying veal brains in the supermarket, other shoppers will ask me how I prepare them and whether they are really worth the trouble, as if I could answer those questions in a word or two. Well, here is the standard way French householders prepare veal brains. And yes! I think they are definitely worth the trouble.

HOW TO PREPARE CALF'S BRAINS

1. Choose only brains that are very fresh, that look whole, compact, and symmetrical. If they are ruptured, they are hard to prepare and difficult to present in an attractive manner. Rinse them carefully under cold running water, but do not use too strong a flow or they will disintegrate. Snip away any untidy bits with sharp kitchen shears. Put the washed brains to soak for an hour in a glass or enamel vessel in

tepid water to which you have added a squeeze of fresh lemon juice. Change the water as it becomes cloudy, adding a little more lemon juice.

2. Drain the brains and pat them dry with paper towels. With your fingers, carefully pull away the network of tiny interlocking veins and threadlike membranes that the water has caused to swell slightly. Rinse and dry the brains.

3. Put the brains to poach in a nonreactive pan—enamel, stainless steel, or Pyrex—containing enough water to cover them to which you have added 1 tablespoon freshly squeezed lemon juice, a bay leaf, and a pinch of rubbed sage. Poach the brains gently for 30 minutes.

4. Allow the brains to cool in the poaching water.

5. When the water has cooled, add 4 or 5 ice cubes so that the brains will chill and firm up.

6. Drain the brains, give them a gentle squeeze to compact them, and pat them dry with paper towels. They are now ready to be used in whatever recipe you choose. If you are not planning to use them at once, put them in a glass or enamel dish, cover them well, and put them in a cold place. You should use them within a few hours.

N O T E : Lamb's brains, when they are available, should be prepared in exactly the same fashion.

Breaded Calf's Brains Burgundy Style

LES CERVELLES PANEES
A LA BOURGUIGNONNE

SERVES 4 OR 5

4 veal brains, cleaned and
   poached as described above
½ teaspoon coarse salt
1 large lemon
½ cup flour
1 large egg
1 teaspoon cold water
½ cup fine dry breadcrumbs

4 tablespoons (½ stick) sweet
   butter
1 tablespoon vegetable oil
1 cup *Sauce bourguignonne*
   (page 277)
3 tablespoons finely chopped
   flat-leaf parsley

1. With a very sharp, small-bladed knife, slice the poached brains into ¼-inch-thick medallions. Sprinkle the medallions with salt and lemon juice.
2. Arrange 3 soup plates in order: the first containing flour, the second containing the egg beaten with the water, and the third containing the breadcrumbs.
3. One by one, dredge the medallions in flour. Make sure that the flour covers every bit of the surface; the breading will fail in those places where there is none.
4. Dip each floured medallion in the egg mixture. Once again, make certain that the medallions are completely covered.
5. Roll each medallion in crumbs. Again, see that the pieces are entirely covered. Pat the breading gently where necessary to see that it adheres. Let the breaded medallions sit for 5 minutes until the breading sets.
6. Heat the butter and oil in a heavy skillet and gently fry the medallions until golden brown, about 3 minutes for each side. Place the medallions on paper towels to drain, but keep them warm.
7. Heat a serving platter and cover the bottom with warmed *Sauce bourguignonne.* Arrange the crisp medallions in the sauce and sprinkle generously with chopped parsley.

N O T E : You will need something crunchy to offset the creamy consistency of the brains. I suggest the Crispy Fried Potatoes on page 103.

Red Wine Sauce

LA SAUCE BOURGUIGNONNE

MAKES ABOUT 1 CUP

Sauce bourguignonne or Burgundian Sauce is one of the sauces used by householders all over France and wherever French cooking is done throughout the world, so it is important to learn how to make it. Often referred to simply as red wine sauce, it is wonderfully adaptable and can be slightly changed to accompany eggs, fish, or meat. It is a robust sauce that can provide the proper balance for strong-tasting fish or variety meats such as liver, kidney, or heart. With the addition of a little vinegar, it can also give just the right fillip to a bland or delicate-tasting dish such as veal brains. If you plan to use it with eggs, it is advisable to substitute shallots for the onion. If you want the sauce to accompany fish, it is good to substitute a nicely reduced fish broth or fumet *for the beef or chicken broth. In any case, after trying it a few times you will discover just how you, your family, and your guests prefer it. All good cooks should learn to use this sauce as an artist uses a principal color to define his or her personal style. After all, that is the principle behind all great "mother sauces" in French cooking.*

3 tablespoons sweet butter
1 thick slice streaky salt bacon (about 2 ounces), poached, rinsed, dried, and cut into ¼-inch dice
1 medium-sized onion, peeled and finely chopped
2 plump cloves garlic, pierced but unpeeled
3 small mushrooms finely chopped (you may even use the stems and peelings)
3 tablespoons finely chopped flat-leaf parsley

2 tablespoons finely chopped carrot
1 bay leaf
1 sprig thyme
2½ cups good red table wine (Beaujolais, Morgon, a California Cabernet Sauvignon, or mountain red)
1 cup unsalted beef or chicken broth
3 tablespoons sweet butter mixed well with
  3 tablespoons flour

1. In a heavy saucepan melt 2 tablespoons of the butter and fry the bacon until it begins to take on color.
2. Add the onion, garlic, mushrooms, parsley, carrot, bay leaf, and thyme and stir them about until the vegetables have wilted and softened.
3. Add the wine and boil at moderate heat until it has reduced to ⅓ its volume.
4. Add the broth and reduce the heat to a simmer. Cook for another 5 minutes.
5. Strain the sauce. Discard everything but the liquid. Rinse the pan and return the liquid to it.
6. Heat the sauce again to a simmer. Make tiny balls of the butter and flour you have mixed. The mixture is called *beurre manié* and is a standard thickener for sauces.
7. Pitch the little balls one at a time into the simmering sauce. Be sure

to stir the sauce very well with each addition, making certain that the little ball has become completely incorporated into the sauce. Add another and another until the sauce has achieved the desired consistency: It should coat the spoon and a finger drawn across it should leave a clean trail that the sauce does not erase immediately. You may not need all of the *beurre manié.* That is the reason it is not all added at once.

8. Turn off the heat and swirl in the last tablespoon of sweet butter. This enriches the sauce and also prevents a skin from forming on the surface while the sauce is waiting to be used. Cover the sauce and keep it warm by putting the pan in hot but not boiling water. (If you are making the sauce to use sometime later, put it in a closed jar or vessel and do not add the final tablespoon of butter until you reheat it for use.)

N O T E : This recipe calls for no salt. Adjust the salt yourself at the last minute. The salt concentrates in reductions, and oversalting cannot really be remedied, so put it off until the last steps of the preparation.

Calf's Brains Thounine
LES CERVELLES EN SALADE
SERVES 4 OR 5

Here is a surprising summer salad in which the veal brains are poached in red wine as if for a Burgundian matelote, *then marinated. They undergo a kind of "sea change" into something rare and strange and very delicious. Serve the salad as an opener or as a main course. I prefer it to many of the seafood salads that are often concocted of toughened squid. I am certain that once you've tried it, it will become a favorite.*

To poach the brains, follow the instructions on page 275 with this important change: Substitute good dry red wine for half the poaching water and add a medium-sized onion, peeled and spiked with 2 cloves. The wine will stain the surface of the brains and give them a slightly different taste.

2 poached veal brains (see above)

6 tablespoons wine vinegar in which has been dissolved ½ teaspoon sugar

1 tablespoon Dijon mustard

½ clove garlic, peeled and crushed into a paste with 1 teaspoon coarse salt

3 scallions, root and green parts removed, finely chopped

½ teaspoon dried leaf thyme

3 tablespoons capers, coarsely chopped

1 tablespoon oil-packed tuna, pounded to a paste

2 flat fillets of anchovy, chopped

6 tablespoons light olive oil

1 firm, medium-sized tomato, unpeeled, seeded, cubed, lightly salted, and drained

3 tablespoons finely chopped flat-leaf parsley

2 hard-boiled eggs, finely chopped

½ finely chopped fennel bulb

3 fresh radishes, trimmed and cut in thin roundels

½ cup thinly sliced celery

Lettuce leaves

Cracked green olives, pitted

½ cup tiny crisp croûtons

1. When the brains are well drained and cold, cut them into ½-inch dice.
2. Combine the sugared vinegar, mustard, garlic paste, scallions, thyme, capers, tuna paste, anchovies, and olive oil. Put the diced brains in a nonreactive vessel and cover them with the marinade. Cover the vessel tightly and refrigerate for at least 1 hour.
3. Just before serving, lightly toss the tomato, parsley, chopped egg, fennel, radishes, and celery with the brains and the marinade.
4. Pile the salad on a nest of lettuce leaves. Sprinkle with the bits of cracked green olives, scatter the croûtons on top, and serve at once.

N O T E : The *thounine* of the title of this recipe is the word used along the southern coast of France for the small variety of tuna caught in the Mediterranean. *Thounine* is greatly prized and eaten in many dishes, the most famous of which is cold, tuna-flavored veal, an exquisite creation.

• • •

Kidneys

LES ROGNONS

American household cooks often ask me how to rid kidneys of their unpleasant odor and strong taste. They usually have eaten them in a good restaurant and liked them, but when they have tried to make them at home for themselves they found them too strong to enjoy. French household cooks use two knacks to purge kidneys of their strong taste and odor:

- Remove and discard any fat and the thin skin that surrounds the kidneys and let the kidneys leach for 2 hours in strongly salted water. Rinse them well and dry them with paper towels. This process tames even pork kidneys, by far the strongest tasting of all the kidneys sold in butcher shops. After drying the kidneys, continue with the recipe you have chosen.
- If you are preparing a fricassee of veal or lamb kidneys, remove and discard any fat adhering to the kidneys and the outside skin. Slice the kidneys top to bottom in 4 or 5 pieces and sauté the slices in hot lard or oil until they are evenly browned. Remove them and drain them on paper towels, discard the lard or oil, and give the frying pan a cursory wipe with a paper towel, but leave the browned bits that have stuck to the pan to be deglazed and used in the recipe. Continue with the recipe.

These two techniques will usually produce a sweeter dish and get rid of the strong taste and odor.

HOW TO BROIL LAMB KIDNEYS

Lamb kidneys are usually mild and need no leaching, so they are ideal for broiling. With a very sharp knife, cut them in half, top to bottom. Skewer them together by running the point of the skewer in, under, and out of the central kernel of interior fat in each half so that the two halves lie alongside each other, cut side up, butterfly fashion. Give each half a good sprinkle of coarse salt, freshly ground black pepper, and a few dried thyme leaves. Broil the kidneys 2 minutes on each side under high heat. Don't cook them longer or they will toughen. They should be rather pink inside.

NOTE: For a good patio lunch in summer, try this mixed grill: Broil one sausage, one thick rasher of smoked bacon, and one lamb kidney done in the fashion I have described above, for each guest. A couple of slices of ripe red tomato, a little mound of freshly fried, cubed potatoes, and a hefty slice of lemon are the right accompaniments for the mixed grill. The sausage, bacon, and kidney can all be grilled over charcoal at tableside, if you wish, doing away with any fuss in the kitchen.

Kidneys in Port Wine Sauce
LA FRICASSEE DE ROGNONS AU PORTO
SERVES 4

There are much simpler ways to prepare kidneys, but this old recipe, a tasty fricassee, rids the kidneys of their strong taste and odor and transforms them into a mouth-watering dish.

2 veal kidneys or 4 lamb kidneys
3 tablespoons coarse salt
4 cups cold water
2 tablespoons light olive oil
2 plump shallots, peeled, trimmed, and finely chopped
2 thick rashers smoked bacon, rind discarded, cut in matchstick-size lardoons
1 plump clove garlic, peeled and finely chopped
2 bay leaves
¼ teaspoon dried thyme leaves

⅛ teaspoon freshly grated nutmeg
½ teaspoon freshly cracked black pepper
3 tablespoons vegetable oil
½ cup port wine (or an equal amount of Cognac or dry sherry)
1 cup water
2 tablespoons tomato purée
2 tablespoons flour
3 tablespoons finely chopped flat-leaf parsley

Leach the kidneys:
1. Remove and discard any fat and the thin outer skin from the kidneys.
2. Dissolve the salt in the water and put the kidneys to leach in the salt water for 2 hours.
3. Drain the kidneys and pat them dry. Discard the leaching water.

Prepare the soffritto:

1. Heat the olive oil in a heavy frying pan and gently sauté the shallots and bacon.
2. When they are almost transparent and sizzling, add the garlic, bay leaves, thyme, nutmeg, and pepper. Fry for 1 minute, stirring the ingredients together, and remove from the fire. Discard the bay leaves.

Sauté the kidneys:

1. Slice each kidney, top to bottom, in 4 or 5 pieces, removing and discarding the tough, center portion.
2. In another frying pan, heat the vegetable oil over medium heat. When it hazes, add the kidneys. Sauté the slices for 5 minutes, turning them so they brown on both sides. (Mind the sputtering oil!)
3. Drain the kidneys on paper towels, discard the oil, and give the pan a quick wipe with a paper towel, but don't clean it.

Finish the kidneys:

1. At high heat, deglaze the frying pan in which you sautéed the kidneys with the wine and water, scraping up and dissolving all the browned bits that have adhered to the frying pan.
2. Add the *soffritto* and the tomato purée, stir in well, and reduce the heat to a simmer.
3. Add the kidneys and sprinkle the flour over the surface, stirring it in to remove any lumps. Simmer for 5 minutes or until the liquid is nicely reduced and thickened. Adjust the seasoning for salt.
4. Dish up the fricassee and sprinkle the top with chopped parsley.

NOTE: Serve the fricassee with plain boiled rice (see page 125) and Bell Peppers Catalan Style (page 44), and serve a good, stout red wine such as Châteauneuf du Pape or a Beaujolais.

• • •

Veal Sweetbreads

LES RIS DE VEAU

Sweetbreads are the thymus and pancreas of very young calves and sheep. They are at their best in the youngest of those animals, and the best are from very young calves. To my mind, they are the finest of all variety meats. In this most French householders concur. The thymus and pancreas are often sold together, and you may easily distinguish between the two by their shape. The thymus is thin and elongated, while the pancreas, considered the better of the two, is a roundish lump that can be held in the palm of the hand. Lamb's sweetbreads are often eaten by households in France, but they are not sold in the United States, as a rule. All sweetbreads need special preparation to maximize their taste and texture. After they are leached in cold water, poached, rid of much of their connective tissue, and pressed for an hour or two under a weight, sweetbreads are ready to be prepared in dozens of ways. Without the special preparation, they are tough, spongy, and strong-tasting. Take the time to prepare them well. They warrant it.

HOW TO PREPARE SWEETBREADS

1. Choose sweetbreads that fit in the palm of your hand. They should be shiny and moist and a clear rose ivory color. Never accept them if they are dry or beginning to turn brownish. (You will need 1 per person.) Rinse the sweetbreads in cold running water, pulling loose from them or snipping off and discarding any fat or untidy bits. Put the sweetbreads to soak in a glass or enamel bowl or pan with plenty of cold water, 1 tablespoon coarse salt, and 1 tablespoon lemon juice. Leave them to leach for at least 1 hour.
2. Rinse them well, pull off any of the viscous connective tissue that will come loose, and put them to poach in cold water to which you have added another tablespoon of lemon juice. Let them poach for 20 minutes over low heat.
3. Allow the sweetbreads to cool in the poaching water. You may hasten this slightly by adding ice cubes. When the sweetbreads are completely cool, carefully remove as much of the tough connective tissue as you can with the help of a sharp paring knife. Unlike brains, which are very fragile and must be handled with the greatest care, sweetbreads are tough and can be pulled at without danger of tearing them

badly. It is important to remove as much of the tough connective tissue as possible.

4. Place 2 or 3 thicknesses of paper toweling on a cookie plaque. Place the poached sweetbreads in one layer toward the center. Cover them with more towels and place another cookie plaque on top of them. Place a heavy kettle or some heavy canned goods on top of the cookie plaque and weight the sweetbreads for 2 hours. The weighting is to press out the rosy liquid at the center of the sweetbreads. The whiter the finished product, the better. The pressing also makes them more compact and easier to slice later.

5. The sweetbreads are now ready to prepare in the manner you have chosen. Pat them dry with clean paper towels and proceed.

Fried Sweetbread Medallions with Bacon and Potatoes

LES MEDAILLONS DE RIS DE VEAU GARNIS

SERVES 4

½ teaspoon coarse salt
4 veal sweetbreads, soaked, poached, pressed, and cut in two, lengthwise
½ cup flour
6 tablespoons (¾ stick) sweet butter

3 tablespoons vegetable oil
3 medium-sized potatoes, peeled and cut in ½-inch dice
4 rashers bacon, cut in two (8 pieces)
1 lemon, cut in quarters
Parsley, to garnish

1. Salt the slices of sweetbreads. Dredge them in flour and brush off the excess.
2. Heat the butter and oil in a heavy frying pan and fry the medallions 3 or 4 minutes on each side, until golden. Take care: sometimes the pieces of sweetbreads retain little pockets of water and will occasionally pop, splattering hot fat, so keep your distance. Remove the sweetbreads and drain them on paper towels. Keep them warm.
3. Rinse the potato cubes and dry them very well. Fry them until they are golden. Remove them, drain them, and keep them warm.
4. Repeat the process with the bacon.

5. Serve the sweetbreads, potatoes, and bacon on a hot platter, garnishing each portion with a lemon wedge and a sprig of parsley.

Old-Fashioned Braised Sweetbreads Normandy Style
LES RIS DE VEAU BRAISES AU CALVADOS
SERVES 4

If you have scored a hit with the fried sweetbread medallions, I encourage you to try this old-fashioned Norman way of braising sweetbreads. The recipe calls for a jigger of the celebrated Norman applejack, Calvados. This powerful distillation of apple fragrance is expensive, but you should, as a good cook and host, have a bottle hidden away somewhere for special dishes and special occasions. A thimbleful of Calvados served along with after-dinner coffee is a greatly appreciated conclusion to a fine meal. As the good folks of Normandy will tell you, however, "a little Calvados tastes like more." In fact, in rural Normandy it has long been the custom, famous as le trou normand, *to down a shot of Calvados between each course at a sumptuous feast to make "a hole" for the next. My point is that you must keep your Calvados hidden away or it has a way of disappearing. A drop of Calvados performs miracles in a modest apple tart, a score of Norman dishes, and in this recipe for braised sweetbreads.*

3 tablespoons sweet butter
1 thick slice streaky salt pork, cut into ¼-inch lardoons, poached, rinsed, and patted dry
1 medium-sized onion, peeled and coarsely chopped
2 plump shallots, peeled and sliced paper-thin
½ cup dry white wine
2½ cups unsalted chicken or veal broth
4 sweetbreads, prepared according to instructions on page 284

1 bouquet garni made of 1 branch each parsley, thyme, and celery, and 1 bay leaf
¼ cup pork lard
¼ cup flour
6 medium-sized white mushrooms, wiped, trimmed, and thinly sliced
1 medium-sized green or half-ripe tomato, skinned, seeded, and finely cubed
1 jigger Calvados
½ teaspoon freshly ground white pepper
1 teaspoon coarse salt

1. Preheat the oven to 375°.
2. In a braising pan or heavy pot melt the butter at medium heat and sauté the lardoons until their edges begin to turn golden. Add the onion and shallots and sauté them until they are transparent, stirring them about with a wooden spatula to see that they do not scorch.
3. Increase the heat and add the wine and ½ cup of the broth. Deglaze the bottom quickly with the spatula. Cook at high heat for 5 minutes.
4. Remove from the heat. Add the sweetbreads and the bouquet garni, cover the pan with a piece of aluminum foil and the lid, and put it in the oven to braise for 30 minutes.
5. Make a dark roux: melt the lard in a heavy frying pan and fry the flour at moderate heat, stirring it and scouring the bottom of the pan constantly with a wooden spatula. See that the flour does not fry too quickly or it will scorch and ruin your roux. The trick is to see that the flour fries evenly (and does not burn) until it has become the color of dark chocolate. A word of caution: Frying roux is like molten lava, so be careful not to flick any of it out of the pan. It burns badly, so take it easy. I use my old cast-iron skillet for this, since it is so heavy it won't budge from the burner when I'm making roux. Novices at roux-making may be aghast at the dark color of this distinctive roux, but interestingly enough, the dark pitchlike substance imparts a wonderful hazelnut quality to the sauce and not the slightest scorched taste, if you have done it slowly and carefully. It takes 20 minutes.
6. Add the mushrooms and tomato to the roux and stir it all together briefly. Add the rest of the broth and stir gently until you have produced a smooth, dark sauce.
7. Remove the braising sweetbreads from the oven, break the seal of aluminum foil and remove the sweetbreads. Discard the bouquet garni. Add the braising liquid and its solids to the dark roux and allow the combined sauce to simmer for 10 minutes. If the sauce is thicker than light cream, add a little water to thin it.
8. Add the Calvados to the sauce and stir it in quickly. Light a match and hold it close to the surface of the sauce so that the Calvados will burn off. Stir in the salt and pepper and taste. Add more sauce if necessary. Return the sweetbreads to the pan and gently simmer them for 3 minutes. Serve in a warmed tureen or baking dish.

N O T E : Tiny sautéed potatoes or plain boiled rice are very acceptable companions for this fine dish. Some cooks like to make the sauce a bit more sophisticated by straining out the solids before adding the mushrooms. I disagree. This dish is obviously a rough braise like a *daube*, and it is certainly of rustic origin. I love to find the braised lardoons in the sauce. That is the way I have learned to make it and present it. You will want to adjust the sauce for saltiness. I undersalt by preference, so suit yourself.

Sautéed Calf's Liver Provençal Style
LE FOIE DE VEAU A LA PROVENÇALE
SERVES 4 OR 5

Of all the variety meats, liver is the most popular in the French household. This is a good, quick, simple way to prepare liver. It takes only 15 minutes.

1 teaspoon coarse salt
1 teaspoon freshly ground black
  pepper
1 pound calf's liver cut in four
  or five ¼-inch slices
1 cup milk
3 tablespoons vegetable oil

½ cup flour
1 tablespoon wine vinegar
3 tablespoons finely chopped
  flat-leaf parsley
2 cloves garlic, peeled and finely
  chopped
Lemon wedges

1. Salt and pepper the liver on both sides.
2. Put the liver slices in a glass dish and cover them with the milk. Let the slices soak for 5 minutes.
3. Choose a frying pan, preferably a heavy one, that will accommodate all the slices at once, and heat the oil at medium heat.
4. Drain the liver slices and dredge each slice carefully in flour, brushing off the excess.
5. When the oil hazes, put in the liver. Allow the slices to cook 3 minutes on each side. If you like liver well done, by all means cook it longer. It will toughen slightly, but it will lose none of its nutritive value.
6. Remove the liver to a warm serving platter. Add vinegar to the frying pan and deglaze the bottom quickly with a wooden spatula. If there seems to be too little sauce to pour over the liver, add a couple of tablespoons water. Pour a little of the resulting sauce over each piece

of liver, sprinkle it with chopped parsley and garlic and serve at once, garnished with lemon wedges.

The lemon wedges are a refinement. On farms and in small village inns in Provence this dish is served up with much more chopped, raw garlic, and no lemon wedges. If your guests are garlic-shy, provide them with plenty of fresh parsley sprigs to chew on afterward.

You may make this dish with beef or pork liver, as well as veal liver. Mashed potatoes, made from scratch, of course, and served with a good-sized knob of unsalted butter, are a natural foil for this aggressively delicious dish.

Marguerite's Baked Chicken Liver Mousse

LE GATEAU DE FOIE DE VOLAILLE

SERVES 4 OR 5

Here is another simple but fine liver dish, this one an old Burgundian family recipe made with chicken livers. It is very easy to make and is more delicate than the usual liver pâté and worlds lighter. It is great as a first course with a light Sauce financière *(following), but I like it as a principal dish accompanied by a salad of bitter greens such as arugula or radicchio in a good mustard vinaigrette.*

½ pound fresh chicken livers
1 plump clove garlic, peeled
1 tablespoon finely chopped
   flat-leaf parsley
3 slices white bread, crusts
   removed, soaked in
    1 cup milk

3 large eggs, separated
2 tablespoons heavy cream
½ teaspoon coarse salt
¼ teaspoon freshly ground white
   pepper

1. With a pair of kitchen shears remove the connective tissue, bits of fat, and any bile spots from the livers. Wash the livers in cold water and pat them dry with paper towels.

2. Crush or food-process the livers, garlic, and parsley until they are the consistency of thick cream.

3. Squeeze the milk from the bread, discard the milk, and add the soaked bread to the liver mixture.

4. Beat the egg yolks with the cream until light and lemon-colored and add them along with the salt and pepper to the liver mixture.

5. Beat the egg whites until they peak and fold them carefully and lightly into the liver mixture. Don't stir the mixture, since the air in the beaten egg whites will determine the lightness of the mousse.

6. Butter or oil an 8-inch soufflé dish and ladle the mixture into it carefully. Place the dish in a pan containing 2 inches of water (a *bain-marie*).

7. Preheat the oven to 450° and bake the mousse 25 to 30 minutes.

8. Serve at once with a light tomato sauce such as *Sauce financière*, to which you have added some tiny poached mushrooms and some small bitter green olives.

Light Tomato Sauce

LA SAUCE FINANCIERE

MAKES ABOUT 1½ CUPS

Sauce financière, *literally "sauce for capitalists," suggests something rich and costly. Fifty years ago perhaps it was. At present it is a light, aromatic tomato sauce, neither rich nor costly, usually containing little bitter green olives and tiny Parisian mushrooms. It is a far cry from the oily, vermilion-colored tomato sauce so often associated with cheap pizza and badly prepared Neapolitan spaghetti in the United States. Everyone in France is familiar with this little sauce, but it is rarely given in recipe books. Here is the version I use. I like its lightness, but I also like the fact that the substitution of 2 tablespoons of capers for the olives, and the addition of 2 tablespoons heavy cream just at the end, make it a perfect sauce for poached fish and steamed mussels.*

2 tablespoons sweet butter
1 small onion, peeled and finely
    chopped
2 shallots, peeled and sliced
    paper-thin
1 clove garlic, peeled and
    crushed to a pulp with
    1 teaspoon coarse salt
1 tablespoon finely chopped
    flat-leaf parsley
1 small carrot, scraped and
    finely chopped
1 small white mushroom,
    wiped and finely chopped
¼ teaspoon thyme leaves
1 bay leaf
3 or 4 rosemary leaves
¼ teaspoon ground white
    pepper

2 medium-sized ripe tomatoes,
    skinned, seeded, and
    coarsely chopped
1½ cups broth or water
1 tablespoon soft sweet butter
    mixed with
    ½ tablespoon flour
6 to 10 small white
    mushrooms, wiped,
    trimmed, and coated with
    1 tablespoon lemon juice
1 tablespoon dry sherry
1 dash Angostura bitters
    (optional)
12 small bitter green olives of
    the niçois or Spanish type,
    not the insipid California
    ones

1. In a heavy saucepan, melt the 2 tablespoons butter gently. When it is foaming, add the onion, shallots, garlic paste, parsley, carrot, the single mushroom, thyme, bay leaf, rosemary, and white pepper. With a wooden spatula, stir the mixture about from time to time, allowing it to soften and sauté but not brown.
2. Add the tomatoes and stir the mixture so that their juice evaporates and the tomatoes are absorbed by the other vegetables.
3. Add the broth or water and increase the heat slightly. Allow the mixture to simmer for 10 minutes.
4. After 10 minutes, add, a tiny bit at a time, the butter and flour mixture, allowing the sauce to absorb each bit before adding another. You will need to help this by stirring the sauce well with a wooden spoon or spatula. The sauce should thicken to the consistency of light cream.
5. Pass the sauce through a fine sieve. Discard the residue.
6. Rinse out the saucepan, return the sauce to it, and reheat it to a simmer. Add the mushrooms and allow them to simmer for 3 minutes.
7. Add the sherry, bitters, and olives and cook for 1 minute only. The sauce is ready to serve.

This light, delicious sauce has dozens of uses. Although the day of the *vol-au-vent*, a puff pastry nest of ham, poached sweetbreads, and poached brains in just this sauce, seems to have passed, it was a wonderful first course thirty years ago, and I see no reason why it could not be revived with success. It would certainly be a relief from too many quiches! Inquire about these patty shells. Your bakery may be able to supply you with them. I have sometimes seen them in amongst the frozen foods in supermarkets. Follow the instructions I have given for preparing sweetbreads and calf's brains. Purchase ½ pound of cooked ham or use leftover ham if you have it. Cut up the poached sweetbreads, brains, and ham into bite-sized pieces, allow them to simmer for only a few minutes in the sauce with the mushrooms and olives, and serve them in the warm pastry cases. The dish often appeared on menus as *bouchées à la reine*, or the queen's tidbit, and it was a royal treat.

Desserts

Les Desserts

The French have invented desserts that are universally admired for their fantasy, their ingenious composition, their lightness, and their beauty. Many of these exquisite desserts require professional expertise and special, sometimes costly, equipment that most French household cooks do not possess. Nor would a French home cook consider competing with the local pastry shop, where many of these special desserts are offered for sale. Instead he or she wisely chooses to make desserts that are simpler and usually cannot be bought anywhere. Every household has its favorites, and every French household cook has mastered a few special homemade desserts that you will only be able to taste if you are lucky enough to be invited for a meal that includes them. I have chosen to present here only a few of the many homemade desserts that I have come to know in France. I have also included the recipes for a couple of cakes passed on to me by old French friends who, alas, left this world a long time ago. I believe that I may be the only person who possesses the recipes for those cakes, and they deserve to be better known, so I pass them on to you.

Norman Apple Tart
LA TARTE AUX POMMES A LA NORMANDE
SERVES 6 TO 8

1¼ cups sifted pastry flour
¾ cup sifted all-purpose flour
½ teaspoon coarse salt
8 tablespoons (1 stick) sweet
   butter at room temperature
1 large egg
3 tablespoons cold water
3 pounds Granny Smith apples,
   peeled, cored (save the
   peelings and cores),
   quartered, and coated with
   3 tablespoons fresh lemon
   juice

½ cup granulated sugar
One 2-inch piece cinnamon bark
1 teaspoon finely grated lemon
   peel
¾ cup dry white wine
½ cup water
½ jigger Calvados applejack

Make the pastry:

1. Mix the flours and salt and heap them in a mound on a hard, clean working surface.
2. Make a crater in the mound and put half the butter (4 tablespoons), the egg, and the 3 tablespoons water in it.
3. Using the ends of your fingers, work all the ingredients into a ball. Work quickly with plenty of additional flour ready to sift over the dough to keep it from sticking to your hands, and do not knead the dough.
4. Wrap the ball tightly in wax paper and refrigerate it for several hours so that the gluten will relax.

Make the filling:

1. Melt the remaining 4 tablespoons butter gently in a large, heavy-bottomed pan and add half the apples, half the sugar, the cinnamon bark, lemon peel, and wine.
2. Cook these ingredients over medium heat until the apples are completely tender, stirring them from time to time to prevent their sticking.
3. Discard the cinnamon bark and purée the apples.
4. Allow the purée to cool.

Assemble the tart:

1. Roll out the dough and line a well-buttered 11-inch tart tin with it, pricking the surface of the dough all over with a fork.
2. Preheat the oven to 400°.
3. Spread the purée evenly over the bottom of the uncooked crust. Slice the remaining apples in very thin pieces and arrange them on top of the purée so each overlaps the next and they form concentric circles.
4. Bake the tart for 35 to 40 minutes, taking care not to let the crust burn. Traditionally the apples should be just slightly burnt at the edges in order to give the tart its distinct taste. If they seem to be browning too quickly, cut a piece of foil to cover the surface.

Finish the tart:

1. Boil the apple peelings, seeds, and cores with the remaining ¼ cup sugar and the ½ cup water until the liquid forms a syrup that will set like a jelly. Strain this syrup into a cup and discard all the rest.
2. When the tart has finished baking, place it on a rack to cool and while it is still hot, sprinkle it with Calvados.
3. When the tart is cool, coat the surface with the syrup from the parings. Serve the tart cold or warm (it is traditionally eaten warm) and pass a pitcher of thick cream. The country people of Normandy eat their tart with cream poured over it.

Caramelized Apple Tart
LA TARTE TATIN
SERVES 6 TO 8

This upside-down wonder is everybody's favorite in France. There are many legends surrounding its origin. The best known recounts how two maiden ladies in the Sologne area of central France were left almost destitute by the death of their father and learned to support themselves by making these pies at home and selling them to the local townspeople. It is such an easy dessert to prepare that the fabulous result is never quite explained, so a little of the mysterious surrounds it. Everyone who makes it follows pretty much the same simple recipe, but the result depends entirely upon the degree to which you like the apples to be caramelized. To my taste, most cooks do not allow the apples to caramelize long enough, for fear they will burn. I remember making it once when I allowed the apples to cook so long and so slowly that they became dark like prunes, yet there wasn't the slightest scorched taste about the pie. I don't hold any brief for cooking the apples that much, nor have I ever been served the pie in France with the apples cooked to that extent, but they should be what the French call confies, *that is, completely caramelized, yet holding their shape and very glossy, not simply dark, dull lumps, as they are so often in slapdash versions of this fabulous pie.*

1½ cups all-purpose flour	½ teaspoon coarse salt
½ cup cornstarch	3 tablespoons cold water
2 sticks sweet butter	1½ cups granulated sugar
3 tablespoons cold lard or shortening	6 Granny Smith apples, peeled, cored, and quartered

Make the pastry:

1. Mix the flour and cornstarch together and sift them into a mound on a hard, clean working surface.
2. Cut ½ stick (4 tablespoons) of the butter into ¼-inch cubes. Make a little crater in the mound and place the cubed butter, lard, and salt inside it.
3. Working quickly with 2 forks, combine the ingredients until they resemble meal.
4. Add the water and work the ingredients into a ball. If the dough doesn't combine well, add a little more water. If it seems too sticky, add a little more flour, but do not knead the dough, and handle it as little as possible.
5. Wrap the dough securely in wax paper and put it in the freezer compartment for 15 minutes. Then remove it to the lower part of the refrigerator until you are ready to use it.

Make the filling:

1. Choose a large, heavy, straight-sided frying pan with an ovenproof handle. It should be 10 inches across. I use my old, black, cast-iron skillet and it is perfect.
2. Cut the remaining 1½ sticks butter into pat-size pieces. Place them carefully all over the bottom and some along the sides of the pan. They should cover the bottom like a mosaic.
3. Sprinkle half the sugar over the bottom.
4. Arrange the quartered apples, rounded side down, all over the bot-

tom, wedging them in loosely, filling in the empty spaces as well as you can. Sprinkle them with the rest of the sugar.

5. Place the frying pan on a burner on top of the stove and allow the ingredients to melt and cook at rather low heat until the syrup that is formed begins to turn dark amber. This will take considerable time and you may do other chores in the meantime. However, when the syrup begins to turn dark, watch the apples and syrup carefully and remove the pan from the fire if the mixture seems to be on the point of scorching, and stop the cooking by setting the pan in cold water. With a long-tined fork carefully lift up some of the apples from the bottom to see if they are done to your liking, then put them back in place. When the bottom is pretty uniformly caramelized, the pie is ready for the next step.

Finish the tart:

1. Preheat the oven to 375°.
2. Roll out the pastry in a 12-inch circle. Place this circle over the apples in the frying pan and, using the handle of a wooden spoon, tuck the overlapping dough down into the pan along the sides all around. Make a tidy job of enclosing the apples with this dough covering.
3. With a skewer or toothpick pierce the dough in many places so the steam can escape later.
4. Put the frying pan in the center of the oven and bake the tart for about 20 minutes or until the crust is nicely golden. Remove the tart from the oven and place it on one of the burners on top of the stove to cool.
5. When the tart is still quite warm, invert a serving dish over the frying pan and quickly turn the frying pan over, allowing the tart to come out of the frying pan onto the dish. If some of the apples stay in the frying pan, simply remove them with 2 spoons and place them where they belong.

Serve the tart:

1. Serve the pie warm or cold, cutting it with a very sharp knife dipped in water.
2. Pass a pitcher of cream for those who would like to pour some over their pie.

NOTE: Because of the amount of butter in the filling, the tart will usually unmold quite easily, but take care. Hot caramelized sugar can make a nasty burn, so use oven mitts when you unmold it.

I can guarantee you that this will be an instant favorite. The directions look terribly complicated, but when you have made the tart a few times you will see how simple and logical they are. I must confess that I have sometimes made this with one of the instant crusts that are sold in supermarkets. I brushed the crust with melted butter before unmolding the pie. Not one of my French friends could tell that I hadn't made the crust from scratch.

Celebration Cake
LE GATEAU DE FETE

SERVES 24

Some of the pleasantest memories of my student days in France are of those rare occasions when my late landlady, Hannah Mathieu, would announce a fête and make this exquisite cake. It was always crisp and cake-like on the outside and like a delicate flan inside. She explained to me many times how she made this "fairy cake," yet, like many of the older household cooks I knew in France, never dealt with exact measures. Here is my version of the famous cake. I doubt if anyone still living has the secret formula for Madame Mathieu's wonderful cake except me. Now you have it. Make it and bless her for it as I do!

12 tablespoons (1½ sticks) sweet
    butter, at room temperature
1 cup confectioner's sugar
One 13-ounce tin sweetened
    chestnut purée (found in
    many gourmet food shops)
½ cup ground walnuts
5 eggs, separated
½ jigger dark rum
½ cup strong coffee
1 teaspoon vanilla extract
½ teaspoon freshly grated
    nutmeg

½ cup all-purpose flour mixed
    with
    2 tablespoons cornstarch
2 drops lemon juice
½ teaspoon cream of tartar
1 cup fine granulated sugar
1 teaspoon sweet butter (for the
    cake pans)
½ cup fine breadcrumbs
1 pint heavy cream
A few drops each of vanilla, rum,
    and orange extract
Grated chocolate or grated
    nutmeg, for garnish

1. Cream the butter with the confectioner's sugar until fluffy. Mix in the chestnut purée and the ground nuts.

2. Beat the egg yolks until smooth and lemon-colored. Beat them into the nut mixture. Add the rum, coffee, 1 teaspoon vanilla, and nutmeg and mix thoroughly.

3. Sift the flour and cornstarch over the batter, a little at a time, mixing well with each addition.

4. Beat the egg whites with the lemon juice and cream of tartar until they peak. Beat in ½ cup of fine granulated sugar gradually, making a glossy meringue, and carefully fold this meringue into the nut batter. Do not beat the batter after folding in the meringue or the cake will lose its only leavening.

5. Preheat the oven to 350° and position the baking rack on the middle level.

6. Butter two 9-inch springform pans and coat the butter well with breadcrumbs, tapping out the excess. Divide the batter between the pans. Do not tap the pans thereafter.

7. Place the pans in the oven well away from the sides and bake for 1 hour, or until a skewer inserted in the cakes comes out dry.

8. Remove the cakes from the oven and place them, still in their pans, on a cooling rack. After a few minutes run a thin, sharp knife around the edges of the cakes to see that they are completely free from the sides of the tins, and lift off the sides, leaving the cakes to cool on the metal bottoms. The cakes will shrink a little in cooling and they may even craze across the surface. Don't be upset. This is quite natural in such torte cakes.

9. When the cakes are almost cool, run a slicing knife between the cakes and the pan bottoms and remove the bottoms. Allow the cakes to cool completely before handling them. As they cool the cakes will shrink in such a way that they will form a little rim around the top. This is entirely right.

10. Whip the cream in a very cold metal bowl set over ice. When the cream peaks, whip in the other ½ cup fine granulated sugar a little at a time, add the extracts, and whip a little more.

11. Place the cakes on their plates with fancy paper doilies under each cake and sift a little confectioner's sugar over each. Spoon the whipped cream onto the tops of the cakes, piling it high within the rims. Sprinkle with a little grated chocolate or nutmeg. Serve in modest slices. It is very, very rich!

N O T E : This sumptuous cake is best when made in two small, 9-inch springforms rather than one larger one. If you feel that two are too many for your fête, decorate only one of them and freeze the other for another occasion. In that case, make only half the amount of whipped cream. This staggeringly good cake causes cake lovers to groan with delight, but it is better to serve the cake in modest slices and have them ask for seconds than to serve them large portions and find that they are satiated before finishing it. This cake should be served with first-rate, black, unsweetened coffee.

If you have a food processor, which Madame Mathieu did not, you can shorten the work involved considerably. I have made the cake performing Steps 1 through 3 in the processor in about 5 minutes.

Pauline's Mocha-Rum Torte
LE GATEAU HONGROIS
SERVES 12 TO 16

Pauline was an ancient domestic in an Aixois household where I was often invited to dinner when I was a student. She made this wonderful cake about once a year. She called it her "Hungarian cake," though she hailed from Perpignan and, I suspect, had never known a real Hungarian in her life. However, in all fairness to Pauline, the late, great actress, Lili Darvis, who was certainly Hungarian, used to make a fantastic torte that, in taste but not texture was very much like Pauline's Gâteau hongrois. Here is my version of Pauline's French-Hungarian wonder.

1½ sticks sweet butter cut up
    into pat-sized pieces
½ cup fine breadcrumbs
6 eggs, separated
2 tablespoons instant coffee
    granules
1 teaspoon vanilla extract
1 teaspoon rum extract
1 teaspoon lemon extract
1 teaspoon orange extract
2 cups granulated sugar

1½ cups coarsely ground nuts
    (walnuts, pecans, or toasted
    and hulled hazelnuts, or
    some of each)
½ cup ground blanched almonds
    (blanched almond flour is
    sold in tins by Williams &
    Sonoma)
2 cups cold water
1½ cups all-purpose flour mixed
    with
      ½ cup cornstarch
2 drops lemon juice

1. Preheat the oven to 350°.
2. Take a piece of the butter and generously butter a 10-inch springform

cake pan. Dust the butter with breadcrumbs. Tap out and discard the excess crumbs.

3. Cream the rest of the butter.

4. Beat the egg yolks until they are light and lemon-colored and whip them together with the butter into a fluffy mass.

5. Beat in the coffee granules, the extracts, and the sugar.

6 Mix in the ground nuts, a little at a time. Add the water and the flour and cornstarch mixture a bit at a time.

7. Beat the egg whites with the lemon juice until they hold a peak and gently fold them into the batter, folding from top to bottom. The batter is quite thick, so take your time, and don't beat the batter once the egg whites are folded in.

8. Ladle the batter into the pan and bake the cake in the middle of the oven for 70 minutes, or until a skewer inserted into the cake comes out clean. Remove the cake from the oven and allow it to cool on a rack in its pan.

9. When the cake is completely cool, remove it from the pan and sift confectioner's sugar lightly over the craggy top.

N O T E : This torte, which looks like a relief map of the Alps, is a surprising combination of tastes. When I serve it, someone always asks for the recipe. Serve it in ½-inch slices. It can be dressed up with a dollop of sweetened whipped cream, but Pauline used to serve it with a mixture of *Crème fraîche* (following) and applesauce, which she whipped up to a light froth.

Beware: This torte is almost addictive! It used to be a real chore to make, but with a food processor you can do steps 3, 4, and 5 in 5 minutes, which makes the torte dangerously accessible.

• • •

French Sour Cream
LA CREME FRAICHE

MAKES ENOUGH FOR 4 OR 5

There is no real equivalent for crème fraîche *in United States cooking. I have called it French sour cream because it is used in somewhat the same manner that we use sour cream, which has become a common item in our supermarkets. La* crème fraîche *is both heavier in fat content and lighter in texture than our commercial sour cream. It can sometimes be bought in large cities in the States, but it is often impossible to find because it must be made with unpasteurized milk. Pasteurization kills not only dangerous bacteria in milk, it also kills the bacteria that give many cheeses their special taste. This is the case with* crème fraîche. *You can, however, make a very good approximation at home with pasteurized milk. Here is the recipe I use when I cannot find a supplier.*

1 **pint whipping cream**	½ **pint cultured buttermilk**

1. Bring both the whipping cream and the buttermilk to room temperature by letting them sit for about an hour outside the refrigerator.
2. Mix the cream and buttermilk together in a glass bowl.
3. Cover the bowl loosely with a cloth and leave at room temperature for 8 to 10 hours. If the culture in the buttermilk is still alive and active, the cream will have thickened and taken on a light, slightly sour taste.
4. Cover tightly and refrigerate until ready to use.

N O T E : *Crème fraîche* will keep and continue to mature in the refrigerator for about 10 days, after which it begins to grow strong and cheesy. It will take on any odor or taste that it is exposed to, so keep it tightly closed. The joy of *crème fraîche* is its light, delicate taste, which makes it a perfect accompaniment for berries, pies, and certain dishes that require rich sauces.

• • •

Baked Custard with Caramel Sauce
LE FLAN AU CARAMEL

SERVES 6 TO 8

Instant puddings have almost driven this worthy old standby into oblivion, but many French household cooks still prepare it. No instant pudding will ever take its place, as far as I am concerned. No product I know of can reproduce the honest, straightforward richness of taste in this classic French baked custard.

1 quart whole milk	1 teaspoon orange extract
8 egg yolks (save the whites to make a meringue next day)	1 teaspoon lemon extract
	3 tablespoons granulated sugar
⅔ cup fine granulated sugar	2 tablespoons water
1 teaspoon vanilla extract	

1. Preheat the oven to 325°.
2. Heat the milk to the scalding point and remove it from the heat.
3. Whisk the egg yolks, ⅔ cup sugar, and extracts together for 7 minutes until they are perfectly combined and will fall in a thin ribbon from the whisk. Gradually whisk this mixture into the hot milk.
4. Over high heat caramelize the sugar and water until they turn a very dark amber. Pour this caramel into a deep porcelain baking dish that is made for custards, puddings, or soufflés and coat as much of the bottom of the dish as you can with the caramel while it is still liquid enough to run. If it crystallizes too quickly reheat it with a few drops of water.
5. Pour the liquid custard into the baking dish on top of the caramel.
6. Set the baking dish in a metal pan containing 1 or 2 inches of water and bake the custard in the middle of the oven for 1 hour.
7. Remove the custard from the oven, allow it to cool, and then chill it completely.
8. Run a thin sharp knife around the custard, invert a serving dish over the baking dish and unmold the custard and its caramel sauce onto it by turning the baking dish with the serving plate held close to it upside down.
9. Serve the custard with a little of its sauce spooned over it.

NOTE: This custard may be baked in individual ramekins. Simply put a little of the caramel in each before filling them with the liquid custard, then set them in the water and bake them. Take them out as soon as they are cooked solid. They will require only about 30 minutes' baking time. Little individual baked custards seem to delight children in both France and the United States.

Rice Pudding
LE RIZ AU LAIT

SERVES 4 OR 5

Riz au lait is part of every French household's survival kit. A Jewish mother will usually resort to chicken soup when someone in her household isn't feeling well. The French mother will inevitably suggest riz au lait. *However, you mustn't gather from that that French rice pudding is reserved for the sick. Children like it when they return from school in the late afternoon, and grown-ups love to discover it when they raid the refrigerator. Of course, not the least of French rice pudding's virtues is that it is most economical.*

3 cups fresh water
½ cup short- or long-grain rice, picked over and well washed
3 cups whole milk
Peel of 1 lemon, carefully removed in a continuous spiral

½ vanilla bean or 1 teaspoon vanilla extract
¼ cup granulated sugar
½ teaspoon salt
2 tablespoons sweet butter

1. Bring the water to a rolling boil and add the rice. Cook for only 5 minutes, then drain the rice in a fine colander. Rinse it in cold water and set it aside to drain.
2. Slowly heat the milk with the lemon peel and vanilla in a heavy pot. Simmer for 5 minutes and remove and discard the lemon peel and the vanilla bean, if you have used it.
3. Add the rice, sugar, and salt and simmer at the very lowest heat for half an hour, stirring occasionally to prevent the rice from scorching at the bottom.
4. Swirl in the butter and remove the pot from the fire. Empty the rice pudding into a serving bowl.

5. Serve either hot or cold and set out a jug of cold milk for those who want it.

N O T E : I have found over the years that the French are not as fond as we are of cinnamon. Although my French friends would cry heresy, I often add a 2-inch piece of cinnamon bark along with the lemon peel and vanilla bean, discarding it along with them before adding the rice. I love the ensemble of delicate tastes.

Baked Rice Pudding
LE RIZ AU LAIT GARNI
SERVES 6 TO 8

This is the fancy, baked version of riz au lait. *It is fine enough to serve as dessert at the end of a special meal. If there is any left over, it will disappear the next day as if by magic. Prepare* riz au lait *as in the preceding recipe, following the instructions to the point at which you are ready to empty the pudding into a serving bowl.*

½ cup white raisins
1 jigger warmed dark rum
8 egg yolks (save the whites for
   another purpose)

½ cup granulated sugar
3 tablespoons sweet butter, cut
   into small bits

1. Preheat the oven to 325°.
2. Rinse the raisins in cold water and drain them. Put them in a cup with the warm rum and allow them to plump up for 30 minutes.
3. Beat the egg yolks with the sugar until they are light and lemon-colored. Then add the rum that the raisins have not absorbed, beating it in a drop or two at a time.
4. Using a wooden spatula, fold the egg and rum mixture and the raisins into the rice pudding. Stir as little as possible.
5. Empty the mixture into a well-buttered baking dish that is presentable at table. Distribute bits of butter over the surface of the mixture. Set the baking dish in an ovenproof receptacle containing ½ inch of water and bake the pudding for 30 minutes. If you like you may sprinkle

extra sugar on the surface of the pudding and brown it under the broiler.

6. Serve the pudding hot or cold with a little light cream for those who wish it.

Strawberry Dessert Omelet
L'OMELETTE AUX FRAISES
SERVES 4 OR 5

There are many varieties of sweet or dessert omelets. I have chosen this one because it is relatively easy to make and because it uses beaten egg whites to puff or leaven the omelet. This technique, souffler l'omelette *(to inflate the omelet), can be used in savory or "salted" omelets, as well. It is quite successful with a little grated cheese in the whites. Here it makes the dessert special.*

When working with sweet omelets you must be very quick and control the heat, because sugar browns very quickly. If you use the high heat required for most "salted" omelets, your omelet can easily overbrown or burn. Just be vigilant. Overbrowning causes an omelet to become leathery. You should really try all the other omelets I have suggested before deciding to do this one. I also suggest you try it on your family before undertaking it for guests. It isn't difficult; it is just a little elaborate. You can do it in great style, I am sure, if you go about it coolly and have everything you need ready and at hand.

1 box fresh, ripe strawberries
2 teaspoons wine vinegar
¼ cup granulated sugar
1 jigger kirsch or rum
6 large fresh eggs, at room temperature
3 drops fresh lemon juice
½ teaspoon cream of tartar

½ teaspoon each of vanilla, lemon, and almond extract
¼ cup plus 3 tablespoons confectioner's sugar
2 teaspoons water
½ teaspoon finely milled table salt
2 tablespoons sweet butter

1. Wash the strawberries thoroughly and drain them well. Choose 5 of the most perfect and set them aside. Don't stem them. Stem and quarter the rest, put them in a glass or enamel bowl with the vinegar,

and toss them. After 5 minutes add the granulated sugar and kirsch or rum. Set them aside. (This can be done hours in advance.)

2. Separate 3 of the eggs. Put the whites in a very clean bowl with the lemon juice and beat until frothy. Add the cream of tartar and continue to beat the whites until they stand in soft peaks. Add the extracts and 3 tablespoons of the confectioner's sugar and beat again.

3. Whisk the egg yolks and the remaining 3 whole eggs together with the water, salt, and 2 tablespoons of the confectioner's sugar until they are lemon-colored.

4. Heat the frying pan, preferably a nonstick pan 10 inches wide. Melt 1 tablespoon of the butter in it, swirling the pan to coat the cooking surface as it melts. Be careful not to overheat the pan. You need moderate, not high heat for this omelet.

5. Fold ⅔ of the beaten whites into the yolk mixture. Fold, don't stir. We are not making a soufflé, but the beaten whites should retain as much of their air as possible.

6. Pour the omelet mixture into the pan. Keep lifting the edge and allowing the liquid part to run underneath, using a wooden spatula.

7. Spread the rest of the whites over the center of the omelet. Keep them away from the edges. Remove some of the strawberries from their juice with a slotted spoon and deposit them in the whites. Quickly fold the omelet over the strawberries and the whites.

8. Invert a plate over the frying pan, hold it tightly against the pan, and turn the pan upside down, so that the somewhat fat omelet comes out easily, underside up.

9. Return the pan to the fire, melt the remaining tablespoon of butter, and pour it over the omelet to glaze it.

10. Roll the strawberries you have put aside in the powdered sugar. Sift the rest of the sugar over the omelet.

11. Spoon the rest of the quartered strawberries and their juice into the plate around the omelet. Arrange the sugared strawberries, stems out, along the open edge of the omelet.

12. Serve the omelet with a pie server that can cut through it, and spoon a generous serving of berries and juice, topped off with one of the whole, sugared berries, on each portion.

N O T E : As you can see, this is an ambitious tour de force, but it is entirely feasible in a family kitchen without any special equipment. There is one very important consideration, however: be sure that you can leave your guests in good hands while you disappear for a few minutes to make this surprise. You want to be sure you can bring it off with élan, panache, and success! Be sure your guests are capable of appreciating this dessert and the trouble you have taken to prepare it for them. Otherwise, plan a simpler dessert that can be entirely prepared beforehand.

Thin French Dessert Pancakes
LES CREPES FINES
MAKES ABOUT 24

These are the very thin pancakes that most of the world thinks of as French pancakes. They are an invention of the fabulous nineteenth-century restaurant cooking era, but today in France these little crêpes are part of every good household cook's repertoire. They should be part of yours, as well. Here is the classic recipe.

2 cups sifted flour	1 teaspoon vanilla extract
½ cup granulated sugar	1 teaspoon lemon extract
¼ teaspoon finely milled salt	1 tablespoon Cognac
3 large eggs plus 1 yolk	5 tablespoons melted sweet
2 cups warm whole milk	butter

1. Mix the flour, sugar, and salt together in a large mixing bowl.
2. Add the eggs and the yolk, one by one, alternately with the warm milk, the extracts, and Cognac to the dry ingredients. Unless you are using a food processor, which will do all this in 2 minutes, mix with a wooden spatula, and take your time. In making crêpes and *galettes*, success depends upon the manner in which the flour particles accept and hold the liquid. Mix until the batter is creamy and coats but does not cling to the spatula. I prefer doing the mixing with my hand. I know the batter is right when I grasp it in my palm and it falls back into the bowl along my fingers in narrow, continuous streams.
3. Stir in the melted butter until it disappears.
4. Cover the mixing bowl and chill the batter for 1 hour before using.
5. Heat an 8- to 10-inch nonstick frying pan over moderate heat. Grease the pan ever so lightly with a little melted butter on a piece of old linen or a folded paper towel.

6. Stir the chilled batter and pour just enough onto the frying pan to coat the bottom and a little of the sides when you tilt the pan and swirl it about. If it "catches" too quickly and doesn't cover the entire bottom, the batter may be too thick. Thin it with a little warm milk. If it jumps and sputters and makes lacy holes, the pan is too hot. Reduce the heat before making the next crêpe.

7. With the greasing cloth and a little coarse salt, rub away any bits that may have stuck to the pan. This will prevent the second crêpe from sticking. Wipe the salt out of the frying pan and continue to make your crêpes.

8. Stack the finished crêpes on a lightly buttered plate, cover them with a clean, dry cloth, and place them in a warm oven with the door open. (If you close the door, the stack of crêpes will generate steam and get damp and soggy.)

You now have about 2 dozen dessert crêpes. A very simple way of serving them is to place ½ cup melted sweet butter in a shallow baking dish. Dip each crêpe in the melted butter so that each surface is coated. Spread good, thick apricot jam on one side. Fold it over once, then again. You now have a quarter circle, the classic shape for these crêpes. Line the folded pancakes up so they overlap like feathers in 2 lines. Sprinkle them liberally with granulated sugar. Place them in a preheated 375° oven for 10 minutes, then put them under the broiler until the sugar takes on color. Serve each guest 2 or 3 with some of the melted butter spooned over them.

This is a dessert that children usually adore. If you are serving only adults, warm 2 jiggers of brandy until very hot and pour the brandy over the crêpes as soon as they are removed from the broiler. Light the brandy and stir it about in the melted butter while it is flaming. Serve the crêpes as soon as the alcohol has burned off. If you substitute Seville orange marmalade for the apricot jam and flame the crêpes with Cointreau or Grand Marnier, you have a version of crêpes Suzette to serve your guests!

• • •

Pears Poached in Red Wine
LES POIRES POCHEES

SERVES 6

This is a very simple dessert that the French love. When I make it, it never fails to impress the guests. It is light, beautiful to look at, and exquisitely flavored.

1 bottle light, red wine (I
   recommend a Bordeaux)
½ cup granulated sugar
1 lemon peel—the yellow outer
   skin of an entire lemon
   removed with a potato peeler
   in one continuous piece

3 cloves
6 firm, perfect pears (russets and
   Comice pears are right for
   this; Bartletts are too soft)

1. Heat the wine, sugar, lemon peel, and cloves for 5 minutes, stirring the ingredients until the sugar has completely dissolved.
2. Peel the pears carefully, leaving them whole. Slice a small piece off the rounded end so that they will sit up well. Don't remove the stems.
3. Stand the pears in a deep, noncorrosive pan that will just accommodate them, and gently pour the hot wine over them. Drop the cloves into the pan and let them fall to the bottom. Lace the lemon peel around the pears so that it is submerged in the wine.
4. Cover the pan and poach the pears gently for 40 minutes. If they seem to be getting tender before the time is up, turn off the heat. Discard the cloves and lemon peel. Let the pears cool in the liquid.
5. Remove the pears once they are cool and reduce the wine over very high heat until it is glossy and will coat a spoon. It should not be allowed to cook down to a heavy syrup.
6. Place the pears upright on a glass or porcelain serving dish and spoon the syrup over them. Chill them and serve them quite cold.

N O T E : Serve the pears individually on shallow plates with a little of the syrup spooned over them. Provide dessert knives, forks, and spoons so the cores can be easily dealt with. Some cooks core the pears before cooking them, but that makes them cook far too quickly and often causes them to lose their crisp texture. Out in the country in France the pears are often peeled, cored, and stewed in quarters, making a compote of them. In pear season a large bowl of this compote appears at almost every meal. It is often eaten with yogurt.

Dried Fruit Stewed in Red Wine
LA COMPOTE DE FRUITS SECS
SERVES 4 TO 6

Almost any dried fruit may be used in this compote. In some French households it is customary for the cook to make a large quantity of this dish. It gets appreciably better after a couple of days in the refrigerator; its taste seems somehow to concentrate and grows more delicious. At my house it never goes begging. My family and friends love it for breakfast, and they like it with yogurt for a snack.

1 pound of mixed dried fruit such as apples, apricots, prunes, and pears or 1 pound of just 1 of these	¾ cup honey
	One 2-inch piece cinnamon bark
	1 lemon peel, just the thin, yellow part removed in 1 piece with a potato peeler
1 cup dry red wine	
3 cloves, tied up in a small piece of cheesecloth	¼ teaspoon dried fennel seed (optional)
2 cups water	

1. Soak the dried fruit overnight in water enough to cover it.
2. Rinse the fruit well under cold running water before cooking it.
3. Heat the wine, cloves, water, and honey until the honey has combined completely with the other liquids.
4. Add the soaked fruit, cinnamon bark and lemon peel, cover the pot, and simmer for 40 minutes.
5. Uncover the pot and simmer for 20 more minutes.
6. Discard the cinnamon bark and the lemon peel and cloves.
7. Add the fennel seeds, stir them in, pour the compote into a glass bowl with a cover, and chill it well before serving.

N O T E : Certain fresh fruits such as plums, apricots, and apples may be prepared in the same fashion. Start with Step 2 and reduce the cooking time to 25 minutes or you will produce a purée.

Apple Charlotte with Raspberry Sauce
LA CHARLOTTE AUX POMMES AU COULIS DE FRAMBOISES

SERVES 6

Apple charlotte is a kind of aristocratic bread pudding that French household cooks used to make quite often. It is also one of those good, old-fashioned desserts you are not likely to encounter anywhere nowadays except in someone's home. Here is how it is done.

12 slices white sandwich bread, crusts trimmed away and discarded

6 to 8 Granny Smith apples, peeled, cored, and cut into eighths

2/3 stick (5 1/3 tablespoons) sweet butter, at room temperature

1/2 cup granulated sugar

1 tablespoon finely grated orange peel

1 teaspoon finely grated lemon peel

1 jigger Calvados or rum

1/4 cup good quality apricot jam

2 tablespoons fine granulated sugar

1 cup sieved fresh or frozen raspberries

1. Butter a 1-quart charlotte mold generously, using plenty of butter.
2. Using a very sharp knife, cut diagonally across several slices of bread, fashioning enough triangular shapes to fit closely on to the circular bottom of the mold like sections of a wheel. Trim the outer ends so that they correspond with the curve of the sides of the mold and fit the bread snugly into the bottom.
3. Cut 2- to 3-inch strips the length of the slices. Arrange them vertically against the sides of the mold, allowing them to overlap slightly. Press the bread against the buttered mold to make it stick there. Don't trim off the ends that stick out above the mold. Chill the mold.
4. In a heavy frying pan sauté the apples with the butter, sugar, and the orange and lemon peels, shaking and stirring them so that liquid from the apples cooks away quickly. Stir the Calvados or rum and the apricot jam into the mixture, increase the heat for 2 minutes, and immediately remove from the fire.
5. Preheat the oven to 400°.
6. Pack the apple mixture into the mold. Cut a piece of wax paper to

fit as a cover inside the mold, and press down on the apple mixture to compact it.

7. Bake the charlotte for 35 to 40 minutes.
8. Remove the charlotte from the oven and lift off the wax paper cover. Neatly trim off the protruding pieces of bread that extend past the mold. Put them on the apple mixture. Replace the wax paper cover, press the pieces of toasted trimmings down into the charlotte, and sprinkle the 2 tablespoons sugar over the top.
9. Put the charlotte back into the oven and bake it for another 20 minutes.
10. Remove the charlotte from the oven and allow it to cool in its mold.
11. Slip a thin, sharp knife around the inside of the mold and unmold the charlotte on a serving plate. Serve each guest a slice of the charlotte with some raspberry purée poured over it or deposited in a little pool alongside it on the plate.

Fresh Sugared Strawberries
LES FRAISES AU SUCRE
SERVES 4 TO 6

Try to choose strawberries that are just at their peak and are not hard and pale. Pick through the strawberries very well, discarding any that are overripe, bruised, or discolored. Wash them very well to remove any sand or grit. Strawberries should never be left more than a few minutes in water because they begin to go soft almost immediately, especially if they have been stemmed before they are washed.

2 boxes fresh strawberries, picked over, washed well, dried, and stemmed
2 tablespoons wine vinegar

½ cup fresh orange juice or dry white wine
½ cup granulated sugar

1. Put the strawberries in a glass or ceramic bowl. Sprinkle them with vinegar and toss them so that they are all exposed to the vinegar. (It is magic in coaxing the strawberries to release their natural bouquet.)
2. Add the orange juice or white wine and sugar and toss the strawberries lightly without bruising or crushing them.

3. Cover the bowl and refrigerate until the berries are chilled through.
4. Serve in individual bowls with some of the juice.

   N O T E : In France strawberries are not often served with whipped cream as they are in the United States. They are usually served only with some of their juice.

Sliced Oranges in Cognac
LES TRANCHES D'ORANGE AU COGNAC
SERVES 4

The soul of simplicity, this dessert is elegant and much appreciated at the end of a heavy meal. The oranges should be top quality.

4 small juice oranges such as Valencias or Haifas	¼ cup granulated sugar 2 jiggers Cognac

1. With a very sharp, stainless steel knife peel the oranges so that all the skin is removed as well as the outside integument that encloses the segments. Slice the oranges ⅛-inch thick. Remove and discard any seeds.
2. Layer the orange slices in a shallow glass or ceramic dish and sprinkle them with the sugar.
3. Empty the jiggers of Cognac over the oranges and let them sit for 5 to 10 minutes at room temperature before serving.
4. Serve the orange slices with plenty of their sauce spooned over them.

   N O T E : Obviously this is not a dessert for children or teetotalers, but it has this plus: It is very effective in settling a certain kind of upset stomach.

• • •

Brandied Cherries
LES CERISES A L'EAU DE VIE
MAKES 1 QUART

For special occasions, the French may serve coffee and brandy or liqueurs after a meal. If you are lucky, a very special old Calvados or homemade cordials or liqueurs may be offered to you. Another rare treat that used to be offered along with coffee, especially if you were invited to a meal in the country, was cherries preserved in country brandy. Some household cooks still prepare a jar of these cérises à l'eau de vie at the end of June or the beginning of July, when the regional cherries are at their best. The recipes for these cherries vary from simply putting a pound of cherries in a liter of alcohol to more elaborate ways of preserving the flavor and appearance of the cherries. The following recipe is from rural Provence.

1 pound fresh, ripe cherries, well washed, dried, stems discarded, stones removed
½ the cherry stones, cracked with a hammer
1 teaspoon crushed coriander seeds
One 2-inch piece cinnamon bark
1 orange skin, removed in one piece with a potato peeler, all pith removed
1 liter *marc* (country brandy) or good, unflavored vodka
1 pound fresh, ripe, completely unblemished cherries, well washed, dried, half the length of their stems removed
½ cup granulated sugar (optional)

1. Put the stoned cherries, cracked stones, coriander, cinnamon bark, and orange peel with the brandy or vodka in a tightly sealed glass jar and leave the ingredients to marinate at room temperature for 15 days.
2. Unseal the marinade and strain the liquid through a sieve lined with 2 thicknesses of rinsed, wrung-out cheesecloth. Discard all the solids.
3. Place the prepared new cherries and the sugar in a clean glass jar that has a clasp-type seal. Pour the strained liquid over the new cherries, making sure that the cherries are completely covered.
4. Seal the jar and allow the new cherries to marinate for at least a week before serving any of them.
5. Serve a few of these cherries with a spoonful of their liqueur on a little plate along with the postprandial black coffee and see what a sensation they cause.

NOTE: These are the very best brandied cherries you are likely to find. Because the alcohol becomes sufficiently by impregnated with the flavors of the first batch of cherries, their cracked stones, and the aromatics, the new cherries remain plump and tasty, and are surrounded with a delicious liqueur. When you are served brandied cherries on a farm in France, the cherries are usually simply marinated in country brandy. The strong liquor causes the cherries to shrink and lose their taste to the alcohol.

If you are careful about sealing up the cherries and shaking them gently so that they remain completely submerged in their liqueur after each time you remove any, the cherries will remain first-rate for about 1 year.

Cheese
LE FROMAGE

Cheese is a major part of the French diet and figures prominently in the daily menu in every household I know. Small wonder! France produces more high-quality cheeses than any other country in the world. In fact, France produces so many cheeses that it would be impossible to list all of them, since every region produces its own varieties, many of which are consumed locally and never find their way to any other market. Householders in one region may know little or nothing about other regional cheeses; however, they are excellent judges of the cheeses of their own region and of the cheeses they regularly purchase for their own table.

It takes as long to become an expert on French cheeses as it does to become an expert on the wines of France. It is not my intention to say more than a few words about them here. Books could be written about this great food; indeed, scores have already been written. Here I simply want to call attention to the importance of cheese in planning French household meals. If the French believe that a meal without wine is like a day without sunshine, the same could be said of cheese. Most major meals in a French home end with cheese, or else cheese appears during meal in some form. Like wines, too, you will only find out which cheeses you like by sampling them, trying them out during your own meals. You'll have to be adventuresome and try an unfamiliar French cheese as often as you can. That is the only way to discover the ones that you can really appreciate.

Leave the processed cheeses for a while and try the natural ones. Soon you will know about them and be able to choose them and offer them to your family and your guests. As they say in France, all is not Brie and Camembert!

CHEESE AS DESSERT

Strictly speaking, the French do not think of cheese as a dessert, but the habit of eating it toward the end of a meal makes it seem so. Also, cheese is often eaten with apples, and if the apples are the dessert, it is easy to reason that cheese is, indeed, also a dessert in France. The fact is this: Cheese is served as a course, as savories are in some homes in England. The cheese course usually follows the salad or is served with it. If a sweet is served, it will follow the cheese. Often one cheese will be served *en famille*, but at least two will be served if there are guests. The unwritten law about serving cheeses is this: If two cheeses are served, one should be soft, one hard, or one should be sharp, one bland, and should one of the cheeses be very strong, sweet butter will usually be offered to cut its sharpness. One last detail should be added in this very cursory account concerning the role of cheese in French household meals: to the ordinary Frenchman, eating cheese requires wine. It may be just a *rinsolette*, that is, only a swallow or two of the wine served with dinner to wash down the bread and cheese. Red wine is most often served with cheese and it is usually a safe choice. There are many cheeses that do not go well with white wine. Naturally, custom should always bow to the occasion, and each host should make his or her own choices about wine and cheese.

Beverages

Les Boissons

A substantial part of the French household's food budget is spent on drinks. Most of it goes for wine and mineral water, both of which are traditionally on the table for each major meal. Most homes usually have a favorite *vin ordinaire* or "daily wine," which is often purchased in bulk once a year and stored in a cellar or provision room, though many modern households purchase wine, like milk, on a daily basis. This wine will be red or white, according to the family's preference, but red is generally preferred because it is thought to be less acidic and easier to digest than ordinary white wines. There is widespread belief among the French that white wines, if drunk often, are apt to put the nerves on edge and produce insomnia. The household "daily wine" is usually a local wine of medium quality, containing no more than 9 percent alcohol by volume. Our American wines often contain as much as 13 percent alcohol by volume, and are considered by the French to be a bit stout for everyday meals.

In addition to the *vin ordinaire*, many households in France lay in a smaller supply of a better quality wine, which will be saved for special occasions. Also, there may be a few really good bottles hidden away *derrière les faggots*—literally, behind the cellar woodpile—for extra-special occasions.

Though most French householders know and recognize the great wines, by and large, they do not possess stocks of such choice wines. When great wines are called for, they purchase them from their local liquor dealer, just as we do. Each French home will usually have, in addition to its modestly stocked liquor cabinet, a bottle of Cognac, good Calvados or country brandy, and sometimes homemade cordials or liqueurs hidden away to be brought out for important events.

A long, detailed discussion of the enormous and growing subject of French wines is not appropriate here, but a few words about the traditional French household's attitudes toward wine are in order. It may surprise many Americans to discover that by no means everyone in

France is an expert on French wines. The ordinary Frenchman will know and recognize some of the great wines of France, and the wines of his region. He may even know a great many of the *petits vins*, the unclassified, nontraveling wines of his native region, but not much more. The great, comprehensive connoisseurship of French wines that was the proud possession of the good French bourgeois householders at the turn of the century has declined. Ordinary French homes nowadays seldom serve more than one wine during a meal. The great dinners prepared for Christmas Eve and New Year's are notable exceptions. I remember many Christmas and New Year *réveillons* where there were eight courses and a different wine was served with each. The French are the first to agree that such indulgence is hard on both the pocketbook and the liver. Gone, too, are the days when most self-respecting Burgundians drank a *canon*, a large, spherical glass of red wine, before breakfast.

If you know very little about wine, the main thing to remember when choosing it for a meal, whether it be French or otherwise, is to think carefully about the tastes of the food you are planning to serve. Choose a wine that will complement or balance those tastes, not obscure them or overpower them. The old saw, white wine with fish and light meat, red wine with dark meat, is a simplistic rule of thumb that suffers all sorts of exceptions. It is best to do as most French householders do: Use your own sensitivities and choose the wine accordingly.

There are so many wonderful French and American wines to discover that it would take more than a lifetime to know them all. If you feel overwhelmed, start your own little study. Buy yourself a pocket-size edition of Johnson's *Encyclopedia of Wine* to help you identify the wines you discover. It is a very good idea, too, to keep a personal wine journal. Every time you encounter a new wine, make an entry so that you will recognize it the next time. It isn't necessary to become a wine expert, but it will add immeasurably to your enjoyment to know a little wine lore. There are many books and magazines on wine at present, even a newsletter, if you want to pursue the subject. You don't have to stock a cellar or spend a fortune to become knowledgeable about wine. The very best wines are costly, but much of the fun of a minor connoisseurship in wine is in discovering wines with qualities that please you at a price that is affordable. They still exist, even in these expensive times! Four years ago I discovered an excellent red "daily wine," the price of which in all that time hasn't budged from $3.00 a liter. It is so good, in fact, that I keep fearing it will be discovered by many others and the price will soar. Finding that kind of bargain is exactly the type of winesmanship that pleases ordinary French householders. They always look for good quality at a bargain price.

A WORD ABOUT APERITIFS AND AFTER-DINNER DRINKS

If you are invited for a meal with a French family, you will almost always be asked if you would like an apéritif before lunch or dinner. The apéritif, or *apéro*, as it is commonly called nowadays, is the French premeal drink. Though Scotch whiskey has been adopted in some French households as a fashionable apéritif, it is an interloper. The traditional apéritif or "appetite teaser" is not as strong as our cocktail. It is usually a fortified wine flavored with aromatics or bitters or both. Sometimes it may be a glass of sherry or port. In the Midi it is often *pastis*, an elixer of anise and other aromatics served with lots of cold water. In some households it may be nonalcoholic—a small glass of tomato juice or fruit juice. Usually a small plate of nuts, olives, or salted crackers will be set out to nibble on as you sip your *apéro*, but never more than a little taste of something. The idea is to stimulate the appetite, not kill it with strong drinks and heavy hors d'oeuvre. While the French will drink an *apéro* at the drop of a hat on the terrace of a café, or when there are guests, most French households do not drink an apéritif before their daily meals at home unless it is a special occasion.

It is a common practice in French homes to drink something after a principal meal to aid the digestion. When guests are present, it is usually a tiny cup of black coffee, or a *tisane*, one of their many herbal teas. The French are very sensitive to excitants, and it is an article of faith in a French household that *tisanes* are less stimulating than coffee. Of the *tisanes*, the most popular with French households are *tilleul*, made of linden flowers, and *verveine*, brewed from the leaves of lemon verbena. Mint and camomile are also popular favorites.

One of the joys of my student days was participating in the harvesting of the linden flowers in the small town of Aups in northern Provence with my old friend Denis Gontard, whose family owned a farm and orchard there. Large boughs were cut from the flowering trees and placed on a wagon sheet, and we stripped the limbs of their fragrant, chartreuse-colored blossoms and the two or three tiny leaves below them wh battling off the swarms of honeybees that also flocked to the blossor trees. (A flowering linden tree attracts so many bees that the tree resounds like a cello.) The gathered blossoms and leaves are dried for several days in the sun, then stored in sealed jars or packages. The tea made from linden blossoms is light, delicately perfumed, and a true soporific. It has the power to lull you to sleep after a big meal. A *tisane* made of lemon verbena leaves, on the other hand, has the opposite effect; it seems to wake you up. It is no longer necessary to gather these herbs and dry them. They are now marketed in little paper *sachets* like ordinary tea.

A WORD ABOUT FRENCH COFFEE

The French prefer their coffee roasted a uniform, jet black color. Longer roasting imparts a deeper color and a stronger taste than most Americans are used to. While French coffee looks and tastes stronger, the French claim that longer roasting reduces the caffeine content. I do not know whether the claim is based on scientific proof. In any case, the ordinary Frenchman drinks less coffee than the ordinary American. Coffee is still considered special in France. It is never drunk along with the meal as it often is in the United States. Coffee mixed with heated milk—café au lait—is the preferred breakfast drink all over France. Tiny cups of black coffee are drunk after a principal meal, but the French generally wouldn't think of adding milk or cream to it. Sugar is available and, on occasion, Calvados, country brandy, or a good Cognac for those who wish a *café arrosé*—literally, a "sprinkled coffee." A morning *café arrosé*, once the great favorite of many French workmen and country people, has lost favor in the last forty years.

• • •

Good French Coffee
LE BON CAFE

Because of the high price of coffee in France, thrifty household cooks sometimes add commercially roasted chicory to their coffee to make it go farther. However, coffee lovers in France insist that nothing but pure, freshly roasted, freshly ground coffee should be used for the real thing—le bon café.

1 tablespoon fresh, dark-roasted, medium-ground coffee per serving, plus 1 teaspoon "for the pot"	¾ standard measuring cup fresh cold water brought just to the boiling point and immediately removed from the heat

1. Put the coffee in a freshly scrubbed, rinsed, and dried ceramic pot.
2. Pour the hot (not boiling!) water over the coffee and stir the mixture once.
3. Allow the coffee to brew for 5 minutes.
4. Pour the coffee through a fine sieve and serve it very hot.

To make good coffee, you must begin with the best, freshest coffee available. Insist upon the best water available, as well, even if you have to resort to a good, noncarbonated bottled water. Especially to be avoided are water from a hot water heater and water that has already been boiled and allowed to remain in the tea kettle. Unlike tea leaves, which depend on rapidly boiling water for releasing maximum flavor, coffee grounds produce their finest bouquet when steeped in very hot but not boiling water. Boiling water extracts bitter-tasting oils from the grounds. Reheated coffee should never be allowed to boil or the flavor will become flat and acidic. These instructions may sound fussy to Americans, most of whom use coffeemakers, but it is useful to know how French householders make their coffee from scratch. A final note: the best thing for scrubbing the pot is bicarbonate of soda, and the pot should be scrupulously cleaned, rinsed, and dried after each use.

• • •

French Breakfast Coffee
LE CAFE AU LAIT

Many American visitors to France are delighted at the thought of breakfasting on warm croissants, brioches, and huge cups of café au lait, served up to them on some pleasant café terrace along a busy French boulevard. For all the charming novelty of that experience, many of those same Americans remember that half an hour after their romantic French breakfast they had a sour stomach. Why? Most cafés in France serve reheated coffee at breakfast time. The next time you have the occasion to breakfast in a French café take note of how few Frenchmen drink café au lait unless they are sure the coffee is made to order. The difference is enormous between "un crème"—the French parlance for café au lait—made from freshly made coffee and one made of reheated coffee. A freshly made café au lait will rarely bother your stomach. You can make a perfect one for yourself at home. Here's how:

Freshly brewed dark-roasted coffee	**Whole milk** Sugar

1. Heat the milk just to the boiling point. Remove it from the heat before it boils.
2. Heat the fresh coffee without boiling it.
3. Strain the quantity of hot milk you desire into large cups or "coffee bowls."
4. Add the coffee.
5. Add a lump or two of sugar, if you desire.

   NOTE: There are disagreements about whether the milk should be poured before, at the same time, or after the coffee. I pour the hot milk in first. In the days before pasteurization everyone used to boil the milk. That doesn't need to be done anymore. In fact, watch the milk carefully because it boils over easily and makes a terrible mess of your stove if it does. If you have any leftover café au lait, put it in a glass container in the refrigerator. It makes a delicious mid-morning or mid-afternoon drink. Chilling the café au lait somehow brings out its flavor.

Index

ABOUT THE AUTHOR

JACQUES BURDICK was born in Texas and educated in the U.S., France, Spain, and Greece. Known chiefly as a theatre historian, in his early youth he trained as a restaurant cook to pay for his university studies. He has co-owned, co-managed and cooked in restaurants on the Costa Brava, but he feels that he has learned most of what he knows about regional European food cooking from his French and Catalan friends in their own kitchens at home. He spends his summers in France and Catalonia, cooking. Currently, Burdick teaches cooking and lives in Manhattan.